HERBS IN THE KITCHEN

A CELEBRATION OF FLAVOR

■

CAROLYN DILLE & SUSAN BELSINGER

PHOTOGRAPHY BY JOE COCA

■

INTERWEAVE PRESS

HERBS IN THE KITCHEN
by Carolyn Dille and Susan Belsinger
photography by Joe Coca

Design by Susan Wasinger/Signorella Graphic Arts
Photo styling by Ann Sabin Swanson and Linda Ligon
Production by Marc McCoy Owens
Garden illustration on page 32 by Ann Sabin Swanson
Photography by Joe Coca except as follows: Susan Belsinger pages 37, 63, 83, 127, 139, 153, 173, 185, 221, 237, 255, 271, 287, 301, and 317; Lauren Springer page 99.

Photo accessories on pages 79, 103, and 213 courtesy of The Cupboard, Fort Collins, Colorado.

 Interweave Press, Inc.
201 East Fourth Street
Loveland, Colorado 80537

Library of Congress Cataloging-in-Publication Data

Dille, Carolyn
    Herbs in the kitchen : a celebration of flavor / Carolyn Dille and
  Susan Belsinger : photography by Joe Coca.
        p.   cm.
    Includes index.
    ISBN 0-934026-73-4 : $24.95
    1. Cookery (Herbs)   I. Belsinger, Susan.   II. Title.
  TX819.H4D54   1992
  641.57--dc20   91-46686
                                                    CIP

First printing: 10M:21292:ARC/CL

TO DICK AND TOMASO

With unflagging appetite
and near unfailing cheer
you greeted the next rewrite
and still called us dear.
Then programmed the computers
and tilled the garden earth;
meanwhile, like swains and suitors,
rallied the cooks with wine and mirth.

ACKNOWLEDGMENTS

Our families and friends have our fondest thanks. Through the years, their good nature, wit, and willingness to help have made the pleasures of the table and the work of the cooks light and satisfying. Special thanks to Tom DeBaggio and Linda Ligon, whose generous-spirited help has contributed so much to this book. We much appreciate the work of Joe Coca, Betsy Strauch, and Susan Wasinger, whose respective eyes for detail brought the book so well together. All the staff at Interweave Press has our grateful thanks for their enthusiasm and support. And thanks to Bellwether Herb Farm of Fort Collins, Colorado, for providing an abundance of beautiful, fresh herbs for cooking and photography.

FOREWORD

The world of herbs, once the province of the initiated few, is expanding to become everyone's experience, delight, and recreation. For all these new garden enthusiasts, as well as those who remember the early days of the herb revival, this well-arranged cookbook will be rewarding reading. The arrangement of the book is interesting, clear, and practical. The herbs form the chapter heading; the recipes follow. I find this the simplest and most satisfying way to decide what original and interesting things to do with long rows of fragrant and prolific plants.

Herbs find their way into so many facets of our lives; they have inspired designers, historians, romantics, craftsmen, perfumers, doctors, religious groups, alchemists, witches, astrologers, and scientists, who have all found virtues in these humble plants. The interest of the cook, along with the physician, is probably the oldest and the most vital of all. The kitchen garden is a very ancient form of gardening, often a feature of castles and manor houses in Europe. Many of these that have been neglected for years are being restored and now generate enthusiasm and curiosity in all who visit them. The grounds around our Early American homes are also being planted with these gardens once grown for "Meate and Medicine".

The interest is great, but application of practical uses lags, and many enthusiasts are presented with burgeoning crops that often go unharvested and unused for want of knowledge. For all the gardeners who find an overabundance of the twenty herbs here described, Belsinger and Dille have provided many answers. The multiple ways to season with basil is one example; it becomes no longer common but truly the "King of Herbs". Lemon balm, so prolific and so seldom used, has most intriguing and delicious recipes. Coriander, chervil, and the cresses are presented in a fashion that invites trying new taste experiences. *Herbs in the Kitchen* will expand your conception of herb cookery and certainly enrich your gardening life.

Adelma Grenier Simmons
Caprilands, 1982

PREFACE

It has been a great pleasure for us to return to the material in our previous work, *Cooking with Herbs*. So much has happened since that book was published in 1983, in the realms of both herbs and food, that we welcome the opportunity to present a complete revision.

Herbs have found the general audience in the United States that we have always believed they deserve. Plants and seeds, in a range of varieties that we had known only in Europe, or had read about, are widely available from herb growers, seed suppliers, and even nurseries across the country. New cultivars are continually introduced, from the work of herb growers here and from other countries. We do not think it an overstatement to say that the interest in herbs has mushroomed in the past decade.

This interest has always been part of our culture, but it was confined to a few people whose efforts kept alive the long traditions of herb husbandry and use. Individuals and organizations have worked to preserve and expand herbal knowledge. We would like to acknowledge our debt and gratitude to these. The Herb Society of America has long maintained an active presence and high standards in the herb world. We have been fortunate to meet some exceptional herb growers, whose dedication and hard work through the lean times when fresh herbs were hardly known here have made possible the abundance of herbs we can all share now.

The art of using herbs in the twentieth century has been nurtured by two people we must call pioneers: Irma Goodrich Mazza and Adelma Grenier Simmons. Mrs. Mazza's book *Herbs for the Kitchen* was published in 1939 and has gone through many reprintings and several editions. It is written with intelligence, charm, and respect for herbs and food. For decades it was the "open sesame" to herb cookery for many American cooks.

Adelma Simmons has been, and remains, indefatigable in her herbal work for almost fifty years. Her desire to communicate a love and fascination for herbs turned her private garden, Caprilands, into a national mecca for everyone who wanted to know more. Our visits to Caprilands and chats with Mrs. Simmons remain cherished memories. In her many works, Mrs. Simmons has expanded herbal knowledge for readers in a clear, practical, and interesting way, with researches into the religious, mythical, and medicinal uses of the plants, recipes for their uses, both culinary and decorative, and sensible cultivation and garden information based on experience.

Our own work owes a good deal to these, and others too numerous to mention in this space. That is another reason we enjoy growing and using herbs so much: a real sense of continuity, through the plants themselves, and the naturalists, cooks, and gardeners who have been moved to write about them for centuries.

The past is not the only herb story, however; the present is a fruitful time, and the future holds great prospects, particularly relating to research into the dietary and medicinal properties of the culinary and other herbs. We are frankly excited that more and more people are turning their interests and talents to working with herbs.

We have had several aims in working on this book, which has been greatly expanded from the previous one. One has been to provide the best and latest information on the varieties and cultivation of the plants. During the intervening years, we have each established new gardens and learned much about different growing conditions. And many cultivars of interest to the cook are now available through a variety of sources. This information has been added to the individual chapters.

Another aim has been to add recipes that we have discovered in further travels, and in acquaintance with ideas and cuisines new to us. The whole world uses herbs; we regret only that we have not had the opportunity and time to visit every place where herbs are important. Still, we are fortunate that in the United States we welcome immigrants who share their traditions with us.

Still another aim has been to lighten some of the dishes, principally by using less fat in them. Since many of the recipes are derived from agricultural cultures, goodly amounts of oil, butter, and cream are traditional and without doubt, tasty. But we, being almost ten years older, have found that olive oil, no matter how healthy a fat, still contains the same calories and has the same staying power as other fats. We think that healthy cooking need not be mean-spirited and flavorless and that herbs are especially good allies of moderation. It is beyond our scope to include dietary information in this book, but we do urge those on restricted diets to add herbs, which contain no fat and tiny amounts of sodium, if any, to the dishes they make.

And finally, we have worked to make the recipes more accessible, easier to understand, and simpler in execution, in the hope that every reader and cook will find a place for herbs in the kitchen.

INTRODUCTION

The pride of cooks, ancient treasures,
herbs delight, inform, inspire,
bring to fullness the table's
pleasures without the surfeit of desire,
regale us with their scent and savor,
renew our palates with finest flavor.

Herbs appeal to us for many reasons, but the most important is the magical transformations they work in the kitchen. The simplest ingredients—sun-ripened tomatoes, fruity olive oil, and a little salt—become an extraordinary salad when strewn with fresh basil leaves. A sprinkling of minced sage worked into bread dough fills the kitchen with rich fragrance while the loaves are baking.

The 20 best-known culinary herbs form the foundation of the oldest and finest cooking traditions. This book is a culinary celebration of these herbs and a guide to growing, harvesting, and preserving your own supply.

The rewards of using aromatic plants are many. The variety and combinations of flavor they offer are infinite. The finesse of fine food in restaurants depends partly on fresh herbs; cooks at home can create equally memorable meals using them. Herbs add so much zest and flavor to food that most dishes need less salt. Garnishing with herbs decorates food naturally and palatably. In pots, tubs, planter boxes, or the garden, the liveliness of herbs stimulates the cook's creativity. Growing your own is not only fun, but it also makes possible the use of varieties that cannot be bought.

Cooking with fresh herbs influences us to think of food in new ways. The amounts to use and diversity of foods they flavor encourage improvisation and help each cook develop a personal taste aesthetic. Although we have worked to make our recipes clear and delicious, they still offer possibilities for individual imagination and experimentation.

We believe that herbs are invaluable ingredients in the current renaissance of American cooking. From the everyday cook to the restaurant chef,

Americans continue to evolve their own cuisine, characterized by a new emphasis on fresh foods and herbs, simple but flavorful dishes, and the merging of regional American with ethnic and foreign foods.

Of course, using herbs to enhance the flavor of food is hardly a new idea. One of the most fascinating aspects of culinary herbs is the way various cultures use them. We have had an opportunity to experience this firsthand while living and cooking in Greece, Italy, Morocco, Mexico, and various areas of the United States. Much of this personal involvement is reflected in our recipes.

In addition to recipes, our book provides some special features to make the cultivation of herbs easier, to illustrate specific uses for them, and to bring alive their enchanting legends. The chapter for each herb begins with an introduction discussing herb lore, culinary suggestions, and cultivation information. The opening chapter, "Working with Herbs", summarizes the generally simple requirements for growing herbs in a chart prepared by a professional herb grower. Included is a garden plan for culinary herbs. A chart of complementary herb combinations helps the cook create variety and subtlety in new dishes or old favorites. The substitution of dried herbs for fresh ones is also reviewed.

Nothing else quite captures the essence of fresh herbs, but there are times when these are just not available. We discuss how to harvest, dry, and freeze them to retain the best flavor. The vinegar and oil section elaborates on these wonderful condiments, which greatly expand the cook's repertoire. The shelf in our pantry, lined with jewellike bottles in shades of topaz, rose quartz, and emerald, offers us more than simple infusions. In a real way, these represent kitchen wealth, gladdening as they do the senses of sight, taste, and smell.

We find herbs even more important kitchen tools than good knives or pots (as much as we value these), since they add flavor and soul to our food. A snip of last summer's chives, brought in to winter over on the sill, does wonders for any vegetable. A pot-bound rosemary, blooming indoors as snow falls, cheers the cook and livens the stew.

We hope you find, as we do, that herbal alchemy is a magic every cook should know and one that brings pleasure to all who come under its spell.

WORKING WITH HERBS

CULTIVATING HERB PLANTS

■

When we began growing herbs back in the 1970s, we tried to follow the books to the letter, but often found that this method brought its disappointments as well as its successes. Growing plants depends on so many factors—climate, soil, how the soil is cultivated, light, water, and placement—that general guidelines can prove inappropriate. Our notes on cultivation come from our experience of growing herbs, mainly in temperate climates.

The most important advice we can give you is to talk with professional herb growers in your area. Although the growers may chafe a bit from being asked the same questions over and over, we've found them exceptionally pleasant people who are glad to share their knowledge.

If there is a garden club or botanical garden near you, inquire whether it sponsors lectures on herb growing. Many do and open these to the public for no fee, or a small one.

All successful gardening depends on preparing the earth well. If you have space in the ground, cultivate the soil deeply, adding sand, organic materials, and fertilizers as necessary. A soil test will provide information as to soil type, pH, and recommended additives. Commercial services or county extension agents can conduct these tests; there are home testing kits available as well. We have always had lush, healthy herbs without any pesticides, other than occasional sprays of Safer Insecticidal Soap on the plants.

Herbs will reward you even if you are new to gardening. They are relatively easy to grow and not fussy in the garden. You may want to start with four or five familiar herbs whose flavor you really like and that you will use often.

Much of the information in the chart on page 15 came from Thomas DeBaggio of T. DeBaggio Herbs. Tom grows some of the finest herbs we have seen for sale; we are fortunate to count him as a friend and to have had his advice in preparing this chapter. His chart provides the most important information for growing herbs in the garden or in the house.

Those who live in a cold climate need to know the hardiness of the plants they want to grow. Some herbs, such as basil and summer savory, can experience frost damage even before the temperature reaches the freezing point of water, 32° F (0° C). These should be harvested or moved to a protected area when the temperature reaches 40° F (4° C), or before. Chervil, coriander, dill, and parsley withstand some frost. Bay, marjoram, and rosemary must be wintered indoors every year if the temperature falls below their cold hardiness.

In warmer climates, you may be able to sow annuals such as chervil or coriander two or three times a year for continuous crops, or you might grow a hedge of rosemary plants.

The chart will be useful for those who have limited space, as it is necessary to know how large the herbs will grow to allow adequate space for them. You must also take into consideration how far apart they should be planted, and whether they prefer sun or shade. The chart also indicates which herbs do best as house plants.

We have discussed each herb's culture, as well as its peculiarities, in each chapter introduction. Below are some herb gardening basics. We have divided the herbs into two categories: annuals and perennials; annuals grow, set seed, and die the same year they are sown, while perennials may live for many years. Parsley is a biennial (sets seed in its second year) but is cultivated as an annual; because we eat the first-year leaves, we need to plant seed every year to keep them coming.

ANNUALS

If you want only a few annuals, you may wish to buy plants. However, annual herbs are quite easily raised from seed, and we encourage you to give them a try. Basil, chervil, coriander, dill, parsley, and summer savory can all be sown in the same manner.

Outdoors, seed can be sown directly in the ground after all danger of frost is past. First, work up a bed with compost to enrich the soil. The soil should have a fine texture and good drainage.

Indoors, start the seed in small plastic pots or in flats. Prepare them by filling them with a mixture of half sterile potting mix and half perlite or vermiculite. Dampen this medium thoroughly before sowing seed. It should not be soaking wet. Place two or three seeds in each pot or make rows in a flat. Seeds planted in rows, rather than scattered, are less susceptible to fungus disease following germination because the air circulation is better. Cover the seeds lightly with a thin layer of dampened potting mix. Place germinating containers in a plastic bag or cover them with plastic wrap to preserve moisture.

Most seeds germinate in a warm, dark place in a week to ten days; parsley may take longer. As soon as they have sprouted, move them to the light. A twin-tube fluorescent fixture with one cool and one warm tube will speed sturdy development, but a sunny window or cold frame may substitute, as long as the temperature is not too hot or too cold. Herb seedlings grow best between 55 and 72° F (12–22° C), though continual nighttime temperatures at the lower end of this range usually mean growth is slow, particularly for warmth-loving herbs such as basil.

Water with a fine mist. The soil should be kept evenly damp and never allowed to dry out. Take care not to overwater, though, or the plants may rot at the soil level.

When the seedlings are 1 to 2 inches (2 to 5 cm) tall, fertilize them lightly. After they reach 3 to 4 inches (8 to 10 cm) in height and possess two sets of true leaves, they may be transplanted into pots for further leaf and root growth. Or, if weather and soil are warm and the plants are sturdy, they may be put in the garden. Before transplanting to the garden, annuals should be hardened off. Gradually get them used to outdoor conditions for a week before setting them in the garden when danger of frost is past.

PERENNIALS

Many gardeners find it convenient to buy perennial herb plants—for several reasons. They need only one or two plants of each variety. Some kinds, such as rosemary, are slow starters; many perennials require a year or more to grow large enough to

HERB GROWING GUIDE

COMMON NAME (Botanical Name)	Cold Hardy To Approx.	Life Cycle	Height in Feet	Light Needs	Inches Apart	House Plant
BASIL *(Ocimum basilicum)*	35° F	A	2	FS	18	■
BAY *(Laurus nobilis)*	15° F	P	40	FS		■
CHERVIL *(Anthriscus cerefolium)*	25° F	A	2	PS	9	■
CHIVES *(Allium schoenoprasum)*	−40° F	P	1½	FS	12	■
CORIANDER *(Coriandrum sativum)*	33° F	A	3	FS,PS	18	
CRESS *(Nasturtium officinale)*	−20° F	P	1	PS	6	
DILL *(Anethum graveolens)*	29° F	A	3	FS	12	
GARLIC *(Allium sativum)*	−40° F	P	2	FS	6	
LEMON BALM *(Melissa officinalis)*	−20° F	P	2	FS,PS,S	18	■
MARJORAM *(Origanum majorana)*	30° F	P	1	FS	10	
MINT *(Mentha species)*	−20° F	P	2	FS,PS	15	■
OREGANO *(Origanum vulgare)*	−20° F	P	2	FS	12	■
PARSLEY *(Petroselinum crispum)*	20° F	B	1½	FS,PS	12	■
ROSEMARY *(Rosmarinus officinalis)*	15° F	P	6	FS,PS,S	36	■
SAGE *(Salvia officinalis)*	−10° F	P	2½	FS	24	
SAVORY, SUMMER *(Satureja hortensis)*	33° F	A	1½	FS	12	
SAVORY, WINTER *(Satureja montana)*	−10° F	P	1½	FS	12	■
SORREL *(Rumex acetosa)*	−20° F	P	2	FS,PS	12	
TARRAGON *(Artemisia Dracunculus sativa)*	−20° F	P	2	FS,PS	24	
THYME *(Thymus vulgaris)*	−20° F	P	1	FS,PS	18	■

KEY: P = perennial, B = biennial, A = annual, FS = full sun, PS = part sun, S = shade provide ample harvests. Others, such as French tarragon and some lavenders, either do not produce seed or do not come true from seed; these must be propagated from divisions or cuttings (see below).

If you do decide to grow your own perennials (grow lights, cold frame, or greenhouse are useful), sow the seeds according to the directions for starting annual seeds indoors.

R O O T I N G

If you are fortunate enough to have a friend who grows herbs, you might want to try rooting some cuttings of perennial herbs, a quick and inexpensive way to obtain plants that are true to type. The best time to do this is in the spring when plants are putting forth new growth.

Choose sturdy cuttings, 4 to 5 inches (10 to 13 cm) long, and remove the leaves from the lower 2 inches (5 cm) of the stem. Fill small plastic pots with a medium made from half sterile potting mix and half perlite. Dampen the mix thoroughly. Dip the leafless part of each stem in a rooting hormone, such as Rootone, shake off the excess, and place the stem in the moist medium. Mist the cuttings.

Keep the cuttings in a warm place with filtered sun. Check them once a day to be sure the foliage and potting medium are damp. Misting is the best method to ensure the cuttings get the right amount of water. If they dry out and wither in the first two or three weeks, they will not root.

The cuttings should produce a healthy root system within six weeks. Check the stems for signs of new growth by tugging them gently; the new roots should hold them in the soil. If all danger of frost is past, you can now transplant the herbs to new pots or into the garden after first hardening them off.

COMBINING HERBS IN THE KITCHEN

■

Herbs are used with foods to accent particular flavors or to create new ones. We recognize two main flavor groups of culinary herbs, which we call "robust" and "mild"; they loosely follow the perennial and annual classifications. Mild and robust do not necessarily refer to the taste of the raw leaves. We consider herbs mild if they combine well with most other herbs, or if their flavors become milder in cooking. Examples are basil, bay, chervil, dill, marjoram, and parsley. The flavors of robust herbs stand up well to cooking, and, with the exception of garlic, they combine with just a few other herbs. Examples include garlic, rosemary, sage, sorrel, tarragon, and thyme.

Robust herbs are used together or alone for braised or roasted meat or poultry, grilled foods, and long-simmered dishes, especially soups and stews. Their flavors are subtly altered during cooking, sometimes muting, and sometimes intensifying. They can be combined judiciously with basil, marjoram, and other mild herbs.

The milder-mannered herbs can often be used in larger quantities and with more variation than robust ones can. We frequently combine several if their flavors are complementary. They appear in salads and dishes in which the leaves are used raw or cooked only briefly.

We suggest that you experiment in combining herbs that you like. When using fresh herbs, it is very difficult to ruin a dish, even if you add a little too

A mélange of mild herbs brings flavor excitement to a simple salad of spring greens.

much of this or that herb. Ideally, a combination should blend or marry on your palate. Combinations of two or three herbs provide enough flavor interest and balance for most dishes. Complex dishes, including braises, soups, and stews as well as bouquets garnis may benefit from using several herbs.

Drying an herb usually concentrates some, but not all, of its oils: some flavor elements become more intense while aromas are weaker. Subtlety and balance are not as great as they are in fresh herbs.

When replacing a fresh herb with a dried herb, the amount of dried herb is usually one-third that of the fresh. For example, a teaspoon (5 ml) of dried basil can be used for a tablespoon (15 ml) of fresh, minced leaves. Dried robust leaves should be substituted carefully. Often only a half-teaspoon (2.5 ml) of rosemary, savory, or thyme will be needed in place of a tablespoon (15 ml) of the fresh minced herb.

It is best to add dried herbs in small amounts, and to crumble them just before adding to better release their flavor. If the dried herbs have not been sitting on the shelf for a year, their taste is strong.

Usually a teaspoon (5 ml) is enough to flavor most dishes. Add a small amount, simmer, taste, and adjust accordingly.

Garlic, parsley, sorrel, and watercress should not be dried, as their flavors alter radically. The dried forms of these herbs taste little like the fresh and may even be unpalatable or tasteless. Delicate herbs such as chervil, chives, coriander, and dill tend to lose most of their flavor when dried. Many of the recipes in this book indicate the amount of dried herb when it can be substituted for the fresh. If no substitution is suggested, the flavor of the recipe depends on the fresh herbs. Freezing also weakens the flavor of most herbs, but if the herbs have been frozen only a month or so, use them as you would fresh.

Our suggestions for herb combinations in the chart on pages 34–35 should be used with your culinary preparation in mind. For example, thyme and rosemary go well together in meat dishes, but rosemary would overpower a delicate soup such as Carrot Soup with Thyme (page 321).

ENJOYING HERBS IN SALADS

■

When you pick the tender lettuce you've coddled to perfection, and you wash and dry it with care, then toss it with a bit of good olive oil and sprinkle it with fine wine vinegar, you have what is fairly called a salad. This salad has the essential elements—freshness, earthiness, sweetness, and tartness—that bring you to appreciate how simple food can be elegant and satisfying.

Freshness is the most important quality in a salad, and the hardest to find unless you grow your own vegetables. Commercial lettuce has barely a shadow of the flavor of garden lettuce. Herbs renew some of this flavor, as restaurateurs who grow chervil, basil, and rocket hydroponically in their basements know quite well. A few sprigs of Italian parsley or dill improve even market lettuce. The ready-to-eat lettuce mixes sold under such names as Spring Salad Mix or Organic Garden Mix usually contain several herbs.

If a salad is eaten before the meal, herbs add pleasant flavors that stimulate the palate. If, instead,

a salad is served after the main course, as the Italians do, herbs help to cleanse and refresh the palate.

When we yearn for the variety and freshness of salad greens that we ate in Europe, we begin to plot our salad garden. One of the best lettuces we know, especially for herb salads, is mâche. It has a fine sweetness and some delicacy, so that it is best with the milder herbs. In English, it is known as corn salad or lamb's lettuce.

Some sweet varieties we like for their compatibility with herbs are red leaf and oak leaf. We grow these every season, along with other loose-leaved lettuces such as 'Black-Seeded Simpson' and 'Salad Bowl'. We prefer these to head lettuces because they provide salad greens until the very hottest part of summer. Tender outer leaves are harvested periodically from each plant, or the entire plant can be cut back to about 2 inches (5 cm) from the soil. In either case, new growth is continuous until the plants send up flower stalks. The more leaves you cut, the more salads you will enjoy. Regular cutting also slows the production of flower stalks and inhibits bitterness from developing in the leaves.

Chicory, curly endive, radicchio, young spinach, and rocket are other salad greens we would not be without. Rocket (also known as arugula, ruchetta, roquette, and rucola) is sometimes classified as an herb. These greens add to the flavor range of a salad: peppery rocket, pleasantly bitter curly endive and the chicories, earthy radicchio and spinach.

Winter is the time to pore over seed catalogs while you decide which salads to eat this year. We order from suppliers that import European seeds to get the plants we are fond of and to try new varieties as well. Some seed mixes, notably the French *mesclun* and the Italian *misticanza,* have a variety of the lettuces, herbs, and chicories mentioned above.

Of the herbs we consider most important for salads—basil, chervil, chives, coriander, cress, dill, Italian parsley, salad burnet, and sorrel—we grow all but watercress. We do allow room for garden cress and even grow it indoors occasionally. A few leaves of lovage, lemon balm, mint, and purslane add an unusual spark to our salads sometimes.

All herb flowers are edible, with the same taste, but more perfume, as the herbs from which they come. We especially like using some of the perennial flowers: chives, thyme, marjoram, mint,

oregano, sage, and rosemary. The annual flowers can be bitter, but we find basil, chervil, coriander, and dill blossoms very tasty and pretty.

Sometimes, particularly for festive occasions, we enjoy making rather extravagant herb salads modeled after those of the Renaissance. We use mild greens to allow the herbs to be fully savored. Handfuls of lettuce and smaller handfuls of Italian parsley, dill or fennel leaves, basil, chervil and sorrel, with some sprigs of tarragon, marjoram, chives, cress, or lovage compose a glorious salad. We dress the whole lightly with flavorful olive oil and lemon juice or wine vinegar, then sprinkle it with nasturtiums, violas, and borage blossoms, or perhaps lavender, sage, or rosemary flowers. We have found that such a fanciful salad gives us and our guests a sensual appreciation of fresh green things. Experimenting with the amounts of greens and herbs will lead you to the combinations and balance you prefer.

Just gathering the salad ingredients from the garden can be a modest but genuine aesthetic experience. Choosing the right lettuce and spinach, picking a few peppery leaves of rocket and garden cress, snipping the tips of the new green dill and parsley,

Bundles of herbs picked at their peak of flavor and dried just until crisp will transform simple food all winter long.

PRESERVING HERBAL BOUNTY

◼

Like most other garden produce, herbs are at their best when they are fresh and in season. Herbs reach the height of their flavor in summer, but we yearn for them in the winter, too, when we live in a cold climate. We long for the taste of garden-fresh pesto or fresh tarragon for sauces and vinaigrettes. To prepare for these cravings, we store summer's bounty in our freezers and pantries. We enjoy the time spent preserving our herbs, knowing that we will be glad to have their flavor throughout the year.

and then deciding which blossoms to use for garnish is like preparing a palette for a painting. The salad forms in your mind and hands as it will appear on your table: a feast for the eyes and a relish for the tongue.

HARVESTING

Although we have harvested herbs before, during, and after bloom with satisfactory results, we try to make one harvest before many buds have formed for maximum flavor in the leaves. Most plants can be harvested more than once a season. If you live in a climate with winter freezes, prune perennials about a month before the first frost is expected. Harvesting later will usually weaken the plants' resistance to cold. The last harvest of annuals can be simply pulling up the entire plants.

It is best to choose a sunny morning, after the dew has evaporated, to pick the herbs; their oils are strongest then, and they are less likely to mold. Cut perennials back to about one-third of their height. Herbs benefit from pruning by half or a third several times a season, depending on their growth. Such pruning opens the plants to light and air, encourages growth, and reduces the chance of disease. If you don't want to preserve the harvest, simply save the cuttings as kindling to start the grill, or compost them. For everyday use or small harvests, snip as many tips as you want.

The tips of annuals can also be snipped freely for fresh use. For harvests, and to encourage new leaf growth, cut annuals above the bottom two or three sets of leaves. They can be cut as low as the bottom set of leaves, and will still put out new growth. Do not leave any cut herbs out in the sun; take them into the shade for sorting and tying into bunches.

Remove the brown bottom leaves and any spotted or bug-eaten ones. If the herbs are dirty, brush off the dirt. If you must wash them, rinse quickly and pat them dry.

DRYING

To dry herbs by hanging, tie the stalks into small bundles with string or twine and hang them in a dry, well-ventilated place such as an attic or shed. To dry herbs on screens, pick off the large leaves and lay them on the screens. Leave small leaves of thyme or savory on their stems and spread these on the screens.

If you are drying herbs such as coriander or dill for seed, hang the stalks to dry as directed above, but place a screen underneath to catch any seed that drops. Alternatively, you can hang each bundle in a paper bag with a few air holes cut in the sides.

Herbs may take from a few days to a week or more to dry, depending on the climate and humidity. Check them daily—if left too long, especially in humid weather, they will lose their green color and turn brown. A dried leaf should crackle and crumble when rubbed between your fingers. If it just bends and is not crisp, it has not dried sufficiently and will mold in storage. To remove excess moisture, spread the herbs on baking sheets and place them in a very low oven, not over 200° F (93° C), for three to five minutes.

When the herbs are dried, strip them from their stems and pack them in clean jars with tight-fitting lids. Do not crumble the leaves but pack them whole to retain the finest flavor. Label the jars and store them away from heat and light. Home-dried herbs can be stored in jars or tins for as long as one year, when next season's crop will take their place.

FREEZING

After experimenting for several years, we have come to the conclusion that freezing most herbs does not yield good enough flavor for the effort. The fluids in tender-leaved herbs form ice crystals that make the herbs limp and flavorless after a month or two in the freezer. Sturdy-leaved herbs, such as rosemary and sage, have better flavor when dried. Some herbs are better preserved in vinegar or oil; see "Concentrating Herbal Flavor" for further discussion.

However, if you want to extend the season by a short time or you have an abundance you just can't bear to throw away, we have found that the procedures below give the best freezer results.

Harvest and clean the herbs as outlined above. The simplest method, and the best flavor, come from freezing whole leaves. Remove the leaves from the stems and pack them in pint freezer bags or airtight freezer containers. Label the containers, as the herbs look alike in the freezer. To pack the herbs in larger containers, first freeze the whole leaves individually on baking sheets, then transfer them to the containers. Remove the leaves as you need them. The bright green color of the fresh leaves will turn dark when they are frozen.

Some herbs—basil, dill, coriander, parsley—freeze fairly well when chopped and packed in a little oil. This method is handy when you know how you will be using the herbs: for example, basil and parsley chopped together with oil for salsa verde or pesto. Small amounts of herbs such as marjoram and oregano can be added to these blends when you plan to use them in cooked dishes. Oil-frozen herbs are best tightly-packed in 1/2-cup to cup-sized (118-ml to 237-ml) containers.

CONCENTRATING HERBAL FLAVOR

■

Perhaps nothing, other than shiny little vials of exotic spices, gives such a sense of imminent kitchen alchemy as an array of fresh herbs floating in a fine white wine vinegar. Picking sprigs of different herbs when the plants are at their aromatic peak and putting them into vinegar for a month or so are all that you have to do to evoke this agreeable feeling. Making herbal infusions is pleasurable for the herb gardener as well as being a simple way to concentrate herb flavor and store it for the year. Bottles of opal basil vinegar shining rosy lavender, and tarragon vinegar gleaming pale golden green in the sunlit garden are two of our summer traditions. They en-

The secret of intensly flavored herbal vinegars is using plenty of plant material in your infusions.

hance salads and sauces all through the winter.

Each year, we experiment with different herbs for making vinegars and oils; often a combination of two herbs offers a pleasant surprise to our palates. Our herbal oils are precious to us; we use them for special dishes and give them to appreciative friends. The rewards are worth the small effort it takes to make them.

HERBAL OILS

The best herbs for flavoring culinary oils are basil, bay, lavender, marjoram, oregano, rosemary, and thyme. Pure, mild-flavored olive oil, such as Bertolli or Sasso, absorbs the herbs' flavor best, though extra-virgin olive oil and vegetable oil can also be used.

Cut the herbs of your choice in the morning of a sunny day, bring them inside, and clean them. If you wash them, be sure that the leaves are completely dry before proceeding. Bruise the herb sprigs, then fill clean quart jars with them. Completely cover them with oil and seal the jars. Place the jars in a cool, dark place for two to three weeks.

After two to three weeks, remove the infused herb sprigs from the jars by straining the oil through cheesecloth. Pour the oil into smaller bottles or jars, adding one small fresh sprig or leaf if you like, label, and store in a cool place. A strong, clear herbal flavor is evident for about six months, though the oils may be used for a year.

HERBAL VINEGARS

Some of the herbs that we like for vinegars are basil, especially the purple varieties; chive with chive blossoms; dill; lavender; lovage; marigold; mint; tarragon; and savory.

A good white wine vinegar makes the best herb vinegars. We find red wine vinegar too strong and distilled vinegar too harsh for most herbs. Some people, however, like the robust herbs, such as oregano, with red wine vinegar; experiment if this appeals to you. If you must use distilled vinegar, we recommend that you buy a brand such as Heinz and add one part of distilled water to every three parts of vinegar.

Cut your herbs on a sunny morning, clean the sprigs if necessary, and pat them dry. Fill clean jars full of the herbs you have chosen and cover them with vinegar. Set the jars where they will receive a minimum of four hours of full sun a day; infuse the herbs and vinegar for three to four weeks.

To prepare the vinegars for storage, remove the herbs by straining the vinegar. Pour the vinegar into smaller bottles, adding a fresh sprig of the herb if desired, and label. Store the vinegars in a cool, dark place and use them within a year.

BASIL LEAVES PACKED IN OIL

We learned this method for preserving basil in Italy. The flavor is remarkably close to that of fresh basil, and it can be used in any recipe that calls for the fresh herb. This is the best method we know of preserving basil for pesto. The cheese and garlic can be added fresh to oil-preserved basil, thereby avoiding the off-flavors that characterize frozen pesto.

Though we have been packing basil in oil for fifteen years, we have recently come across reports of botulism in oil-packed herbs. Botulism is an anaerobic bacterium that requires an air-free environment in which to live. If you are concerned about botulism, do not use this method, or contact your county or state health department to see if there has been any botulism poisoning in your area.

In humid parts of the country, we have encountered mold on the top layer of basil leaves. We remove the top layer and use what we need; sometimes the mold will grow again, but we have never found off-flavors or -odors.

Cut the basil on a sunny morning before buds form. Brush the leaves free of dirt. Rinse only if absolutely necessary and pat dry. If the leaves aren't completely dry, they will mold and spoil the oil. Remove the leaves from the stems.

Add enough olive oil to cover the bottom of a half-pint (273-ml) canning jar. Place six or eight basil leaves in the jar and press them down lightly with a wooden spoon. Add a little more oil and another layer of leaves. Repeat this process until the jar is filled. It is surprising how much herb will be needed when packing the leaves in this manner. Place the lid on the jar and keep it in the refrigerator for up to one year. Once refrigerated, the leaves may turn a bit darker and the oil will coagulate. Use the leaves as you need them, whole or chopped; the oil can be used as well.

USING THE RECIPES

■

The recipes in this book have been carefully tested to give results that we are proud to put our names to; many of the dishes are part of our everyday cooking and we have made them countless times. Some recipes have special techniques that need to be followed carefully. Homemade egg pasta is one of these: it is not difficult to make, but reading the explanations as to why and when to follow certain procedures will give you a deeper understanding of pasta. When we provide detailed instructions, developed through the years for our classes and publications, it is to further understanding and confidence for the novice and experienced cook.

We compare recipes to blueprints and encourage readers to tailor the recipes to their styles. This happens naturally in any case. Even when two cooks are in the same kitchen, making a dish with the same recipe and ingredients, the dishes will not taste the same. For us, this variability is one of the great and interesting things about cooking.

The topics that follow cover our standard practices in this book. When specific techniques, ingredients, or tools are important to a recipe, they will be mentioned in that recipe.

HERBS

A little more or less of a fresh herb will not make a difference to a dish in most cases. You will quickly discover how much of an herb you and your family like. Pickling usually intensifies herb flavor. Cooking may mute flavor or intensify it. Consult "The Culinary Herbs", pages 34–35, for reference to particular herbs.

SIZE OF HERB SPRIGS: When a recipe calls for sprigs, it always means the fresh herbs. Leaves are removed from the sprigs unless the recipe directs otherwise. Annual sprigs (basil, summer savory, etc.) and parsley are from 8 to 12 inches (20 to 30 cm) long. Most perennial sprigs (rosemary, sage, winter savory, etc.) are from 3 to 4 inches (8 to 10 cm) long. Lemon balm sprigs and chive and garlic chive leaves are from 6 to 12 inches (15 to 30 cm) long. The size of the sprig will depend on the growth stage and variety of the plant. Any herb may need to be cut longer or shorter. If, for example, a thyme has sparsely set leaves, you will want to cut sprigs about

Heads of fresh, plump garlic cloves figure importantly in the authors' repertoire of herb-laden dishes.

6 inches (15 cm) long. If the leaves are thickly set and plump, cut 3- to 4-inch (8- to 10-cm) sprigs. Because peppermints taste strong, making small sprigs is advisable, while spearmints can be used with a freer hand and cut in longer sprigs.

Sorrel leaves should have the stems and ribs removed, unless they are small and tender. Large sage leaves should also have the stems and ribs removed. An easy way to do this is to fold the herb leaf in half lengthwise, following the natural bend of the leaf. Hold the leaf in one hand and the stem in the other and pull the stem toward the leaf tip. Or run a small sharp knife between the leaf and the stem, again toward the leaf tip.

Garlic cloves in this book are good-sized healthy ones, about 1½ inches (4 cm) long, and 3/4 inch (2 cm) in diameter. If you have smaller ones, use more, or adjust the amount of garlic to your taste.

DAIRY PRODUCTS: Use any low-fat version of cream cheese, sour cream, and yogurt you prefer. We have not made the recipes with margarine or butter substitutes but see no reason why these would not work. As we have included no recipes, such as puff pastry, that depend on butter's fat and water content, the difference will be in flavor. In cream soups, milk or low-fat milk can be used for whipping cream (double cream) and/or half-and-half (single cream). We do not know any low-fat version of crème fraîche.

OILS: We prefer the taste of olive oil with most herbs; still, any oil you like may be used for sautéing and sauces. For deep-frying, use a pure vegetable oil with no preservatives, or peanut oil. Olive oils have several designations. "Extra-virgin", "virgin", and "pure" are labels controlled by the Italian and French governments, so if you buy these, you may be reasonably sure of getting a reliable product. A rich green color and a full, fruity flavor characterize extra-virgin, and frequently virgin, olive oil. Naturally, these are more expensive, sometimes as much as $50 a litre. We have had good luck with Greek and Spanish extra-virgin olive oils, which are much less expensive. Because the flavors of extra-virgin and virgin olive oils change during heating, we reserve these mostly for salad dressings and uncooked sauces. "Pure" olive oil is golden and lightly flavored. It is stable at sautéing temperatures and is the oil we have used for most cooking in this book. We have not tried the recently available "light" olive oils. We assume "light" refers to flavor, since any pure oil, olive or otherwise, has the same number of calories.

CHEESES: The parmesan cheese used here is parmigiano reggiano, the finest quality imported from Italy. Its price is an expense we are willing to bear, as the flavor is incomparable. It keeps well in blocks or wedges and should be grated just before use. Another, less expensive, parmesan from Italy is called grana or grana padana, and is widely available. American and Argentine parmesans are waxy and gummy and will ruin sauces. Asiagos and romanos from Italy can be used in place of parmesan, but taste them before buying; sometimes they are quite sharp, even biting, without the sweet nuttiness of parmesan.

BREAD AND BREAD CRUMBS: We have used European-style country bread and crumbs for sauces, croutons, and sandwiches. This kind of bread is made of flour, salt, yeast or natural leavening, and water only, with no fat and no additives. It is slow-risen and often hearth-baked. Most American breads become pasty when used to thicken sauces, cooked or uncooked. If country bread is not available in your area, try using a bread with the fewest additives possible, and drying it in an oven at 200° F (93° C) until it is crisp but not colored. Then proceed with the recipe.

VINEGARS AND LEMON JUICE: White wine vinegar and lemon juice go well with all herbs. Certainly you can use any vinegar you like, including distilled, apple cider, red wine, balsamic, sherry, and rice. Bear in mind that distilled vinegar is strong and rice vinegar is mild if you substitute these. Sometimes the fullness of red wine vinegar, the sweetness of balsamic, or the nuttiness of sherry is particularly appropriate. As with olive oil, the more you spend on a vinegar, the higher quality you usually get.

HONEY: Use light-colored, mild-flavored honeys such as clover, sage, fruit, or berry blossom.

SALT AND PEPPER: We have left the seasoning up to the cook because palates vary so much. Specific amounts of salt are called for in legume dishes, which taste insipid without some salt, and in breads, in which salt plays a part in leavening. Most people find that dishes flavored with herbs need less salt. We use kosher or sea salt, with no additives, for pickling and preserves, as they do not cause clouding. Freshly ground pepper is almost as good a cook's helper as fresh herbs. Black and white pepper can be used interchangeably as you prefer; when white pepper is called for, it is mostly for the appearance of the dish.

TOMATOES: Tomatoes are a seasonal

crop and used that way in this book. When canned tomatoes can be substituted, it is indicated in the recipe. Two pounds (908 g) of fresh tomatoes equals a 28-ounce (800-g) can of tomatoes, or 1 quart (1 litre) of home-canned tomatoes. Canned plum tomatoes, whether imported or domestic, can be very acidic. We have found consistently sweet canned tomatoes in the S&W brand.

TOASTING HERBS AND SPICES: Dry-toasting dried herbs and spices brings out their flavor, especially for complex and long-simmered dishes and baked goods. Place the herb or spice in a small, heavy-bottomed frying pan or saucepan over low heat. Toast just until the aroma is released, usually 2 or 3 minutes. Take care not to overtoast the spice or herb, or it will taste burned. Remove the herb or spice to a plate to cool, then crumble or grind.

NONCORRODIBLE PANS: The acids in many foods react with some metals, causing discoloration and/or off-flavors. Aluminum and cast iron pans are corrodible; in other words, they will react with acids. Most aluminum-alloy pans, and all stainless steel, glass, porcelain-enameled iron, and tin-lined copper pans are noncorrodible.

A CULINARY HERB GARDEN

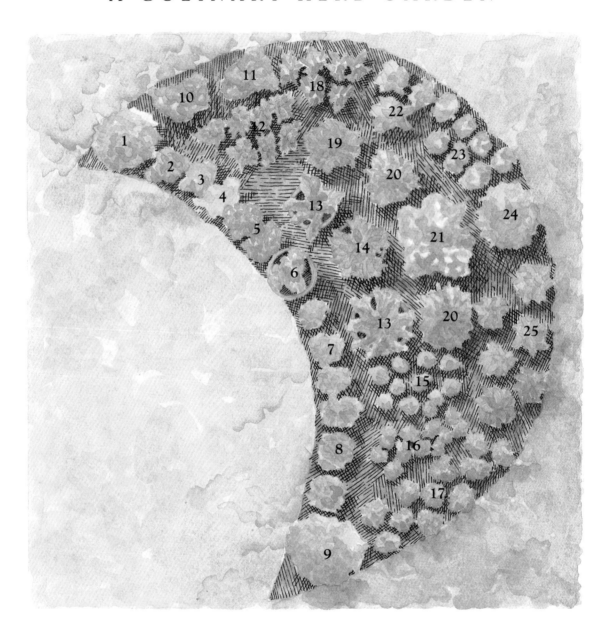

The beauty of planning an herb garden is that you can tailor it to your space and your style. Beginning gardeners are sometimes intimidated by plans, but there is no need to be. We suggest first deciding if you are a gardener who likes the fun of planning and the symmetry of the finished plot. Some prefer a loose garden arrangement throughout, whether they are growing flowering perennials or herbs for the kitchen.

Certainly it is convenient to have culinary herbs together, and close to the kitchen if possible. Just seeing them in close proximity, and sniffing sage, for example, while you are cutting parsley for a particular dish, can suggest new possibilities for their use. Both of us, however, started by simply sowing some annuals next to the vegetable and cut-flower plots. This is an easy way to begin if you don't have the time to work up a plan.

Herb gardens, for most of their long history, were planted for medicinal as well as culinary use. There are a great many traditions for their design in many cultures, and many people today like to incorporate these in their gardens. A variety of excellent suggestions for and approaches to planning can be found in *The Herb Book, Park's Success with Herbs, The Complete Book of Herbs and Spices,* and *Herb Gardening in Five Seasons,* listed in the bibliography.

We like this crescent-shaped plan for its slight asymmetry and because it is not traditional. There are many other plans to be found for square, rectangular, and round gardens. The design here can be adapted to other patterns—triangular, sinuous, or cross-shaped—just remember to allow plenty of space between plants since herbs spread rapidly.

The taller herb plants run along the back side of the crescent curve, while low-growing border-type plants are in the front of the crescent, and the medium-sized herbs are in the middle. We've placed annuals at one end of the crescent and perennials at the other end. This avoids disturbing perennial roots when you replant annuals every spring.

Tender perennials are left in pots and grouped in the center of the garden. Bay, marjoram, and most rosemaries are considered tender perennials and will not survive through cold winters. If you live in a warm climate, these plants can be planted directly in the ground. Bay trees can grow to thirty feet in favorable climates, and rosemary can likewise become a thick, wide hedge. Check your local growing conditions before permanently placing these plants.

The mints are kept separate from one another so that they do not cross-pollinate. Garlic and watercress are not included here. Garlic could be planted along the back side of the curve, but we feel it is better placed in the vegetable garden since its leaves fall to the ground and die as the plants mature.

Watercress needs constantly running water to grow, a requirement beyond the scope of most gardens. For more detailed growing information on individual herbs, read the chapter introductions. For general cultivation information, refer to pages 12–16.

LEGEND
1. PEPPERMINT
2. ENGLISH THYME
3. FRENCH THYME
4. LEMON THYME
5. WINTER SAVORY
6. MARJORAM
7. CURLY PARSLEY
8. FLAT-LEAF PARSLEY
9. ORANGE MINT
10. GREEK OREGANO
11. ITALIAN OREGANO
12. COMMON CHIVES
13. ROSEMARY
14. BAY
15. CHERVIL
16. SUMMER SAVORY
17. CORIANDER
18. GARLIC CHIVES
19. TARRAGON
20. SAGE
21. LEMON BALM
22. SORREL
23. DILL
24. SPEARMINT
25. BASIL

THE CULINARY HERBS

HERB	DESCRIPTION OF FLAVOR	DESCRIPTION OF AROMA
BASIL	robust, intense, spicy when fresh; sweet and mild cooked; cultivars vary in taste	base of sweet grasses, clove, orange, mint, and hyacinth; cultivars vary in fragrance
BAY	sharp and slightly peppery, slightly bitter	blend of balsam and honey with hint of rose, clove, orange, and mint; sweet and strong
CHERVIL	delicate mixture compounded of parsley and mild anise with undertones of pear	very delicate; slightly green grassy with hint of anise
CHIVES	versatile, onion-like with hint of garlic	slightly garlicky; green tasting; flowers are sweet and oniony
CORIANDER	grassy, a bit oily; a bittersweet aftertaste; faintly citron-like; becomes muted when cooked	distinctive and pungent elements of wet grass, forest humus, and wild mushrooms; becomes deeper and expansive when cooked
CRESS	peppery green taste; hot to the tongue; cooked has an herby vegetable taste with overtones of spinach, parsley, and mustard greens	very slight aroma; like salad greens
DILL	green tasting with camphor, anise, parsley, and celery	combination of mint, citrus, and fennel with touch of sea air
GARLIC	robust, pungent, spicy, strong; cooked becomes milder and sweeter	mild in the bulb, strong peeled and cut; nose-tingling
LEMON BALM	sweet citrus; mild when cooked; subtle, sweet grassy with a hint of lemon	very aromatic; tart lemon and sweet honey
MARJORAM	sweet, green, and herby with a hint of mint; slightly bitter resinous flavor; cooked subtle and sweet	sweet broom and mint; slightly spicy
MINTS	peppery to sweet, cultivars vary; can be mild menthol to hot and spicy	cultivars vary in fragrance; sweet and slightly menthol to strong and balsamic
OREGANO	spicy, slightly peppery with a hint of mint, pine, and clove; cooked becomes milder and less spicy	spicy with hints of clove and balsam
PARSLEY	most versatile fresh green taste; faint peppery tang, green apple aftertaste; mild yet piquant	clean green aroma
ROSEMARY	strong components of tannin and camphor; moderate bitterness and pepperiness	highly aromatic; refreshing fragrance of sea coast, pines, fir, and balsam
SAGE	pungent, lemon rind tones over resin, then camphor with pleasant muskiness, similar to silage; cultivars vary in taste	strong muskiness, camphor-like with hints of lemon
SORREL	tart, lemony, sour, leafy green aftertaste	not much aroma, salad-like with hint of citrus; slightly sour
SUMMER SAVORY	mild, sweet and spicy; rather like marjoram and thyme together	sweet grass scent with touch of marjoram-like perfume
WINTER SAVORY	peppery, hot, and resinous; spicier than summer savory	strong grassy smell with hint of thyme; slightly resinous
TARRAGON	piquant, anise-like, peppery; heat brings out pungency; cooked dishes need less	freshly cut hay, mint, and licorice
THYME	sweet, spicy, subtle taste compounded of mint, bay, and marjoram; cultivars vary in taste	fragrance varies with cultivars; sweet and pungent, earthy; almost plummy

COMBINES BEST WITH THESE HERBS	USE FRESH WITH	USE IN COOKED DISHES
bay, chives, cress, dill, garlic, marjoram, mint, parsley, oregano	salads, cheeses, tomatoes, pastas, vegetables, vinegars, oils	marinades, sauces, meat; cooked briefly— soups, vegetables, eggs, seafood, pastas
compatible with all	bouquets garnis, marinades	meat, fish, fowl, stuffings, breads, puddings, soups, stews
chives, cress, dill, lemon balm, parsley, sorrel, tarragon	salads, eggs, avocados, vegetables, melons, cheeses	cook only briefly—fish, oysters, poultry, eggs, sauces, vegetables
bay, chervil, coriander, cress, dill, lemon balm, marjoram, oregano, parsley, sorrel, tarragon, thyme	salads, cheeses, eggs, vegetables, butters, mayonnaise, vinegars, sour cream	needs little cooking—sauces, soups, stews, eggs, vegetables, potatoes, seafood
chives, garlic, marjoram, oregano, parsley; often used alone	salads, sauces, salsas, cheeses, escabeches	fish, shellfish, curries, fowl, pork, lamb, sauces, soups, beans, stir fries, Mexican dishes
chervil, chives, dill, garlic, parsley, sorrel, tarragon	best raw in salads; with vegetables, grains, pastas	cook briefly—soups, sauces, fish, chicken, pasta, grains, potatoes
basil, bay, chervil, chives, cress, garlic, mint, parsley, sorrel, tarragon	best raw in salads; with vegetables, pastas, grains, seafood, eggs, slaws, sour cream, cheeses	cook briefly—soups, sauces, vegetables, fish, potatoes, baked goods, pickles
compatible with all; but use sparingly with chervil, chives, lemon balm, mint	rubbed on bread, in salads, sauces, marinades; with pastas, grains, seafoods, cheeses	goes well with every type of food except desserts and sweets
chervil, chives, mint, parsley; use sparingly with garlic	salads, fruits, macerated fruits, beverages, butters, sorbets	vegetables, grains, fish, chicken, desserts, tea
basil, bay, chives, coriander, garlic, oregano, mint, parsley, rosemary, sage, summer savory, tarragon, thyme, winter savory	salads, eggs, rice, pastas, cheeses, vegetables	sauces, soups, stews, pasta, meat, fish, poultry, vegetables, cheeses
basil, cress, dill, lemon balm, parsley, tarragon	beverages, salads, vegetables, desserts, ices, ice creams, fruits	tea, sauces, jellies, preserves, baked goods, meat, soups, vegetables, fish
basil, bay, chives, coriander, garlic, marjoram, mint, parsley, sage, summer savory, tarragon, thyme, winter savory	salsas, pastas, cheeses, tomatoes, vegetables	sauces, soups, stews, pasta, meat, beans, vegetables, cheeses
compatible with all	salads, dressings, bouquets garnis, sauces, cheeses, pastas, vegetables	soups, stews, vegetables, poultry, fish, meat, pasta, grains; everything but desserts
bay, garlic, marjoram, oregano, parsley, sage, summer savory, thyme, winter savory	cheeses, breads, marinades, beverages, vegetables, oils	roast meats, game, poultry, fish, soups, stews, potatoes, legumes, bread
bay, garlic, marjoram, oregano, parsley, rosemary, summer savory, thyme, winter savory	cheeses, marinades	tea, soups, stews, meat, poultry, breads, vegetables, beans, apples
basil, chives, dill, garlic, parsley, tarragon	best raw in salads; mayonnaise, grains, legumes	lightly cooked soups, sauces, eggs, vegetables, shellfish, fish, poultry
basil, bay, garlic, marjoram, oregano, parsley, rosemary, sage, tarragon, thyme	beans, tomatoes, bouquet garnis, salads, vegetables, cheeses	vegetables, soups, beans, corn, eggs, potatoes
basil, bay, garlic, marjoram, oregano, parsley, rosemary, sage, tarragon, thyme	beans, bouquet garnis, marinades	soups, stews, meats, poultry, beans, vegetables
bay, chervil, chives, cress, dill, garlic, mint, sorrel, summer savory, thyme, winter savory	salads, dressings, eggs, vegetables, seafood	sauces, fish, eggs, chicken, meats, soups, vegetables, vinegars, pickles
basil, bay, chives, garlic, marjoram, oregano, parsley, rosemary, sage, summer savory, tarragon, winter savory	grains, vegetables, bouquet garnis, salads, cheeses	soups, sauces, stews, meat, poultry, fish, shellfish, vegetables, mushrooms, breads, marinades

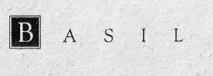 BASIL

BASIL *is summer's prince,*

with jeweled leaves and sweetest scent.

■ Richly fragrant and handsome, basil inherits its name from the Greek word for king. Its aroma is as complex as a perfume, with a base of sweet grasses that grow by meadow streams, clove, orange, mint, and hyacinth. Of the sixty-odd varieties, most are cultivated for use in perfumes. Basil's scent probably inspired the stories of romantic and sensual love in European herb lore. The villagers of Crete, southern Italy, and Spain used to give pots of it to newly-weds and placed its sprigs around the doors and windows of their houses. On a more homely note, basil was given as a house gift in Renaissance England to keep flies away.

Cooking with fresh basil has been recognized as a special treat for hundreds of years. Its cultivation as a potherb was noted in tenth-century France, where it is still called *l'herbe royale*. Recipes old and new call for the flavorful leaves with all varieties of meats including game, in soups, with cooked vegetables and salads, in egg dishes, with fresh cheeses or seafood, and for flavoring vinegars and oils.

Italians seldom eat tomatoes, cooked or raw, without basil; there, field or greenhouse basil is available throughout the year. It is now available year-round in the coastal regions of the United States, too. Our first dish of summer pesto in Italy so captivated us that basil remains one of our favorite herbs. Every summer, we have to restrain ourselves from adding it to everything. This abandoned use can have intriguing results: try substituting it for dill with

THERE ARE

MORE THAN SIXTY

VARIETIES OF BASIL.

cucumbers or fish or using it in place of lettuce on cheese sandwiches. Lavish basil over vegetables and green salads and add it to marinades and sauces.

To retain the aroma and flavor of the fresh herb, cook it only briefly, or cut it in fine shreds and add as a garnish to dishes that require long cooking. A simple butter with lots of minced basil is excellent with all fresh vegetables and seafood, especially lobster and salmon.

Growing basil is relatively simple. The main culinary varieties have a range of aromas and uses. Bush basil (*Ocimum basilicum* 'Minimum') is a fine small variety that can be grown in pots. Of the sweet basils (*O. basilicum*), we like Genoa Green for its especially clean and strong perfume and flavor; it is an easy plant in the garden. Lettuce-leaf basil has a less intense flavor than sweet basil but is still very aromatic. Purple, or Dark Opal, basil (*O. b.* 'Purpurascens') has a more pungent perfume and is slightly more bitter than the others; it is the best for vinegar.

BASIL'S RANGE IN AROMA AND FLAVOR IS QUITE REMARKABLE . . .

Many new cultivars have been introduced for sale in the United States in recent years. The range in aroma and flavor is quite remarkable and delicious: from lemon and cinnamon to anise and spicy Thai basil. As these names suggest, their perfumes are striking, and this characteristic is most prevalent when the herb is used fresh rather than cooked. Choosing among these and other cultivars such as

Spicy Globe (a kind of bush basil), Piccolo (an intermediate form of sweet basil), and Purple Ruffles (a cross between lettuce-leaf and Dark Opal basil), appeal to both the cook and gardener in us. When we see a cultivar new to us, we rub the leaves and sniff to discover if the perfume appeals. Frequently, we order seed that we have not planted before and sow it for a basil surprise.

Basil may be sown directly in the ground after the danger of frost is past. The soil must be warm, rich, and well drained. Basil also is easily transplanted and may be started indoors in cold climates. Transplant 12 to 24 inches apart, depending on the variety. Ample water, sunshine, and light fertilization once a month cause basil to flourish outside, whether in the ground or in pots. For us, basil has not been a successful indoor herb, a languid grower with poor leaf production, and prone to whitefly infestation. Some growers get good results by placing indoor basil well, where it has some fresh air and plenty of light, for example, in a greenhouse window, or similar situation. Pinch back the growing points so that flowers do not develop, unless you plan to eat them. Though the flowers do make a tasty and attractive garnish, the leaves tend to turn bitter after the plants flower. Cutting the plants when they are 12 inches (30 cm) or more tall, just above the lowest set of leaves, stimulates new leaf growth and provides a plentiful harvest as well.

Continual harvesting and maintenance of your established plants is one way of ensuring a supply of basil throughout the growing season. If your growing space is limited, consider buying some during the season to preserve for use during the winter. In the market, look for shiny deep green leaves with no dark spots, full bushy growth, and pronounced aroma.

To keep fresh bunches of basil for more than a day, do not rinse the leaves, as water tends to turn them dark. Put the stems in a glass or jar of water and keep it out of sunlight. The magic of sniffing a freshly cut bouquet of basil from your own garden or balcony is one of the small enchantments which seduces herb growers.

Although summer ends, basil devotees need not despair. There are several good ways to preserve the herb. Mincing two parts basil with one part parsley leaves and freezing them in convenient amounts—1 tablespoon (15 ml) to 1/2 cup (240 ml)—gives moderate flavor and color for a variety of uses. A little olive oil may be stirred in; this is especially good if the mixture will be used for pesto. Whole leaves may be laid on a baking sheet, frozen, and then packed in convenient-sized containers. Although basil loses much of its characteristic aroma when dried, it is a pleasant and useful herb in that form. To dry, hang bunches upside down in a warm place away from direct sunlight until the leaves are dry and crackly.

THERE ARE SEVERAL GOOD WAYS TO PRESERVE BASIL.

Our favorite way to preserve basil is to layer whole leaves with olive oil. The procedure for this method is discussed on page 26. The basil may darken a little, but the flavor is very close to fresh.

TOMATOES WITH MOZZARELLA AND BASIL

■

THIS SUMMER APPETIZER is one of the best we know: on a hot day, the refreshment of cool, flavorful tomatoes, soft, mild cheese, and spicy basil is palpable. The best-tasting tomatoes and the finest fruity extra-virgin olive oil are essential here. Mozzarella di bufala, made from buffalo milk, is the cheese of choice in Italy. If you can't find it, try locally produced fresh mozzarella or an imported Italian fontina. If neither is available, use a domestic whole-milk mozzarella that you have sliced and soaked in milk for a few hours or overnight. The soaking improves the texture and flavor of American-style mozzarella.

SERVES 6 TO 8

4 large firm-ripe tomatoes

1 small sweet onion such as Maui, Walla Walla, or Vidalia

1/3 cup (80 ml) olive oil

Salt and freshly ground pepper to taste

1/2 cup (120 ml) packed fresh basil leaves

1/2 pound (225 g) mozzarella di bufala or Italian fontina, or whole-milk mozzarella, sliced and soaked in milk

Cut the tomatoes into rather thick slices, 3/8-inch to 1/2-inch (8 to 10 mm). Cut the onion in half lengthwise, then into very thin slices crosswise. Sprinkle the vegetables with the olive oil and salt and pepper to taste. Cut the basil in fine shreds and toss it gently with the tomatoes and onions.

Have the cheese well chilled to cut it easily into slices about 1/4 inch (5 mm) thick. Add the cheese to the tomatoes and basil, coating it well with the oil. Arrange the vegetables and cheese on a platter and marinate them in the refrigerator for an hour or two. Bring to cool room temperature before serving.

BASIL MAYONNAISE

■

GOOD MAYONNAISE MAY BE MADE even in a soup bowl with a fork to blend the egg and oil. We think the finest-textured, most silken mayonnaise is made in a mortar and pestle using just the egg yolk. Using a food processor results in a stiffer texture, closer to that of commercial mayonnaise. Herbed mayonnaises are particularly appropriate accompaniments to grilled foods, especially chicken, fish, artichokes, eggplant (aubergines), potatoes, onions, and peppers. They are also good with mixed vegetable salads such as potato and green bean, and, of course, as sandwich spreads. We have been making mayonnaise for twenty years with no harmful effects from raw eggs. If you are concerned about solmonella bacteria in eggs from your region, we suggest buying eggs from a reliable salmonella-free source, or else not making preparations that use raw eggs. Eggs, and dishes containing them, should always be stored in the refrigerator.

MAKES ABOUT 1 CUP (240 ML)

1 garlic clove	*Salt*
1/2 cup (120 ml) basil leaves	*3/4 cup (180 ml) olive oil or*
1 large egg yolk, at room temperature	*vegetable oil*
1 lemon	

Peel the garlic and slice it thin. Put it in the mortar and pound it to a paste. Chop the basil leaves and pound them in the mortar with the garlic until they make a paste.

Stir the yolk into the basil and garlic mixture along with about a teaspoon (5 ml) of lemon juice and a pinch of salt. Begin to add the oil a few drops at a time, stirring constantly. When about 1/4 cup (60 ml) has been added, pour the oil in a fine stream. Continue until the oil has been used and the mixture has emulsified. Season to taste with salt and lemon juice.

To make the mayonnaise in a food processor or blender, place the sliced garlic and chopped basil in the processor bowl or blender jar. Add the egg yolk, a little lemon juice, and a pinch of salt. With the motor running, add the oil in a very fine stream, until the mixture has emulsified. Finish the seasoning with lemon juice and salt.

CUCUMBER BASIL TEA SANDWICHES

■

THE THIN-SKINNED SEEDLESS CUCUMBERS marketed as English or Japanese cucumbers are best for this dish because of their mild flavor and the uniformly round slices they yield. Trimming the bread to rounds is a nice decorative touch, especially if you are serving the sandwiches with other canapés at a tea or baby or bridal shower. These are good too as regular-sized sandwiches, and can be packed in a lunch box if they are topped with another piece of bread. For a different flavor, use 3 or 4 ounces (about 100 g) of soft mild goat cheese in place of some of the cream cheese.

MAKES 24 TEA SANDWICHES OR 4 REGULAR-SIZED SANDWICHES

1/2 pound (225 g) cream cheese, softened

1 or 2 tablespoons (15 to 30 ml) half-and-half (single cream)

1 small bunch chives, snipped

1 small loaf rye or whole wheat bread, trimmed to round slices, or 8 slices whole wheat bread

1 English cucumber

24 basil, or lemon basil leaves

Thin the cream cheese with the cream until it is the consistency of soft butter. Mix the snipped chives with the cheese. Spread the cheese on the slices of bread.

Wash the cucumber and slice it thinly. Arrange the cucumber slices on the bread slices and top with a whole large leaf of basil.

BASIL ALMOND DEVILED EGGS

■

THOUGH EGGS GO WELL with many herbs, they are especially good with basil, tarragon, and sorrel. The almonds add texture and flavor not usually found in deviled eggs. As with any of the recipes in the book, low-calorie versions of sour cream, cream cheese, or yogurt may be used.

MAKES 12 DEVILED EGG HALVES

6 large eggs	1/2 teaspoon (2 ml) paprika
1/4 cup (60 ml) toasted almonds	1/2 teaspoon (2 ml) salt, or to taste
1/3 cup (80 ml) sour cream	1/4 cup (60 ml) packed fresh basil leaves
1 1/2 teaspoons (8 ml) Dijon-style mustard	12 small basil leaves

Cover the eggs with warm water in a saucepan. Bring them to a simmer and cook for 10 minutes. Cool the eggs under cold water, then shell them and cut them in half lengthwise. Remove the yolks and press them through a sieve into a small bowl.

Chop the almonds until they are about the size of tiny peas. Mix the sour cream, mustard, paprika, and salt well. Add this mixture and the nuts to the sieved yolks and combine thoroughly. Taste the mixture for seasoning.

Mince the basil leaves and add them to the yolks; chill, covered, for 1 hour. Fill the egg whites with the yolk mixture with a teaspoon or pastry bag with a wide tip. Garnish each egg with a basil leaf.

P O T A T O   P E S T O   P I Z Z A

■

THIS PIZZA BRINGS TOGETHER one of our favorite food combinations. We first ate potatoes and pesto together in Liguria with trenette noodles, a very old dish in that region. In our opinion, it is worth heating up the oven for pizza during the summer when the basil and potatoes are at their peak; but it is wonderful in the winter too, with frozen or preserved basil substituting for the fresh. The pizza dough recipe yields enough for four 9-inch (23-cm) pizzas. The potato pesto topping covers two of these pizzas. You may wish to freeze the remaining dough, which it accommodates beautifully, or try another topping. We often vary the flavor and color of the dough by replacing 1/2 cup (120 ml) of unbleached white flour with 1/2 cup (120 ml) of whole wheat flour, or with 1/4 cup (60 ml) each of whole wheat and rye flours.

The best homemade pizza is cooked on a baking stone or on tiles. The porosity of the stone allows the water in the dough to be converted to steam efficiently, producing a crisp outer crust and a light, bready top layer. Because the stone is preheated, it is necessary to have a baker's peel (or pizza paddle) to slide the pizza onto the stone in the hot oven. We have achieved good results with this dough in pizza pans, too. The oven needs to be set a little lower when the pizza is baked on metal.

P I Z Z A   D O U G H :

THIS RECIPE YIELDS ENOUGH DOUGH FOR THE FOLLOWING QUANTITIES OF PIZZA:

6 pizzette, each about 6 inches (15 cm) in diameter OR
4 pizzas, each about 9 inches (23 cm) in diameter OR
2 pizzas, each 12 to 13 inches (30 to 33 cm) in diameter OR
2 schiacciate or foccacie, each about 9 by 12 inches (23 by 30 cm) OR
4 calzone, each 8 inches (20 cm)

2 teaspoons (10 ml) active dry yeast

1½ cups (360 ml) water

3½ cups (830 ml) unbleached white flour

1/2 cup (120 ml) whole wheat flour, or use another 1/2 cup (120 ml) white flour

2 tablespoons (30 ml) olive oil

1 teaspoon salt

POTATO

PESTO

PIZZA

Dissolve the yeast in about 1/4 cup (60 ml) warm water. When the yeast has softened and become foamy, in about 10 minutes, add it to the rest of the water.

Mix the flours and make a well in the center. Gradually stir the water and yeast into the well. Add the olive oil and salt. Gather the dough and knead it for 7 or 8 minutes, or until it is soft and lively.

Let the dough double in bulk in a lightly oiled bowl. It is ideal to do this first rise in the refrigerator overnight. Punch the dough down, divide it into portions, and roll these lightly into balls or pat into rectangles, depending on the finished shape. Let them rest, covered with a towel, on a lightly floured surface for 20 minutes, or until the dough is at room temperature if it has been refrigerated.

Stretch the dough gently with your hands on lightly oiled baking pans, or on floured bakers' peels if you will be using a baking stone to bake it. If the dough resists, let it rest a few minutes longer.

P I Z Z A   T O P P I N G :

POTATO PESTO TOPPING FOR TWO 9-INCH (23-CM) PIZZAS, SERVING 3 OR 4 AS AN APPETIZER

6 to 8 new potatoes, about 2 inches (5 cm) in diameter

1/2 cup (120 ml) olive oil

5 or 6 garlic cloves, 2 unpeeled and mashed

1 cup (240 ml) packed basil leaves

3/4 cup (180 ml) freshly grated parmesan cheese

1 small red onion

Salt and pepper to taste

Scrub the potatoes, dry them, and rub with a little olive oil. Place them in a baking dish with the mashed garlic and roast them in a preheated 350° F (180° C) oven for about 25 minutes, until they are just tender. Remove from the oven and cool to room temperature.

Slice the remaining garlic thin. Put the garlic, basil, and about 1/4 cup (60 ml) olive oil in a large mortar or in a blender or food processor. Pound or blend to a smooth paste. Add the cheese and more olive oil little by little. Taste for balance and consistency, adding more cheese or olive oil if necessary.

Slice the potatoes into 1/4-inch-thick (5-mm) rounds. Cut the onion in half lengthwise, then into 1/8-inch (3-mm) slices. Preheat a baker's stone for 15 minutes in an oven set at 500° F (260° C). If you do not have a stone, preheat the oven to 450° F (239° C).

Form one piece of dough into a 9-inch (23-cm) round on a lightly floured baker's peel, or on a lightly oiled pizza pan or baking sheet. Brush the top of the dough lightly with olive oil and arrange half of the potato and onion slices on it. Salt and pepper lightly.

Slide the pizza onto the preheated baker's stone, or place the pizza pan on the lowest oven shelf. Bake the pizza for 5 to 6 minutes, or until the crust is puffed around the edges and light golden brown. Remove the pizza with the paddle, or remove the pizza pan, and spread the pesto over the potatoes.

Return the pizza to the oven for 1 to 2 minutes, until the bottom crust is done and the pesto just begins to bubble. This may take a little longer if you are baking in a pizza pan. Remove the pizza to a cutting board and slice. Serve immediately. Make the second pizza in the same manner.

PASTA WITH FRESH TOMATO AND BASIL SAUCE

■

THE TRICK TO THIS DISH is to have everything ready to serve: the pasta hot from the water and the uncooked tomato sauce very cold from the refrigerator. When the pasta and sauce are mixed together immediately, the resulting wonderful perfume and refreshing flavor make a perfectly satisfying summer pasta. We have eaten many variations of this dish in Italy. Food-loving Italians will argue about the name of the dish, what kind of pasta to use, how much garlic and basil to add, in fact, almost any aspect of the dish. We always make this with garden tomatoes and extra-virgin olive oil.

SERVES 3 OR 4

1 ¼ pounds (560 g) firm-ripe tomatoes

2 or 3 garlic cloves

About 1/4 cup (60 ml) olive oil

1 tablespoon (15 ml) red wine vinegar, or to taste

Salt and freshly ground pepper to taste

Pinch of red pepper flakes, optional

3 or 4 large basil sprigs, or 5 or 6 Piccolo basil sprigs

1/2 pound (225 g) imported pasta shells such as rotelle or other shaped pasta to catch the sauce

Rinse the tomatoes, core them, and cut them into about 1/2-inch (1-cm) cubes. Mince the garlic. Mix the tomatoes, garlic, olive oil, and red wine vinegar in a bowl. Season with salt and pepper, and red pepper flakes, if you like. Refrigerate the sauce for at least 30 minutes.

Cook the pasta in abundant boiling salted water. When the pasta is nearly al dente, tear or shred large basil leaves, or pluck Piccolo basil leaves, and add them to the sauce.

When the pasta is just done, drain it and mix it with the sauce. Serve immediately.

SPINACH   BASIL   SOUP

■

SPINACH AND BASIL are a surprisingly good flavor combination. We like this soup best in early summer when the first basil and the end-of-spring spinach coincide. The brilliant green color fades, so serve the soup as soon as it is ready.

SERVES 4 TO 6

3 tablespoons (45 ml) unsalted butter	*1½ cups (360 ml) milk*
1 medium onion, diced	*Salt and freshly ground white pepper*
3 garlic cloves, minced	*Dash cayenne pepper*
1 pound (450 g) fresh spinach leaves	*Freshly grated nutmeg*
1 cup (240 ml) packed fresh basil leaves	*6 tablespoons (90 ml) freshly grated parmesan cheese*
3 cups (710 ml) chicken or vegetable stock	*6 basil leaves, shredded*

Melt the butter in a frying pan over low heat and soften the onion in it for 3 or 4 minutes. Add the garlic and cook for a minute or two longer.

Wash and stem the spinach. Wilt the spinach with the water that clings to the leaves in a covered noncorrodible pot over low heat. Remove from the heat and add the spinach and its cooking liquor to a soup pot along with the basil leaves, onions, garlic, and stock. Simmer over moderate heat for 5 minutes, then add the milk and season with salt and pepper, cayenne, and nutmeg.

Puree the soup, 1 cup (240 ml) at a time, in the blender or food processor. Return the pureed soup to the pan and stir in 4 tablespoons (60 ml) parmesan cheese. Heat the soup over low heat for 2 or 3 minutes, stirring occasionally. Ladle the soup into warm bowls or a soup tureen and garnish with the remaining cheese and shredded basil.

SALSA ITALIANA
■

THERE ARE SO MANY VARIATIONS of bread-crumb sauces in Italian cooking that we have given this recipe a generic name. Good bakery bread is still available in Italy, as it has been for millennia, and Italians have ways to use leftover bread aside from feeding it to the birds. A very herby sauce such as this one is served with poached or fried meats, variety meats, poultry, and fish. We like it as well with simply cooked vegetables, particularly artichokes, broccoli, chard, and potatoes, and with raw tomatoes and fennel. In fact, we like this sauce so much we eat it on hard-cooked eggs, on bread, and even by the spoonful. Using a rough-textured, hearth-style bread for the crumbs makes a much superior sauce. If you have very dry leftover bread cubes (which we keep on hand for sauces and soups), soak them just the same as day-old bread. You may have to toss the bread occasionally and let it soak a little longer so that it is evenly moist. If your bread is very fresh or moist, dry the cubes for 15 minutes in an oven set at 250° F (130° C), then let them stand until completely cool before soaking.

MAKES ABOUT 2½ CUPS (600 ML)

1 cup (240 ml) cubed day-old or two-day-old Italian or French bread, crusts removed

1/4 cup (60 ml) white wine vinegar

1/2 cup (120 ml) water

2 garlic cloves, sliced

1 cup (240 ml) packed basil leaves, chopped

1 cup (240 ml) packed Italian parsley leaves, chopped

3/4 cup (180 ml) olive oil

Salt and freshly ground pepper to taste

Red pepper flakes to taste, optional

Soak the bread in the vinegar and water for 15 minutes. Squeeze it as dry as possible.

Pound the bread and garlic to a paste in a mortar and pestle or puree it carefully in a food processor. Do not overprocess. Stir in the chopped basil and parsley.

Add the oil as for a mayonnaise, a few drops at a time, increasing the amount of oil as the sauce emulsifies. Season to taste with salt and pepper, and red pepper flakes if desired. The thin film of oil on top of the sauce is traditional. Stir the sauce just before serving, if desired.

ROASTED RED PEPPER AND BASIL BUTTER

■

BUTTERS ARE SOMEWHAT OVERLOOKED culinary resources; they can be made with little effort and freeze well because the butterfat coats the ingredients. This one makes a simple pasta sauce or a garnish for any kind of poached or grilled finfish, especially salmon, and most vegetables, particularly potatoes. It will also keep, tightly covered, in the refrigerator for as long as a week. Since other ingredients than butter make up most of the recipe, it is not even wickedly caloric.

MAKES ABOUT 1½ CUPS (120 ML)

1/2 cup (120 ml) unsalted butter, softened

1 red bell pepper, roasted, peeled, and seeded

1 garlic clove

1/2 cup (120 ml) packed basil leaves

1/4 cup (60 ml) flat-leaved parsley leaves

Salt and freshly ground white pepper

Combine the butter, pepper, and garlic in a food processor and process until almost smooth. Add the herb leaves and pulse until they have been minced and incorporated into the butter. Season with salt and pepper to taste.

Pack the butter in a small crock or bowl and refrigerate until ready to serve. Remove from the refrigerator and let stand at room temperature for about 10 minutes before serving.

BASIC BASIL TOMATO SAUCE

■

THIS ALL-PURPOSE TOMATO SAUCE is made in the Italian manner, but it is good in any dish which calls for tomato sauce and, of course, with pasta and pizza. The Italians who taught us this sauce add carrot for sweetness, to cut the acidity of the tomatoes, which makes the sauce bright orange. Passing the sauce through a food mill gives it the best texture. If you chop the sauce in a food processor, do it in two batches, using the pulse button to make a sauce with some body.

This sauce is delicious canned. Double or triple the recipe and when the sauce is finished, pack it into hot, sterilized canning jars. Follow the manufacturer's directions for processing.

MAKES ABOUT 1 QUART (1 LITRE)

1 medium carrot

1 small onion

2 pounds (900 g) fresh red plum
  tomatoes, or 1 28-ounce (800-g)
  can plum tomatoes

1/2 cup (120 ml) packed basil leaves,
  or 1 tablespoon (30 ml) dried basil

2 garlic cloves

1 teaspoon (5 ml) salt, or to taste

Grate the carrot and coarsely chop the onion. Combine them in a heavy noncorrodible 2-quart (2-litre) saucepan with the tomatoes, basil, and garlic. Add 1/2 teaspoon (2 ml) salt, cover, and simmer over moderate heat for 30 minutes.

Remove from the heat and taste for salt. Pass the sauce through a food mill. If you are not using the sauce immediately, cool to room temperature, then store in a jar in the refrigerator for as long as 5 days.

PESTO ALBERTO

■

WE NAMED THIS SAUCE FOR OUR FRIEND who made the first pesto we ate in Toscana. Pesto is a wonderfully simple sauce that depends on the best ingredients, combined carefully to produce its classic flavor. The origin of true pesto is claimed most fervently by the Ligurians, though other regions in Italy have quite old versions. In this country, almost any green chopped herb sauce may be called pesto, though it has little or nothing to do with real pesto and should really be called something else.

Parmigiano reggiano makes the best pesto, but a younger Italian parmesan such as grana padana can also be used. Italian, Spanish, or western U.S. pine nuts are all good, but be sure they are fresh; they go rancid quickly. Fruity-flavored extra-virgin olive oil gives the authentic pesto flavor. Basil and garlic vary in strength according to season and variety, so you may have to add more of one or the other. If the pesto tastes sharp, add more parmesan cheese. A bit of pesto makes a good sauce for grilled or roasted fish and vegetables, especially salmon, eggplant (aubergines), tomatoes, and squash, as well as a flavorful garnish for minestrone-style vegetable soups. Leftover pesto is still tasty after 3 or 4 days if kept tightly covered in the refrigerator. The top layer will darken some; just stir it in.

MAKES ABOUT 2½ CUPS (600 ML), ENOUGH FOR 8 PORTIONS OF PASTA

1 cup (240 ml) packed Piccolo, Genoa, or lettuce-leaf basil leaves

1 cup (240 ml) packed Italian or curly parsley leaves

1/2 cup (120 ml) pine nuts

6 garlic cloves, sliced thin

3/4 cup (180 ml) freshly grated parmesan cheese

3/4 cup (180 ml) olive oil

If you make the pesto in a food processor or blender, add all the ingredients and pulse the motor to make a homogeneous sauce which is not as fine as a puree.

If you use a mortar and pestle, pound the garlic first, then add the pine nuts. Finally, chop basil and parsley, and pound the herbs in, a handful at a time. Stir in the cheese and oil. Serve over hot pasta, with minestrone, or any foods suggested in the recipe introduction.

T H A I - C A M B O D I A N   C H I C K E N W I T H   B A S I L

■

THAI AND CAMBODIAN CUISINES resemble each other in several respects: basic ingredients, the complexity of flavor in dishes, and the absence of European influence. The subtlety of both cuisines is rather surprising, considering how many strongly flavored ingredients are combined in a single dish. To our taste, Thai food is more assertive, especially in its use of chilis. This recipe came about after enjoying similar dishes in many Thai and Cambodian restaurants. Basil is a popular herb in these cuisines and is almost always added during the last minute or two of cooking or used as garnish. We use cinnamon, anise, spice, or holy basil, all of which we have seen sold as Thai basil. Aromatic Italian basils such as Genoa and Piccolo or Compatto work well, too. For variation, try substituting boneless snapper or cod fillets cut into about 2-inch (5-cm) pieces for the chicken. You may add a few roughly chopped coriander sprigs or use them in place of the basil.

SERVES 4

1 ½ pounds (675 g) boneless, skinless chicken breast, cut into 1/2-inch (1-cm) strips on a diagonal

3 tablespoons (45 ml) peanut or vegetable oil

4 green onions, including about 4 inches (10 cm) of green, sliced in 1-inch (2-cm) lengths

2 garlic cloves, minced

1-inch (2-cm) piece of ginger, peeled and grated

1 tablespoon (15 ml) soy sauce

1 tablespoon (15 ml) lemon juice

2 teaspoons (10 ml) Thai, Cambodian, or Vietnamese fish sauce

1 (5 ml) teaspoon sugar

1 or 2 small fresh red chilis such as Thai or serrano, stemmed, seeded, and cut in thin slices

4 cinnamon or other basil sprigs, leaves coarsely chopped

Heat the oil in a wok or large sauté pan over medium-high heat. Stir-fry the chicken until lightly browned, and just cooked, 2 to 3 minutes. Remove the chicken to a warm serving dish.

Add the green onions, garlic, and ginger to the pan and cook over low heat until the ingredients begin to give off their aroma, about a minute. Add the soy sauce, lemon juice, fish sauce, and sugar. Stir-fry for about a minute, then add the chilis, basil, and chicken, and just heat through. Serve hot with rice.

CANNELLONI WITH CHEESE AND BASIL

■

CANNELLONI ARE MADE WITH HOMEMADE PASTA similar to that we learned to make in Italy. It has a tender yet resilient texture and a delicate flavor. When we first moved back from Italy, fresh pasta was hardly available in the United States; after trying many locally made and commercial pastas, we still prefer this kind. How much liquid to add is always the important question in pasta making. So many factors come into play—the brand of flour, the size and temperature of eggs, the relative humidity—that it is difficult to specify an amount without having the pasta right in front of us. If you use a food processor, you will usually need to add a teaspoon (5 ml) or so of water. If you mix the dough by hand, the eggs may not absorb all the flour, and you won't need to add water. For the ideal combination of toothsomeness and workability, the dough should neither be so wet that it is very pliable and soft nor so stiff that it crumbles apart when you try to knead it. Add either flour or water, according to the temperament of your dough. Making cannelloni takes several steps, but they can be made ahead and refrigerated for a day or two. In this case, do not cover them with sauce until ready to bake them.

MAKES 16 CANNELLONI, SERVING 8 AS A MAIN COURSE

P A S T A :

3 cups (710 ml) unbleached flour   3 large eggs

Heap the flour and make a well in it. Break the eggs into the well and beat them together with a fork. Stir them into the flour from the bottom of the well with the fork until the dough in the center is smooth and shiny. With your hands, gradually incorporate the flour from the outside of the well toward the center, kneading gently until the mass of dough comes together.

Knead the dough until it is smooth and resilient. You may need to add more flour, or you may not be able to incorporate all of the flour. If the dough is sticky, or very pliable, keep kneading flour into it.

Divide the dough into three portions and cover it with plastic wrap or an overturned bowl. Let it rest for at least 30 minutes before putting it through a pasta machine.

To mix the dough in a food processor, put the flour in the work bowl with the steel blade and pulse. Add the eggs and process about 30 seconds. The dough should just turn over itself at the top of the bowl. Test by stopping the machine and pinching a bit of the dough together. If it coheres readily, turn it out and knead it. If not, add water, a teaspoonful (5 ml) at a time, and process. Be careful not to add too much water.

Processor dough is stiffer than hand-worked dough. Cover and let it rest for at least 45 minutes before rolling.

Begin rolling one portion of the dough through the machine at the widest setting of the rollers. Fold it, and run it through the widest setting another time or two. Always put an open side into the machine when adding folded dough. If the dough feels wet or sticky, dust it lightly with flour before you roll it through the machine.

Advance the rollers and put the dough through the machine without folding. Continue rolling the dough once through each setting without folding. The final setting of pasta machines varies; the ideal thickness for cannelloni is a little less than a millimeter, the last setting on some machines, the next to the last on others. The pasta will be difficult to handle if it is rolled too thin.

When the pasta has been rolled to the correct thickness, trim the odd-shaped pieces from the ends, reserving them for another use, and cut the pasta into about 5-inch (13-cm) lengths. Set the pieces of cut pasta on a smooth, lightly floured surface so that they do not touch. Roll and cut the remaining two pieces of dough.

FILLING:

2 large eggs

1 pound (450 g) ricotta cheese

1 cup (240 ml) packed fresh basil leaves

2 cups (475 ml) freshly grated parmesan cheese

1 teaspoon (5 ml) salt, or to taste

About 1 teaspoon (5 ml) freshly grated nutmeg

Beat the eggs well and mix with the ricotta. Shred the basil and stir it into the ricotta along with the parmesan. Season with salt and nutmeg.

ASSEMBLING THE CANNELLONI:

2 tablespoons (30 ml) olive oil

3 quarts (3 litres) cold water

At least 5 quarts (5 litres) well-salted boiling water

1 recipe Basic Basil Tomato Sauce (page 51) or 1 recipe Simple Tomato Sauce (page 191)

Use 1 tablespoon (15 ml) of the oil to oil two 9-by-13-inch (23-by-33-cm) lasagna pans or casseroles. Place the cold water and remaining oil in a pot or large bowl. Drop the pasta, four sheets at a time, into the boiling water and cook for 15 seconds. Do not overcook. Transfer the pasta with a large strainer or slotted spoon to the cold water. Repeat until all the pasta is parboiled. Preheat the oven to 375° F (190° C).

Gently spread a sheet of parboiled pasta in the lasagna pan and blot excess water with a tea towel or paper towel. Spread about 3 tablespoons (45 ml) of filling across the upper third of the pasta sheet. Roll it so that the seam side is down. Continue filling and rolling.

Eight cannelloni will fit in each casserole. Cover them with sauce, dividing it evenly between the casseroles, leaving about an inch of pasta on each side uncovered. Bake the cannelloni for 25 minutes. The edges should be slightly brown and crunchy. Serve hot.

HERBED WILD RICE AND BULGUR PILAF

■

THIS FLAVORFUL PILAF is best with simply roasted or grilled poultry, especially duck and squab. The quality of wild rice varies greatly. If you can find a source of clean, whole grains rather than broken bits, it is more economical to buy the rice in bulk. As the cooking time can also vary greatly, it's best to stick with one source so that you can establish a consistent cooking time. Any basil can be used here, but a spice basil such as cinnamon or Thai adds an unusual touch.

SERVES 8

1 cup (240 ml) wild rice

2 cups (475 ml) coarse bulgur wheat

6 cups (1.5 litres) chicken or vegetable stock

5 tablespoons (75 ml) unsalted butter

1 large carrot, diced

1 large celery rib, diced

1 medium onion, diced

1 teaspoon (5 ml) salt, or to taste

1/2 cup (120 ml) packed fresh basil leaves or 1 tablespoon (15 ml) and 1 teaspoon (5 ml) dried basil

1 tablespoon (15 ml) fresh oregano leaves or 1 teaspoon (5 ml) dried oregano

1/2 cup (120 ml) raw cashew nuts

Salt and freshly ground pepper

Cook the rice in 3 or 4 cups (about 1 litre) of lightly salted boiling water for 15 to 30 minutes, until the rice just begins to open. Drain it and cover. In another pan, bring the stock to a simmer and keep it hot.

Sauté the bulgur in 3 tablespoons (45 ml) of the butter over medium heat for 2 or 3 minutes. Add the drained rice and sauté for another 2 or 3 minutes. Remove the grains to a large pan or earthenware casserole.

Sauté the carrot, celery, and onion in the remaining butter over medium heat for 5 minutes. Mix the vegetables and grains together and add 3 cups (710 ml) of stock. Season lightly with salt and pepper. Cover and simmer for 15 minutes, adding more stock a little at a time, as necessary.

While the grains are cooking, chop the fresh herbs or crumble the dried herbs. Toast the cashews in a small pan over medium-low heat until they are lightly browned, about

10 minutes.

Add the herbs and cashews to the pilaf. Cook over low heat until all liquid has been absorbed and the grains are tender, about 5 minutes.

B A S I L   S T E W E D   T O M A T O E S

■

STEWED TOMATOES WERE FAVORITES in both of our families. We have added basil, which our parents didn't use, and replaced the pinch of sugar with a little honey. The best tomatoes for this recipe are round, juicy ones that have been vine-ripened. For a homey American dinner, roast chicken, mashed potatoes, and stewed tomatoes cannot be bettered.

SERVES 4 TO 6

1 medium onion, diced

1 medium celery rib, diced

2 tablespoons (30 ml) olive oil

2 pounds (900 g) ripe tomatoes, or a 28-ounce (800-g) can of tomatoes

8 lettuce-leaf or cinnamon basil leaves or 1/2 teaspoon (2 ml) crumbled dried basil

1/4 cup (60 ml) packed parsley leaves

3 garlic cloves, minced

2 teaspoons (10 ml) honey

1/4 teaspoon (1 ml) cayenne pepper

Salt

1 cup (240 ml) coarse day-old whole grain bread crumbs

Sauté the onion and celery in the olive oil for about 8 minutes over medium heat. Cut the tomatoes into wedges, or coarsely chop the canned tomatoes, and add them to the vegetables.

Coarsely chop the basil and parsley leaves and add them to the tomatoes with the cayenne, garlic, honey, and salt to taste. Simmer uncovered for 20 minutes, then stir in the bread crumbs and simmer 5 minutes longer. Cover and let stand for 5 minutes. Serve in a heated serving dish.

BASIL POTATO SALAD

■

BECAUSE WE LOVE POTATOES AND HERBS, we are always trying new combinations. Lemon basil adds a nice touch here. As it contains no mayonnaise, this salad is particularly good for picnics: pack the garnishes separately. Steaming is a good method of cooking potatoes for salad; they can be cooked with their skins (which we like) and do not become waterlogged. If sweet onions are not available, you may substitute ordinary ones, after first soaking them in ice cold salted water for 15 or 20 minutes, draining, and patting dry.

SERVES 8 TO 10

3 pounds (1.4 kg) new potatoes

1½ pounds (675 g) fresh small peas in the shell

1/2 cup (120 ml) packed fresh basil leaves

8 salt-packed anchovy fillets

5 small, firm-ripe tomatoes

1 small, sweet onion such as Vidalia or Walla Walla

1/4 cup (60 ml) white wine vinegar or lemon juice

1/2 cup (120 ml) olive oil

Salt and pepper to taste

Leaf lettuce

Basil sprigs or flowers

Scrub the potatoes well. Cut them in half and steam them, cut side down, until they are just tender, about 15 minutes. Remove the steamer from the pan and let the potatoes stand at room temperature while you prepare the rest of the salad.

Shell the peas and simmer them, covered, in a little water over low heat until they are tender, about 5 minutes. Spread them on a plate to cool.

Chop the basil and four anchovy fillets coarsely. Split the remaining anchovies lengthwise and reserve them for garnish. Cut four of the tomatoes into wedges. Halve the onion lengthwise, then cut it crosswise into thin slices. Reserve about one-quarter of the slices for garnish. Peel the potatoes, if desired, and dice them or cut them into wedges or chunks. In a large bowl, mix the potatoes, tomatoes, peas, onion slices, anchovies, and basil.

Place the vinegar or lemon juice in a small bowl and whisk in the olive oil. Season with salt and pepper. Toss the dressing with the salad vegetables. Adjust the seasoning.

Cover a large salad platter with lettuce leaves. Arrange the salad on the lettuce and scatter the reserved onion slices over it. Cut the remaining tomato into wedges and arrange them on the salad. Complete the garnish with the remaining anchovy fillets and basil sprigs or flowers.

B A S I L   L I M E   M A R M A L A D E
■

YOU WILL HAVE TO DO A LITTLE PLANNING to make this recipe, as the fruit must soak overnight twice, but this old way to make marmalade gives the finest texture and flavor. Lemon basil is best, though other varieties may also be used. However very spicy ones, such as Thai or cinnamon basil, add aromatic notes that overpower the lime perfume.

FILLS ABOUT 6 HALF-PINT (240-ML) JARS

6 limes

3 lemons

Water

Sugar

10 lemon basil, Piccolo basil, or other basil sprigs 6 inches (15 cm) long

12 basil leaves

Scrub the limes and lemons well and remove the colored part of the rind with a vegetable peeler or a sharp knife. Cut the rinds into very fine slivers. Cut the fruit into very thin slices, removing the seeds and reserving the juice.

Measure the rind, fruit, and juice and transfer it to a large bowl, covering it with three times as much water. Let stand at room temperature for 24 hours.

Transfer the fruit and water to a large noncorrodible pan. The mixture should come no more than halfway up the side of the pan. Bring to a boil and cook for 15 minutes. Remove the pan from the heat and let the mixture stand overnight, or as long as 24 hours.

Measure the mixture again and return it to the pan with an equal volume of sugar. For example, if you have 6 cups of fruit and juice, you would add 6 cups of sugar. Add the basil sprigs. Boil the mixture 15 to 30 minutes, or until it reaches the soft-jell temperature of 222° F (106° C) or a teaspoon (5 ml) of marmalade stays put on a chilled saucer.

A good way to test for jelling without a candy thermometer is to use the cold saucer test. Chill two or three saucers in the refrigerator. Start testing after boiling marmalade for 15 minutes. Place about a teaspoon (5 ml) of the hot mixture on a saucer and return it to the refrigerator for 2 or 3 minutes. If the marmalade is runny when you tilt the saucer, it is not yet jelled. You will see a thin skin on top of the marmalade when it has reached the soft-jell stage. This skin keeps the marmalade from spreading over the saucer. You may cook marmalade a few minutes longer if you like a firm spread, but remember that it will firm up further when it cools.

Remove the basil from the marmalade. Let the marmalade cool to room temperature, then stir it gently to distribute the pulp and rind.

Sterilize six half-pint jelly jars, with lids and rings added separately, in boiling water for at least five minutes. Remove one jar at a time and add a basil leaf to it. Half-fill with marmalade, add another basil leaf then fill with marmalade to within 1/4 inch (5 mm) of the top. If necessary, wipe the rim of the jar with a paper towel dipped in hot water. Close the jar tightly with the lid and ring. Fill the remaining jars in the same way.

Store in a cool, dry place and refrigerate after opening. If any jars have not made a vacuum seal, refrigerate immediately, and use within a month.

B AY

A crown of bay good fortune brings

to poets, cooks, scholars, kings.

Bay (*Laurus nobilis*) is the superlative herb for many herbalists: the most beautiful, the most fragrant, the most versatile, the most useful medicinally. About bay nothing bad is said; cooks and herbalists from early civilizations on have been unanimous in recording its virtues. The classical legend of bay's origin was Daphne's transformation into a laurel tree during her pursuit by Apollo. Apollo was so astounded by the tree's beauty that he claimed the laurel as his own and dedicated it to reward the highest achievements of Greek civilization. Bay was first an herb of poets, but also of oracles, warriors, statesmen, and doctors.

Because bay was so strongly associated with the gods and people of high esteem, it gained the reputation of protecting against all manner of natural and manmade disasters. Sorcerers and poisoners could not harm the person who carried bay, and it was widely held that lightning would not strike where bay was planted. The Caesars appropriated bay as their special protector against accidents and conspiracies. Though not notably successful, its efficacy in this field was maintained even in sixteenth- and seventeenth-century England. Witches and devils were supposed to be rendered helpless by it.

Bay, along with rosemary, was taken to weddings and funerals, being "good for the unborn, living and dead". It was the symbol of wisdom, both acquired and intuitive. The word "baccalaureate" is from the Latin for laurel berries, which were given

COOKS . . . FROM EARLY CIVILIZATION ON HAVE BEEN UNANIMOUS IN RECORDING BAY'S VIRTUES

to Greek students of the classical period. As bay is a narcotic and stimulant in large amounts, it was an important part of the Delphic rites. Apollo's priestesses chewed bay before prophesying. Later, even placing bay leaves beneath pillows was thought to bring prescient dreams.

The medicinal uses of the herb were always

important; it was used as often as garlic to protect against epidemics. Considered an antirheumatic, it was drunk as a tea and used in baths. The Romans used bay leaves and berries for the treatment of liver disorders. Culpeper said that bay berries were "effectual against the poisons of all venomous creatures and the sting of wasps and bees." Oil from the berries was rubbed on sprains and dropped into aching ears.

BAY IS . . . SWEET BUT NOT CLOYING, PERVASIVE BUT NOT OVERPOWERING.

The culinary history of bay has been even more constant; it is still an essential herb in European cuisines. Though bay is widely thought to have originated in Asia Minor (present-day Turkey), it is strange that the Chinese, who had trade with this region for thousands of years, do not use bay in their cuisine. In those periods when people appreciated more and stronger herbal flavors, bay was commonly ground fine and sprinkled over fresh vegetables and cooked or marinated in fruit compotes. Now it is cooked with every variety of meat and most kinds of fish and shellfish. Bay leaves are in the stuffings of or simply alongside many roasted fowl dishes. Its sweet balsamic aroma wafts from freshly baked breads and puddings. It is essential to bouquets garnis for soups and stews. We believe that bay adds depth and warmth to most kinds of sweets and savories.

The main contribution of bay to foods is its fragrance, sweet but not cloying, pervasive but not overpowering. If you have ever walked through a forest of bay trees, you will understand the almost incredible refreshing power of bay's scent. Its blend of balsam and honey, with faint tones of rose, clove, orange, mint, and other more ethereal echoes must be an ideal of master perfumers. Bay's aroma peaks between three days and a week after it has been picked; this brief drying time concentrates the oils just enough.

The taste of bay is sharp, slightly peppery, and of medium bitterness. Most cooks now use the whole leaves and remove them before serving, though traditionally, the guest who found the leaf in his portion was due to receive some minor or major fortune. Crumbled or crushed bay leaves have very sharp edges; they should be enclosed in a bouquet garni bag or tea ball so that diners don't eat them. In general, the leaves should be added when the cooking begins.

Be sure that the commercially dried bay that you buy is *Lauris nobilis*. California bay (*Umbellularia californica*) is often sold as bay in the supermarkets, though it must be identified as such somewhere on the container. We have picked California bay in the woods there and used it in camp cooking, but the aroma has eucalyptus overtones, and the flavor is decidedly bitter. We do not recommend picking bay in the wild, as some plants commonly called bays or laurels are highly poisonous.

The effort to grow this noble herb is well paid with a beautiful evergreen bush or tree which enhances any garden or home that provides the necessary growing conditions. The plants are expensive because seed germination is chancy and other methods of propagation are slow. We prefer to buy well-rooted plants from a grower.

We have found that bay prefers to spend the warm season outdoors, rather than being kept in all year. Potted plants require special attention to light, moisture, and fertilization. Keep the plants in a sunny place, make sure the pots have good drainage, and allow the soil to dry slightly between waterings. Fertilize once a month while the plant is outdoors with liquid 10-10-10 fertilizer, in a solution half the recommended strength. Reduce fertilization to once every two months once the plant is inside. A permanent planting of bay likes a sunny spot, good drainage, occasional fertilization, and a good supply of water while it is getting established. Once the tree is two or three years old, it is fairly drought-hardy. Given that its other requirements are met, it grows well even in the meager seasonal rainfall of coastal California.

In the following recipes, we have capitalized on bay's intensity by using it a few days after it has been picked from our plants. If you use commercial dried bay, you will need to add more leaves, as the recipes indicate. Since fresh bay is such a rewarding herb, we encourage you to grow it.

THE EFFORT TO GROW
———
THIS NOBLE HERB
———
IS WELL PAID. . . .

S P I C E D   M U S H R O O M S

■

BAY PLAYS AN IMPORTANT ROLE in several spice mixtures, from American-style pickling spice to Greek and Cypriot marinades for meat and poultry. In this dish, bay picked two or three days before using is noticeably more aromatic than just-picked or dried leaves. The mushrooms are an excellent appetizer, stimulating to the palate because of the spices and bay but not overpowering or filling.

SERVES 6 TO 8

1 ½ pounds (675 g) medium-sized cultivated mushrooms

1/3 cup (80 ml) olive oil

1 tablespoon (15 ml) lightly toasted coriander seed

1 teaspoon (5 ml) fenugreek seeds

6 black peppercorns

1 teaspoon (5 ml) pickling spice

1 garlic clove, crushed

1 cup (240 ml) dry white wine

2 large fresh bay leaves, or 3 dried bay leaves

1 teaspoon (5 ml) salt, or to taste

1/4 cup (60 ml) red wine vinegar

Brush and stem the mushrooms. Reserve the stems for another use. Heat the olive oil in a large frying pan over moderate heat and sauté the mushrooms for 3 minutes, shaking the pan to coat them all over with oil.

Tie the coriander seed, fenugreek seed, peppercorns, pickling spice, and garlic in cheesecloth, or put them in a bouquet garni bag. Add the spice bag, wine, bay leaves, salt, and red wine vinegar to the pan with the mushrooms. Simmer the mushrooms for 10 minutes, turning them once.

Remove the mushrooms to a glass or ceramic dish and cool them to room temperature, turning them occasionally. Chill them, covered, for at least 4 hours or overnight. Let the mushrooms come to cool room temperature and remove the spice bag and bay leaves before serving.

FOUR-MEAT TERRINE

■

THE PORK FAT THAT ENCASES A TERRINE is necessary to keep the forcemeat moist; it also adds flavor and helps keep the terrine fresh by preventing oxidation of most of its surface. Little of the fat melts into the terrine, and in any case, it is usually removed by the eater. It's easiest to have the butcher slice the fat for you, about 1/16 inch (1 mm) thick. The finest imported Italian prosciutto is quite expensive, but that level of quality is not strictly necessary for this recipe, in which the prosciutto is cooked. If there is an Italian delicatessen in your area, choose a local prosciutto that does not taste too salty. A Canadian prosciutto, available in cheese and gourmet shops, is good for cooked dishes and is less expensive than Italian prosciutto. Failing these alternatives, substitute half boiled ham and half fresh salt pork for the prosciutto. Serve the terrine with baguettes or a crusty country-style bread and cornichons or Tarragon Pickles (page 315).

MAKES ABOUT 1½ POUNDS (675 G), SERVING 12 TO 16

1 pound (450 g) fresh pork fat, very thinly sliced

5 fresh bay leaves, or six dried bay leaves

1/2 cup (120 ml) whipping cream (double cream)

1/4 pound (115 g) prosciutto, very thinly sliced

1/2 pound (225 g) ground veal

1/2 pound (225 g) ground pork

1/2 pound (225 g) chicken livers

2 eggs

3 tablespoons (45 ml) Armagnac, Cognac, or brandy

2 teaspoons (10 ml) salt

1 teaspoon (5 ml) freshly grated nutmeg

1 teaspoon (5 ml) freshly ground black pepper

Fresh bay sprigs

Slice the pork fat very thin and line a 1½-quart (1.5-litre) rectangular terrine with it. Scald three fresh bay leaves, or four dried, in the cream and set the cream aside to cool with the leaves still in it.

In a food processor, make a paste of the prosciutto, veal, pork, and chicken livers. The paste should not be completely smooth. Remove the bay leaves from the cream and blend the cream, eggs, Armagnac, salt, nutmeg, and pepper with the meats. The forcemeat should be well seasoned. Check by frying a spoonful of the mixture; taste and adjust seasoning.

Place one of the reserved bay leaves in the center of the fat in the terrine. Spread the forcemeat in the terrine. Put the other bay leaf on the mixture and cover the forcemeat with foil. Cover the terrine and bake in an oven preheated to 350° F (180° C) for 1 hour and 15 minutes.

Take the terrine from the oven and remove the cover. Place a weight, such as a brick or 3 14-ounce (400-g) cans, on the terrine and cool to room temperature. Chill the weighted terrine for 24 hours, then remove the weight and carefully unmold the terrine. Garnish the top with fresh bay sprigs. Slice it 1/4 to 3/8 inch (5 to 8 mm) thick. The terrine will keep, well wrapped and refrigerated, for 3 or 4 days.

C H I C K E N   B R O T H

■

LONG SIMMERING releases more of bay's flavor than dishes cooked for just a half hour or so. One bay leaf is enough for most broths or stews, but if you like a pronounced bay flavor, add half a leaf more. Carolyn learned to add chicken feet to broth in Italy, something even her grandmother didn't do; they add richer taste and more body. Stewing hens make the best broth, but are hard to come by. Backs and necks produce good broth and are inexpensive.

MAKES ABOUT 2 QUARTS (2 LITRES)

1 4-pound (1.8-kg) chicken, with feet
   if possible

2 pounds (900 g) chicken backs and
   necks

1 whole clove

1 medium onion, peeled and quartered

1 medium carrot, peeled and
   quartered

1 medium leek, washed well, white
   and light green parts chopped, and
   2 dark green leaves reserved

Leaves from 1 celery rib, or 2 or 3
   lovage leaves

3 parsley sprigs

1 bay leaf

1 teaspoon (5 ml) black peppercorns

Remove the feet from the chicken, or have the butcher do this. Wash the feet and the chicken well. Remove extra fat from the chicken. Wash the backs and necks.

Add the chicken, chicken feet, backs, and necks to a 10 quart (10-litre) stockpot and cover by an inch (2 cm) with cold water. Bring the liquid just to a boil over high heat, then reduce heat immediately to a simmer. Skim the broth and simmer for about an hour, skimming occasionally.

Insert the clove into one of the onion quarters. Add the onion, carrot, and white and light green parts of the leek to the broth.

Make a bouquet garni with the dark green leaves of the leek by wrapping them around the celery or lovage leaves, parsley sprigs, bay leaf, and black peppercorns, then tying securely with kitchen twine or unwaxed dental floss. Add the bouquet to the broth.

Alternatively, add the dark leek leaves directly to the broth and make a bouquet garni of the celery or lovage leaves, parsley sprigs, bay leaf, and peppercorns by wrapping them in a 12-inch (30-cm) square of the rinsed fine-weave cheesecloth. Gather the ends up and tie the bag securely about 3 inches (8 cm) from where the ends meet. Add the bouquet to the broth.

Simmer the broth for about an hour and a half, skimming occasionally. Taste the broth; if the flavor is weak, simmer for another 30 minutes.

If you want very clear broth, strain it through a colander lined with rinsed fine-weave cheesecloth. Otherwise, strain the broth through a colander. The chicken will have given most of its flavor to the broth, but the meat is good in well-seasoned dishes. Cool the broth to room temperature, then store it in the refrigerator or freezer. The broth will keep in the refrigerator for 5 days. Bring it to a rolling boil for 5 minutes before using it. The broth will keep in the freezer for 6 months, but it is best during the first 2 months.

PECAN TOMATO SAUCE WITH BAY

■

GROUND PECANS THICKEN THIS PASTA sauce (a change from thickening with cream that we like) while adding a pleasantly nutty flavor and texture. You could use hazelnuts or walnuts instead, but we think pecans are best with the bay.

SERVES 4 TO 6

2 pounds (900 g) plum tomatoes, or a 28-ounce (800-g) can of plum tomatoes

1 small red onion, diced

3 tablespoons (45 ml) olive oil

2 garlic cloves, minced

2 fresh bay leaves, or 3 dried bay leaves

Pinch of cayenne

Salt to taste

2/3 cup (160 ml) shelled pecans

2 to 3 tablespoons (30 to 45 ml) unsalted butter

Freshly grated parmesan cheese

Blanch the fresh tomatoes for 10 seconds, then peel, seed, and dice them, or remove most of the seeds from the canned tomatoes and dice them. Cook the onion in the olive oil over moderate heat for about 10 minutes.

Add the tomatoes to the pan along with the minced garlic, bay leaves, cayenne, and a little salt. Simmer the sauce for 20 minutes.

Make a medium-fine meal of the pecans in a food processor, blender, or nut grinder, and stir it into the sauce. Adjust the seasoning and simmer for 3 or 4 minutes. Serve over "Straw and Hay" Pasta (recipe follows) or other hot pasta, garnished with unsalted butter and freshly grated parmesan cheese.

"STRAW AND HAY" PASTA

∎

THE ITALIAN TERM for this combination is *paglia e fieno*, the egg pasta being the "straw" and the spinach, the "hay". Delicious with the Pecan Tomato Sauce with Bay, it is also good with Basic Basil Tomato Sauce (page 51), Tomato Cream Pasta Sauce (page 168), and Simple Tomato Sauce (page 191), as well as cream, butter, and parmesan sauces. Since you will need only half of each kind of pasta for one recipe of sauce, you will have the bonus of homemade pasta for another meal. To store the remaining pasta, you may dry it, store it on a covered baking sheet in the refrigerator for a day or two, or freeze it. Be sure the noodles are not sticking together before storing. If they are sticking, the best thing to do is to separate them carefully, dust them with semolina flour or a granular flour such as Wondra, and let them air-dry a few minutes before storing. The pasta may be used for any fresh pasta dish you like, including lasagna, or other noodle shapes with different sauces.

EGG PASTA

MAKES ABOUT 1 POUND OF FRESH PASTA, ENOUGH TO SERVE 4 TO 6 PEOPLE

3 cups (710 ml) unbleached flour   *3 large eggs*

Heap the flour and make a well in it. Break the eggs into the well and beat them together with a fork. Stir them into the flour from the bottom of the well with the fork until the dough in the center is smooth and shiny. With your hands, gradually incorporate the flour from the outside into the center, kneading gently until the mass of dough is coherent but still soft.

Knead the dough until it is smooth and resilient. You may need to add more flour, or you may not be able to incorporate all of the flour. If the dough is sticky, or very pliable, keep kneading flour into it.

Divide the dough into three portions and cover it with plastic wrap or an overturned bowl. Let it rest for at least 30 minutes before putting it through a pasta machine.

To make the dough in a food processor, put the flour in the work bowl with the steel blade and pulse. Add the eggs and process about 30 seconds. The dough should just turn over itself at the top of the bowl. Test by stopping the machine and pinching a bit of the dough together. If it coheres readily, turn it out and knead it. If not, add water, a teaspoonful at a time, and process. Be careful not to add too much water. Processor dough is stiffer than hand-worked dough. Cover and let it rest for at least 45 minutes before rolling.

Begin rolling one portion of the dough through the machine at the widest setting of the rollers. Fold it, and run it through the widest setting another time or two. Always put an open side into the machine when adding folded dough.

If the dough feels wet or sticky, dust it lightly with flour before you roll it through the machine.

Advance the rollers and put the dough through the machine without folding. Continue rolling the dough once through each setting without folding. The final setting of pasta machines varies; the ideal thickness for "straw and hay" is a little less than a millimeter, the last setting on some machines, the next to the last on others. The pasta will be difficult to handle if it is rolled too thin.

When the pasta has been rolled to the correct thickness, run it through the fettuccine cutting blades on the machine. Cut the pasta across in about 6-inch (15-cm) lengths. If the pasta is very moist, toss it with a little flour to prevent it from sticking. Set the pieces of cut pasta on a smooth lightly floured surface so that they do not touch. Roll and cut the remaining two pieces of dough.

S P I N A C H   P A S T A

MAKES ABOUT 1 POUND OF FRESH PASTA, ENOUGH TO SERVE 4 TO 6 PEOPLE

1/2 pound (225 g) tender spinach   *2 large eggs*

*3 cups (710 ml) unbleached white
     flour*

Wash, dry, and stem the spinach. Puree it as fine as possible in a food processor or blender. This takes about 2 minutes; stop and scrape the sides of the bowl or jar occasionally.

Sift the flour into a mound on a smooth surface and make a well in it. Add the spinach mixture to the well and make the dough in the same way as the egg dough. Follow the kneading, rolling, and cutting directions for Egg Pasta.

C O O K I N G   A N D   S A U C I N G
T H E   P A S T A :

6 to 8 quarts (6 to 8 litres) boiling
water

Salt

1/2 recipe Egg Pasta

1/2 recipe Spinach Pasta

Pecan Tomato Sauce with Bay (page
70)

Salt the water well and bring it to a boil. Add the pasta and cook it al dente, about a minute. Drain it well and place it in a large warm serving bowl. Toss it with half of the Pecan Tomato Sauce with Bay. Pour the rest of the sauce on top and serve immediately.

C O R N   A N D   P O T A T O   C H O W D E R

■

THOUGH THIS SOUP is relatively quick to prepare, we have made the recipe a large one so we can have leftover soup for lunch or a cup before dinner later in the week. It is hearty enough to serve as a main course, especially when accompanied by homemade bread such as Parsley Batter Bread (page 227), Marjoram Corn Bread (page 194), or Rosemary Biscuits (page 245).

SERVES 8 TO 10

2 large celery ribs, diced

3 large leeks, white and tender green
parts sliced

4 large waxy potatoes, peeled and
diced

4 tablespoons (60 ml) unsalted butter

1½ quarts (1½ litres) chicken or
vegetable stock

2 fresh bay leaves, or 3 dried bay
leaves

4 ears of corn, husked, or 2 cups
(475 ml) frozen corn kernels

2 cups (475 ml) half-and-half (single
cream)

1/3 cup (80 ml) chopped parsley

Salt and freshly ground pepper to taste

Curry powder to taste, optional

1/2 cup (120 ml) freshly grated
parmesan

Place the celery, leeks, and potatoes in a soup pot and sweat them in the butter over low heat for 10 minutes. Add the stock and bay leaves, bring the soup to a boil, then reduce the heat to a simmer, cover, and cook for 10 minutes or so.

Cut the corn kernels from the cobs and add them to the soup, or add the frozen corn kernels. Cook for 2 or 3 minutes, then stir in the half-and-half and parsley and season the soup with salt and pepper. Add the curry powder, if desired.

Heat the soup over low heat until just hot. At serving time, stir in the grated parmesan cheese. Serve in warmed soup bowls.

S A L T   C O D   I N   T O M A T O   S A U C E

■

WE REMEMBER WHEN, in the not-too-distant past, salt cod was a neglected food in the United States and hard to find but reasonably priced, befitting a peasant's and fisherman's staple. Since then, the price has tripled, making it a delicacy. We still enjoy it greatly, if less frequently, for its special flavor and the wealth of ways to prepare it in Italian, Spanish, Portuguese, and French cooking. Buy the fleshy white salt cod, marketed sometimes as baccalà in Italian delicatessens, rather than the very desiccated yellow cod known as stockfish that is sold with the skin and bones. Skinless and boneless Canadian salt cod in 1-pound (450-g) wooden boxes is also available in many fish markets and supermarkets.

SERVES 4

1 pound (450 g) salt cod

1 medium onion

4 whole cloves

3 tablespoons (45 ml) olive oil

1 large fresh bay leaf, or 2 dried bay leaves

1 pound (450 g) plum tomatoes, diced or a 14-ounce (400-g) can plum tomatoes, diced

2 garlic cloves

Freshly ground black pepper to taste

1/4 cup (60 ml) chopped parsley

Soak the cod in 6 to 8 quarts (6 to 8 litres) of cold water for 24 hours in the refrigerator. Change the water three times. Before cooking the cod, remove any small bits of skin, bones, and dark spots.

Cut the cod into 1-inch (2-cm) strips. Peel and cut the onion into quarters. Stud each quarter with a whole clove. Heat the olive oil over moderate heat in a large frying pan; sauté the onion with the bay leaf for 5 minutes.

Add the tomatoes, cod, garlic, and pepper. Simmer, covered, for about 15 minutes. Add the parsley and simmer 5 minutes longer. Serve hot with plain rice or boiled potatoes.

BRISKET OF BEEF WITH BAY MUSTARD SAUCE

■

SOMETIMES AN OLD-FASHIONED STEW is the most appealing dish for a fall or winter dinner. This one is good to serve to meat and potatoes people.

Edible juniper berries come from *Juniperis communis* and related species. The berries are blue-black, and are picked for commercial use in the fall when they are ripe, and their oils are concentrated. If you have a suitable shrub, just pick the berries in the fall and use them fresh from the bush, or dry them for future use.

SERVES 6 TO 8

2 fresh bay leaves, or 3 dried bay leaves

2½ to 3 pounds (1.1 to 1.4 kg) brisket of beef

2 quarts (2 litres) beef stock

6 juniper berries

10 black peppercorns

1 pound (450 g) green cabbage

6 medium-sized russet potatoes

24 pearl onions

Salt and freshly ground pepper

Place one bay leaf in the center of the brisket. Roll and tie the brisket. Add the brisket and the stock to a large pot and bring the stock to a boil. Reduce the heat to a simmer.

Make a small bouquet garni by tying one bay leaf, the juniper berries, and the peppercorns in cheesecloth. Add the bouquet garni to the pot and simmer for 2½ hours, skimming as necessary.

Wash the cabbage and discard the outer leaves. Core the cabbage and cut it lengthwise into eighths. Peel the potatoes and cut them lengthwise into eighths. Peel the onions and slash the stem ends.

Remove the brisket from the stock, cover it and keep it warm. Season the stock with salt and reserve 1 cup (240 ml) of it for the sauce. Add the potatoes to the remaining stock. Cover and simmer for about 5 minutes, then add the onions. Simmer for another 5 minutes, then add the cabbage. Cook the vegetables until the potatoes are just done.

While the vegetables are cooking, make the mustard sauce.

M U S T A R D   S A U C E :

2 tablespoons (30 ml) unsalted butter

2 tablespoons (30 ml) flour

1 cup (240 ml) reserved beef stock

1 fresh bay leaf, or 1½ dried bay leaves

1/2 cup (120 ml) half-and-half (single cream)

3 tablespoons (45 ml) Dijon-style mustard

Salt and freshly ground pepper

Melt the butter in a heavy saucepan over low heat. Whisk in the flour and cook for 3 or 4 minutes to make a roux. Simmer the reserved stock with the bay in another pan for about 5 minutes. Add the stock to the roux, whisking or stirring constantly. Add the cream to the sauce and whisk or stir to incorporate. When the sauce is smooth, add the mustard. Cook over very low heat for 10 minutes. Remove the bay and adjust the seasoning with salt and pepper before serving.

Remove the vegetables with a slotted spoon and arrange them on a warm serving platter. Remove the string from the brisket and slice it into 1/2-inch (1-cm) slices on a slight diagonal. Discard the bay cooked with the meat. Arrange the sliced meat in the center of the platter. Spoon some of the mustard sauce over the meat and vegetables and serve the rest of the sauce separately. Serve hot.

HUNGARIAN BAKED VEGETABLE STEW

■

HUNGARY GROWS MANY KINDS and great quantities of sweet and chili peppers and produces some of the world's finest paprika from them. This hearty vegetable stew blends the subtle flavors of bay and paprika with the robust flavors of chili and red wine to create an intriguing medley. We like this in the fall, with bread, a simple salad, and, of course, Hungarian red wine. It is a good dish to make ahead, as the flavor mellows and deepens on standing.

SERVES 8

4 tablespoons (60 ml) olive oil

4 large shallots, diced

1 medium red or green sweet pepper, diced

1 medium red onion, diced

3 garlic cloves, minced

3 bay leaves

1 pound (450 g) waxy potatoes

2 large carrots

2 rutabagas, about 4 inches (10 cm) in diameter

1 tart green apple

4 medium-sized firm-ripe tomatoes

About 1½ teaspoons (8 ml) salt

1 tablespoon (15 ml) light honey

2 teaspoons (10 ml) Hungarian sweet paprika

1 teaspoon (5 ml) medium-hot ground chili pepper

1/2 cup (120 ml) chopped parsley

3 cups (710 ml) Hungarian red wine, or other rich red wine

1/2 cup (120 ml) sour cream

Heat the olive oil in a large frying pan over moderate heat and add the shallots, pepper, and onion. Stir in the minced garlic and bay leaves and cook for about 5 minutes. Preheat the oven to 350° F (180° C).

Wash, peel if necessary, and roughly chop the potatoes, carrots, rutabagas, apple, and the tomatoes. Add these to the frying pan and cook for about 5 minutes.

Stir in the salt, paprika, chili pepper, parsley, and red wine. Mix the ingredients thoroughly and transfer them to a 2½- to 3-quart lightly oiled earthenware or ceramic casserole. Cover the casserole and bake for 1 hour.

Reduce the heat to 300° F (150° C) and bake 1 hour longer. Remove the casserole from the oven and let it stand, covered, for about 15 minutes. Serve from the casserole into individual bowls, and pass the sour cream.

BAY HOT CROSS BUNS

■

THOUGH HOT CROSS BUNS are a traditional Easter and Lenten bread, we like these handsome buns so much we make them several times a year. We have found that all yeast breads except batter breads benefit by an overnight rise in the refrigerator. The slow rise allows the yeast to interact thoroughly with the gluten in flour, which produces an evenly spaced structure and a light crumb. In addition, a slow rise allows the yeast to ferment very well, thereby releasing carbon dioxide and alcohol (by-products of fermentation), which results in fewer off-flavors in the bread. If you like a wheatier flavor, substitute up to 2 cups (475 ml) of whole wheat flour for the same volume of white flour.

MAKES ABOUT 36 BUNS

1 cup (240 ml) milk	2 tablespoons (30 ml) active dry yeast
3 fresh bay leaves, or 4 dried bay leaves	About 8 cups (1.9 litres) unbleached white flour
1/4 cup (60 ml) light honey	2 large eggs
1/2 cup (120 ml) unsalted butter, melted	1 teaspoon (5 ml) salt
2/3 cup (160 ml) currants	1/2 cup (120 ml) water
2½ cups (590 ml) warm water	1 egg white

Scald the milk with the bay leaves. Remove it from the heat and dissolve the honey in it. Let the bay steep in the milk for 30 minutes, then remove the leaves. Soak the currants in 2 cups (475 ml) of the warm water for 15 minutes, then drain and squeeze the excess water from them. Discard the soaking water.

Dissolve the yeast in the remaining 1/2 cup (120 ml) warm water. Sift 8 cups (1.9

BAY
HOT CROSS
BUNS

litres) of flour into a large bowl. Beat the eggs lightly and add them, along with the salt and 1/2 cup (120 ml) water, to the milk and honey.

When the yeast is bubbly, add it to the flour along with the milk mixture, melted butter, and currants. Stir the liquid with a wooden spoon to incorporate about half of the flour. Remove the dough to a smooth surface and knead in the flour, a cup at a time, to form a soft but not-too-sticky dough. Knead for about 5 minutes after the last addition of flour. The final dough should be smooth, soft, and elastic.

Place the dough in a lightly oiled bowl and cover tightly with plastic wrap. Let the dough rise in the refrigerator overnight or for as long as 24 hours, or let it rise in a warm place until doubled in size, 1 to 2 hours.

Punch the dough down and divide it in half. Knead each portion for 3 or 4 minutes, then cover the dough and let it rest until it is relaxed enough to roll, 20 to 30 minutes. Roll each portion into a long cylinder about 3 inches (8 cm) in diameter.

Cut the cylinders into 1-inch (2-cm) slices and roll each slice into a ball. Place the balls on lightly buttered baking sheets. Cover them with a tea towel and let them rise in a warm place until almost doubled in size. Preheat the oven to 375° F (190° C).

With a sharp knife, slash a cross in the top of each bun. Beat the egg white until frothy and brush each bun lightly with it.

Bake the buns for 15 to 20 minutes, until they are a rich golden brown. Remove the buns from the oven and let them cool on a rack to room temperature. Drizzle them with Simple Icing (recipe follows) following the slash marks, if desired.

S I M P L E   I C I N G :

MAKES ABOUT 1/2 CUP (120 ML) OF ICING

1 tablespoon (15 ml) lemon juice   *1 cup (240 ml) confectioners sugar*

1 tablespoon (15 ml) water

Combine all ingredients in a bowl and whisk until smooth. Drizzle the icing over the cooled Bay Hot Cross Buns or other sweet rolls or cookies.

BAY RUM CUSTARD

■

THOUGH WE HAVE ALWAYS BEEN custard lovers, we don't make them as often as we used to before the age of cholesterol awareness dawned. This is one of our favorites, and very popular in our herb classes. The bay adds a wonderful aroma and moderates the egginess that some object to in custards.

SERVES 6

1 ½ cups (360 ml) milk	4 egg yolks
1 cup (240 ml) half-and-half (single cream)	1/4 cup (60 ml) light honey
	A large pinch of salt
2 large fresh bay leaves, or 3 dried bay leaves	2 tablespoons (30 ml) dark rum

Scald the milk and half-and-half in a saucepan with the bay leaves. Remove from the heat and let cool to room temperature. Preheat the oven to 350° F (180° C).

Whisk the egg yolks, honey, and salt together in a bowl. Remove the bay leaves from the milk and whisk the milk into the yolk and honey mixture. Stir in the rum.

Pour the custard into six lightly buttered custard cups, or pot de crème pots, or into a 1-quart (1-litre) soufflé dish. Place the dishes in a pan of very hot water and place this in the oven. The individual custards will take about 25 to 30 minutes and the soufflé dish, about 45 to 50 minutes to cook. Shake the dish slightly to see if the custard is set.

Remove the dish(es) from the hot water and cool to room temperature. Chill the custard 3 to 4 hours or overnight. Remove from the refrigerator 30 minutes or so before serving.

CHERVIL

Like lace it looks
and tastes divine;
God send to cooks
fair chervil fine.

hervil (*Anthriscus cerefolium*) is one of the herbs whose absence distresses us. As the fresh herb is difficult to find for sale (though some is grown for the restaurant trade), we are careful to grow plenty of it for salads, which always seem a little dull without its sprightly sprigs. We vigilantly cut it back to prolong our seasonal enjoyment. We put up with its fickle temperament as we might indulge a favorite finicky aunt who comes for a short visit. The pleasure of chervil's company at dinner is well worth the effort of accommodating its special needs for water and shade. The fragile foliage lightens a shady corner in the garden and rewards the gardening cook with a graceful, amiable beauty which pleases the palate and eye equally.

In the cook's realm, chervil has been treasured beginning with the Romans, who probably transplanted it throughout England and France. It was prized as the "finest salade herbe" in medieval times. Its lively delicate flavor, compounded of parsley and mild anise with undertones of pear, continues to find favor, especially in France, where chervil shares the reign with parsley and tarragon. It is much used there with fish, oysters, poultry, and eggs, and in salads and sauces, especially rémoulades and ravigotes. It is also excellent with carrots, cucumbers, asparagus, avocados, mushrooms, and potatoes.

In spite of its lacy, romantic appearance, chervil's history contains little fanciful lore. Because of its alleged powers of rejuvenation, many Europe-

THE PLEASURE

OF CHERVIL'S COMPANY

AT DINNER IS WELL

WORTH THE EFFORT . . .

ans sipped chervil broth on Holy Thursday to symbolize the resurrection of Christ. Although not considered a powerful medicinal herb, chervil had its advocates. Evelyn recommended it as a spring tonic and "chearing of the spirits", and Pliny thought it good for stomach disorders. During the time of the plague, chervil roots were boiled and eaten as a preventative. Another popular folk use of the herb was as cure for hiccups.

Chervil is a bit fussy about its place in the garden, but when established, it will do quite well and will self-sow readily. In most climates, choose a partially shaded spot with very finely worked soil.

Sow the slender black seeds freely as soon as the soil is warm and cover them lightly with fine soil. They must receive some light and be kept moist until they germinate, in 10 to 14 days. It is best to sow directly in the ground. However, you may sow the seeds in flats and transplant in the same manner as parsley. We find several herbs of the family Apiaceae (Umbelliferae)—chervil, parsley, dill, coriander—tricky to transplant and get the best results by sowing directly in the ground.

CHERVIL, LIKE CHIVES, BENEFITS FROM CUTTING.

In climates with fairly mild winters, chervil can be wintered in a cold frame. In coastal California and in the South, sow it in the fall for winter gardens. Chervil does poorly even in the shade in strong summer heat. Brussels Winter is a slow-flowering variety, a good choice for hot summers. In very hot climates, sow the seed in the fall and very early spring. Where summers are cool, chervil does well in full sun.

During the summer, water and harvest continuously to keep the plants from going to seed; they have a way of setting seed all too soon regardless of the attention they receive. Chervil, like chives, benefits from cutting. Begin when the chervil is 3 to 4 inches (8 to 10 cm) tall and keep some of it at that height during the hottest summer months. The leaves will turn orange or red from too much heat and light.

If you do find chervil in the market, look for glossy, medium-green leaves without a hint of yellow. Many of chervil's essential oils evaporate in drying, so shop carefully for the dried herb and store it away from light in tightly closed glass jars. If you are successful in growing a large patch of chervil, you can freeze your surplus in small batches, either as tiny sprigs or chopped coarsely with a bit of parsley.

S A U C E   R A V I G O T E

■

RAVIGOTE IS A CLASSIC FRENCH SAUCE that is a year-round favorite in our kitchens for three reasons: it uses herbs lavishly, it is easy to make, and it goes well with a great variety of foods. We like to make French and Italian herb sauces in a mortar and pestle because the pounding releases herb flavor better than any other method and because the final texture is finer. But perfectly tasty sauces may be made in a blender or food processor. Ravigote is good with hard-cooked eggs and with steamed or boiled vegetables, especially artichokes, asparagus, carrots, cauliflower, and potatoes. It is commonly served with plain fish dishes, poached, baked, or grilled, as well as boiled beef, veal, and variety meats such as tongue. It is also good with poached chicken, and elevates leftover roast chicken and beef. You may vary the character of ravigote by adding leaves from a few sprigs of salad burnet, savory, sweet marjoram, or tarragon.

MAKES ABOUT 2 CUPS (475 ML)

1 cup (240 ml) packed chervil leaves	*1/2 cup (120 ml) olive oil*
1/2 cup (120 ml) packed parsley leaves	*1 tablespoon (15 ml) capers*
	Salt and freshly ground pepper to taste
1/2 cup (120 ml) packed watercress leaves	*2 or 3 salt-pack anchovy fillets, optional*
1 hard-cooked egg	*2 or 3 cornichons, optional*

Roughly chop the chervil, parsley, and watercress leaves. Add a small handful at a time to a mortar and pestle and pound until the herbs release their juices, and the mass is reduced. Keep adding until all the herbs have been used.

Sieve the egg yolk into the herbs. Add the olive oil a few drops at a time, as for mayonnaise, stirring continually until the sauce begins to emulsify. Add the rest of the oil in a thin stream. The sauce will not emulsify completely.

Chop the egg white very fine and stir it, along with the capers, into the sauce. Season with salt and pepper. If you wish to use the anchovies and/or cornichons, chop them very fine and stir them into the sauce.

To make the sauce in a food processor or blender, place all the roughly chopped herbs in the bowl or jar along with the sieved egg yolk. Add the olive oil in a thin stream, stopping to scrape the sauce down occasionally, until all the oil has been absorbed. Stir in the remaining ingredients and season as above.

CHERRY TOMATOES WITH CHERVIL SALMON MOUSSE

■

WE OFTEN SERVE THESE with the following recipe, Snow Peas with Chervil Goat Cheese. Together they make a festive spring appetizer. Because this dish has few ingredients, its success depends on a full-flavored salmon; choose one of the varieties listed below.

MAKES ABOUT 40 STUFFED TOMATOES

1/3 pound (150 g) very fresh salmon: king, silver, or Norwegian

2 tablespoons (30 ml) crème fraîche, or yogurt

1/4 cup (60 ml) chopped chervil

1/2 teaspoon (2 ml) Dijon-style mustard

Salt and white pepper to taste

1 pint basket (about 500 ml) firm-ripe cherry tomatoes, about 40 tomatoes

Skin and remove bones from the salmon, and cut into 1-inch (2-cm) chunks. In the food processor or in the blender in batches, puree the salmon with the crème fraîche or yogurt, chervil, mustard, salt and pepper.

Carefully cut 1/8 inch (3 mm) from the tops of the cherry tomatoes and gently scoop out the centers with a grapefruit knife or spoon, or small paring knife. Transfer the salmon puree to a pastry bag fitted with a medium star tip and pipe it into the tomatoes. Refrigerate the tomatoes until ready to serve.

CHERRY
TOMATOES
WITH SALMON
MOUSSE, AND
SNOW PEAS
WITH
CHERVIL
GOAT CHEESE

SNOW PEAS WITH CHERVIL GOAT CHEESE

■

POURING BOILING WATER OVER THE PEAS makes them pliable and easy to handle, as well as giving them a bright green color. Fresh goat cheese can be quite dry: you might need to add a little more half-and-half to have a soft consistency.

MAKES ABOUT 30 STUFFED SNOW PEAS

1/4 pound (115 g) snow peas, about 30

5 ounces (140 g) mild fresh goat cheese, softened

2 tablespoons (30 ml) half-and-half (single cream)

2 tablespoons (30 ml) minced chervil

1 tablespoon (15 ml) minced chives

1/8 teaspoon (0.5 ml) paprika

Salt to taste

Chive blossoms, if available

Place the peas in a colander. Pour abundant boiling water over them and toss them, then refresh with cold water. Drain the peas and pat them dry. Carefully slit each pod open along a rib and set them open side down.

Combine the goat cheese, cream, chervil, chives, paprika, and salt. Stir the mixture well.

To stuff each pea, hold it open at one end, then take about 1½ teaspoons (8 ml) of the cheese mixture on the tip of a small blunt knife and spread it inside the pea. Or put the cheese mixture in a pastry bag fitted with a medium star tip and pipe it into the peas. Refrigerate the stuffed peas until ready to serve. To serve, place on a platter and garnish it with whole chive blossoms, or snip the chive florets and scatter them over the peas.

EGGPLANT CAVIAR WITH CHERVIL

■

WE HAVE MADE THIS LIGHT APPETIZER for so many years that we've forgotten its origin, but a similar dish is made in Georgia (a republic of the former U.S.S.R), and its name acknowledges the superficial resemblance of poppy seeds to caviar. When chervil is out of season, the dish is good with 3 tablespoons (45 ml) chopped parsley and 2 tablespoons (30 ml) chopped tarragon. If you don't have both kinds of nuts on hand, use a cup (240 ml) of the kind you do have; pecans lend a nice sweetness. Serve with pita bread, crusty country-style bread sliced thin, and lightly cooked or raw vegetables.

MAKES ABOUT 2½ CUPS (600 ML), SERVING 8 TO 12 PEOPLE AS AN APPETIZER

1 large eggplant, about 1½ pounds (700 g)

1 lemon

1/4 cup (60 ml) olive oil

2 garlic cloves, minced

1/2 cup (120 ml) shelled walnuts

1/2 cup (120 ml) shelled pecans

1 cup (240 ml) sour cream or yogurt, or a mixture

1/2 cup (120 ml) packed chervil leaves

Cayenne pepper

Salt

2 tablespoons (30 ml) poppy seeds

Cut a lengthwise slice about 1 inch (2 cm) thick from one side of the eggplant. Scoop the pulp out carefully, leaving a 1/4-inch (5-mm) shell. Rub the inside of shell with lemon juice to prevent darkening.

Cut the eggplant meat into chunks and sauté over low heat in the olive oil with the garlic for about 15 minutes until the eggplant is tender and lightly browned. Stir the eggplant frequently for even cooking.

Grind the nuts to a meal in a food processor, or in a blender in batches. Add the eggplant and puree. Add the sour cream, chervil, and a dash of cayenne. Process or blend to a smooth paste. Season with salt and lemon juice, and more cayenne if desired. Blend in the poppy seeds.

Fill the eggplant shell and chill for at least 3 hours. The caviar and eggplant shell may be kept for 3 to 4 days in separate containers in the refrigerator. Remove from the refrigerator about an hour before serving.

CHERVIL AND ASPARAGUS SOUP

■

APRIL AND MAY ARE WHEN WE FIND the best local asparagus and the nicest chervil in our gardens. This light soup, given body with potatoes, brings them together. The pale jade color and refreshing taste make it an inviting beginning to any spring meal.

SERVES 6

2 medium russet potatoes, peeled

1½ pounds (675 g) asparagus

4 cups (1 litre) chicken or vegetable stock

1 medium shallot, minced

3 tablespoons (45 ml) unsalted butter

1/2 cup (120 ml) chopped chervil

Salt and freshly ground pepper

Chervil sprigs

Cut the potatoes in half and bring them to a boil in 3 cups (about 700 ml) lightly salted water. Reduce the heat and simmer uncovered until the potatoes are fork tender. Drain and set aside.

Wash and break the tough stems from the asparagus. Bring the stock to a simmer. Break the tender stalks into three pieces and add them to the simmering stock. Reduce heat, cover, and cook the asparagus until just tender. Puree it with the stock and potatoes in batches in the food processor or blender, leaving some asparagus in pieces.

Soften the shallot in the butter over low heat. Return the pureed soup to the pan, add the shallot with the butter and the chervil, and season with salt and pepper. Bring the soup just to a simmer over low heat and ladle into warm bowls. Garnish each bowl with a chervil sprig.

SCALLOPS IN PASTRY SHELLS

■

WHEN WE ARE FEELING EXTRAVAGANT, we like to celebrate a spring birthday or other special occasion by making these elegant, rich little appetizers. They may be prepared ahead, up to the point of sautéing the scallops and filling and glazing the shells. We buy frozen puff paste from bakeries that make it in the French way, with only real butter and flour. Commercial puff pastry, available in the freezer section of many supermarkets, can be used; it puffs well, but the flavor is not as fine because it is made with other fats. You could also substitute croustades for the shells; the directions for making them are given on page 291.

MAKES 12 SMALL PASTRY SHELLS

1/2 pound (225 g) puff paste

1 cup (240 ml) whipping cream (double cream)

1/2 pound (225 g) scallops

1 tablespoon (15 ml) clarified butter

3 tablespoons (45 ml) minced chervil

1 tablespoon (15 ml) capers

Salt and white pepper to taste

Preheat the oven to 450° F (230° C). Roll the puff paste into a 10-by-8-inch (25-by-20-cm) rectangle. Cut out 12 pastry shells with a 2¼-inch (6-cm) round cutter.

Place the shells on a lightly buttered baking sheet and bake for 8 to 10 minutes, until they are golden brown. Remove the shells from the oven and cool to room temperature. Cut a 1/8-inch (3-mm) slice from the top of each shell and remove the uncooked center dough.

Reduce the cream to 3/4 cup (180 ml) over very low heat, about 35 to 40 minutes. Remove any fibrous tissue from the scallops, rinse them well, and pat dry. Cut them into bite-sized pieces and sauté them in the butter over medium-high heat until they are just done, about 2 minutes.

Transfer scallops and their pan juices to a small bowl. Stir in the reduced cream along with the chervil, capers, salt, and pepper. Divide the scallop filling equally among the pastry shells and glaze for 2 minutes, 5 inches (13 cm) from a preheated broiler. Serve immediately.

CHICKEN BREASTS WITH CHERVIL

■

REFRIGERATING ANY BREADED FOOD, whether it is to be sautéed or deep-fried, helps the breading to adhere. About 30 minutes in the refrigerator is ideal, but 10 or 15 minutes in the freezer makes a difference. Clarified butter is a good fat in which to sauté breaded food as it contains no milk solids, which burn easily. To clarify butter, simply melt it over very low heat. Pour off the clear golden clarified liquid and leave the milk solids in the bottom of the pan. One-half cup (240 ml) of butter yields 5 or 6 tablespoons (about 80 ml) of clarified butter; it keeps well in the refrigerator.

SERVES 2

2 medium shallots, diced

3 ounces (85 g) mushrooms, chopped fine

2 tablespoons (30 ml) unsalted butter

About a dozen chervil sprigs

Salt and freshly ground pepper

1 large egg

1 whole chicken breast, about 1 pound (450 g)

Large pinch salt

About 1/2 cup (120 ml) flour

About 3/4 cup (180 ml) fine dry bread crumbs

3 tablespoons (45 ml) clarified butter

Chervil sprigs

Soften the shallots and mushrooms in the butter over low heat for 5 minutes; remove from heat. Mince the dozen chervil sprigs; there should be about 1/2 cup (120 ml) loosely packed chervil.

Combine the chervil and the mushroom and shallot mixture in a bowl. Season with salt and pepper. Bone and skin the chicken breast. Divide each half breast into two pieces by slicing through the thickness with a sharp knife held parallel to the work surface. Flatten each piece between waxed paper to about 3/8 inch (8 mm) thick.

Spread the mushroom chervil mixture evenly on two of the pieces. Cover these with the other pieces, and flour them well, patting off any excess flour.

Beat the egg lightly with about 1/4 teaspoon (1 ml) salt, and dip the floured breasts into the egg, coating them evenly. Coat the breasts in the bread crumbs, patting the crumbs onto the egg coating and sealing the edges well.

Cover the breasts with plastic wrap or waxed paper, and place them in the freezer for 10 to 15 minutes or in the refrigerator for up to 8 hours.

Sauté the breasts in the clarified butter over medium heat for 4 to 5 minutes on each side. If the breasts have been refrigerated longer than an hour, lower the heat and increase the cooking time by about 2 minutes on each side. When the breasts are a rich golden brown, serve them immediately on warm serving plates garnished with chervil sprigs.

C H E R V I L   A V O C A D O   P A P A Y A   S A L A D

■

MÂCHE IS THE FRENCH NAME for lamb's-lettuce, which we discuss in "Enjoying Herbs in Salads" on page 19. Limestone lettuce is grown in areas fed by limestone springs; this gives it a subtle earthy flavor. Chervil complements these mild greens and has a special affinity for avocados, too. Lacking mâche or limestone lettuce, use small leaves from Boston or butter lettuce. The salad has a slightly exotic look and taste because of the alternating avocado and papaya slices and the tangy raspberry vinegar and hazelnut oil. If the French full-flavored hazelnut oil is not available, use pure olive oil. The hazelnut oil is worth a small investment as it adds interest to many salads and marinades; it keeps well in the refrigerator for up to a year.

SERVES 4

1 ripe avocado

1 ripe papaya

12 or 16 mâche or limestone lettuce leaves

Large bunch chervil sprigs

2 tablespoons (30 ml) raspberry vinegar

2 tablespoons (30 ml) hazelnut oil

2 tablespoons (30 ml) olive oil

Salt

Chervil blossoms, if available

Peel the avocado and papaya carefully. Halve them lengthwise, and remove the avocado pit and the papaya seeds. Carefully slice each half lengthwise in 1/4-inch (5-mm) slices. Gently alternate papaya slices with avocado slices to form four multi-striped "halves". Arrange a few lettuce or mâche leaves and a small handful of chervil sprigs on each of four plates. Place a striped fruit "half" on each plate.

Pour the raspberry vinegar into a small bowl and whisk in the hazelnut and olive oils. Season the dressing lightly with salt. Drizzle the dressing over the salads. Garnish each salad with a chervil blossom or two if you have them.

P A S T A   A N D   C H E R V I L   S A L A D
W I T H   S P R I N G   V E G E T A B L E S
■

THIS IS A LIGHT FIRST COURSE, created to take advantage of special spring vegetables. If you don't have fava beans, make the salad without them, and use three artichokes and 1½ pounds of asparagus. A tasty hot variation will serve three or four people. To make the latter, sauté the shallots with the artichoke hearts. Cook the pasta al dente, drain it, and add it, along with the fava beans and asparagus, to the pan with the artichokes and shallots. Add the olive oil and a little lemon juice, and season with salt and pepper. Pass freshly grated parmesan cheese.

SERVES 6

2 artichokes	3 medium shallots, diced fine
1 lemon	3 tablespoons (45 ml) white wine vinegar or lemon juice
1/3 cup (80 ml) olive oil	
2 pounds (900 g) fresh fava beans	1/2 cup (120 ml) loosely packed chervil leaves
1 pound (450 g) asparagus	Salt and freshly ground pepper
1/2 pound (225 g) angel hair or other fine pasta	

Pare the artichokes to the hearts. Remove the chokes. Slice the hearts about 1/8 inch (3 mm) thick. Rub slices with a cut lemon as you work with them to keep them from darkening. Sauté them over medium heat in 1 tablespoon (15 ml) of the olive oil for 3 to 4 minutes, and salt and pepper them lightly. Remove to a plate and cool to room temperature.

Shell the fava beans and blanch them for 15 seconds. Refresh them with cold water and drain. Remove the tough outer skins. Snap the tough ends from the asparagus stalks and peel the stalks about halfway to the tips with a sharp paring knife or a vegetable peeler. Place the asparagus in a sauté pan with about a cup (240 ml) of water. Cover the pan and pan-steam the asparagus until it is just done, about 3 minutes. Turn the stalks once for even cooking.

Cook the pasta al dente in abundant boiling, well-salted water. Immediately add 2 cups (475 ml) of cold water to the pot to stop the cooking. Drain the pasta very well and toss with a little olive oil.

Mix the shallots with the white wine vinegar or lemon juice in a small bowl. Whisk in the remaining olive oil, and season the dressing with salt and pepper.

Toss the vegetables and chervil with the pasta. Dress the salad and toss again. Let the salad stand at room temperature for about 30 minutes before serving.

CARROTS IN CHERVIL VINAIGRETTE

■

SOMETIMES WE ADD A HALF POUND (225 g) or so of pan-steamed asparagus to this salad for a pretty and pleasant variation.

SERVES 4 TO 6

1 pound (450 g) baby carrots, peeled and trimmed

1/2 cup (120 ml) packed chervil, chopped

3 tablespoons (45 ml) white wine vinegar

1 tablespoon (15 ml) lemon juice, or to taste

1/3 cup (80 ml) olive oil

Salt and freshly ground pepper

Several chive blossoms or a small bunch of chives

Pan-steam the carrots in about a cup (240 ml) of lightly salted water for 3 to 4 minutes, until they are crisp-tender. Refresh them under cold water and pat dry.

Place the chervil in a small bowl. Add the vinegar and lemon juice, and whisk in the olive oil. Season the dressing with salt and pepper. Toss the carrots in the vinaigrette and cover and chill for at least 2 hours. Remove from the refrigerator about 30 minutes before serving. Scatter the chive blossoms over the salad, or arrange the whole chives around the salad.

BAKED YAMS WITH PARMESAN AND CHERVIL

■

WE HAVE ANECDOTAL EVIDENCE that few people care for sweet potatoes or yams. Giving the tubers an herbal accent has caused some actually to admit enjoying these vegetables (see also Sweet Potato and Parsley Salad, page 232). We are glad to see that creative restaurant cooks are presenting them in tasty and unusual ways.

SERVES 6 TO 8

2 pounds (900 g) yams or sweet potatoes

3 tablespoons (45 ml) unsalted butter

1/2 cup (120 ml) freshly grated parmesan cheese

1/3 cup (80 ml) chopped chervil

Salt and freshly ground pepper

Preheat the oven to 350° F (180° C). Wash the yams and split them lengthwise. Place them, cut side down, in a lightly oiled baking dish and bake for 40 minutes, or until they are fork-tender. Remove the yams from the oven and let them stand at room temperature until they are just cool enough to handle. Scoop the pulp into a large bowl, leaving 1/4-inch (5-mm) shells.

Mix the pulp with the butter, cheese, and chervil, and season with salt and pepper. Mound the mixture into the yam shells and return to the oven for 10 minutes. Serve hot.

HONEYDEW CHERVIL SORBET

■

THE COLOR OF THIS SORBET reminds us of the palest celadon glazes on antique Chinese porcelain. The flavor is one of those special marriages between foods: in this case, the honeyed, perfumed melon with the angelica and pear notes of chervil. Because it is not too sweet, it can be served as a palate-refreshing course for an elaborate meal, or as a dessert, perhaps with late-summer pears or crisp cookies. Any good sparkling wine with some sweetness could be substituted for the Asti Spumante. This dish is one reason we make a midsummer sowing of chervil in a semishady spot.

SERVES 8 TO 10

1/3 cup (80 ml) sugar

1 cup (240 ml) boiling water

1 large honeydew melon, about 2
    pounds (900 g)

4 tablespoons packed chervil (60 ml)

1 cup (240 ml) Asti Spumante

Violets or borage blossoms, or chervil
    sprigs

Dissolve the sugar in the water and let the syrup cool. Remove the seeds from the melon and scoop enough pulp to measure 3½ cups (830 ml). Puree the melon with the syrup and chervil in a food processor, or in a blender in batches.

To make the sorbet in an ice cream machine, follow the manufacturer's instructions. Add the Asti Spumante when the sorbet is about half-frozen. Some ice cream machines have a pour spout to facilitate this addition. If your machine lacks a pour spout, shut the motor off, remove the lid, and add the Asti Spumante.

To make the sorbet in a freezer, pour the puree into a thin metal bowl or pan and freeze for 1 hour. Remove the sorbet and break it up with a spoon, whisk, or mixer. Repeat the freezing twice more, stirring in the Asti Spumante after the sorbet has been broken up for the third time.

About 10 minutes before serving, break up the sorbet and process or blend to a smooth puree. If you have made the sorbet in an ice cream machine, this step will not be necessary. Transfer the sorbet to chilled serving glasses or dishes and return to the freezer for 5 minutes. Garnish with flower blossoms or chervil sprigs.

C H I V E S

No one grows a single chive
who wants his table's grace to thrive.

The gentle spark of chives is a tonic that any busy cook, in cold climates or warm, in city, suburbs, or country can use. The slender dark green leaves require minimal care and thrive on constant snipping to sprinkle over the plainest salad or the simplest soup. The history of chives is not one of great medicinal purpose, grand myth, or charming folklore, yet chives have been respected for at least 3000 years for their compatibility with virtually every kind of food other than desserts. Their flavor, with the sweetness of a platonic onion and the echo of very young garlic, is ideal for refined palates and delicate foods.

Chives have found a niche in all cuisines of the Northern Hemisphere, though they are used differently according to the taste and genius of each. In Japanese food, they are often a contrasting garnish for clear delicate soups. Russians favor them with fermented creams and milks and with beets and lamb. The Italians use them exclusively in summer green salads. For the French, they have an affinity with egg dishes, light sauces, and lightly cooked vegetables. The English use of chives is concentrated on fresh cheeses and salads. German cooks use them in mayonnaises and rémoulades. Egyptians and Lebanese garnish spicy meat stews and sauces with chives. Persian cuisine uses chives and garlic chives lavishly: in herb salads, meat sauces, and soups.

Once the flavor of fresh chives is established in the cook's palate, it will suggest itself as a pleasing

CHIVES' FLAVOR HAS THE SWEETNESS OF A PLATONIC ONION AND THE ECHO OF VERY YOUNG GARLIC . . .

touch to many classic and impromptu dishes. An especially tasty green rice may be made by adding equal amounts of snipped chives and minced parsley to taste. A chive butter made of 1/2 cup (120 ml) of snipped chives and 1/2 pound (225 g) of softened unsalted butter should not be restricted to potatoes; it is excellent with grilled garden tomatoes, fresh corn, sweet peas, and summer squash. With the addition of a tablespoon (15 ml) or so of lemon juice, it adorns the finest fresh lobster or grilled meat.

Fresh chives have nothing to do with dried ones, and even frozen chives lose their liveliness in the freezer after a few months. As chives are easy to grow indoors and out, insect and cold resistant, they add much for little to the essential herbal variety that stimulates the imagination and the taste buds. We find two varieties essential. The most common, *Allium schoenoprasum*, has slim, tubular leaves and 1-inch (2-cm) lavender blossoms, whereas garlic chives, *A. tuberosum*, have flat, broad leaves and larger white flower heads. We like the finer taste of common chives with lighter foods and the garlic flavor with robust dishes.

Last year, we discovered another chivelike plant at an herb grower's. Society garlic belongs to the family Liliaceae, though not to the genus *Allium*. Its horticultural name is *Tulbaghia violacea*; the plant is native to the tropics and therefore not winter-hardy in cold climates. The flavor is between those

CHIVES NEED A LIGHT SOIL, VERY GOOD DRAINAGE, AND PLENTY OF LIGHT AND MOISTURE.

of common and garlic chives: stronger than the first, but not as garlicky as the second. Society garlic can be used instead of chives as a pleasant variation; like the latter, it is best raw or cooked briefly. If you live where winters are mild, it is a handsome plant in the herb garden, with flat leaves edged with white stripes and an unusual and pretty lilac bloom. It grows to about 2½ feet (75 cm). Though we have not grown society indoors, we have learned from *The Herb Companion* that it winters well on a sunny windowsill. Some people find the oniony aroma unpleasant indoors.

Though chives are easily grown from seed, we find it convenient to buy a potted plant or two from a nursery. Whether in the garden or pots, chives need a light soil, very good drainage, and plenty of light and moisture. Although they cluster, they prefer ample space to produce lush, upright leaves. If potted chives become potbound, knock the plant out of the pot, pull it apart into clumps about 1 inch (2 cm) in diameter, and replant them in separate pots filled with fresh potting medium. This is best done in the spring or fall. Clumps of chives in the garden can be divided in the same way. Potted chives should be moved to a colder, darker place in the winter, as they require a dormant period. Under a greenhouse bench, in a cool back porch or other room, or shaded in a cold frame are good places to keep potted chives. Water the plants sparingly; there should not be much growth. Bring the pots into the light in late winter or early spring, depending on how cold it is. The tops of garden chives die back during cold winters, but they are one of the first herbs to reappear in the spring.

The leaves should be snipped from the bottom, about 1/2 inch (1 cm) above soil level. The blossoms should be snipped off as they form to maintain the best flavor and tenderness in the leaves. We always allow some chives to bloom so that we can use the flowers in salads. If you have abundant chives, cut the lavender blossoms (or the white ones of garlic chives later in the summer) and steep them in white wine vinegar for a flavored salad vinegar. Common chive blossoms give a lovely lavender-pink color to vinegar. A rare garden treat is garlic chive blossoms dipped in a light batter and fried gently until golden brown.

Fresh chives are usually available in markets through spring and summer. These are often a large variety, which has a slightly coarser flavor than that of home-grown chives. Entire leaves can be frozen for up to three months; the flavor is acceptable. Snip off what you want, straight from the freezer.

CHIVES . . . ARE ONE

OF THE FIRST HERBS

TO REAPPEAR

IN THE SPRING.

C A V I A R   A N D   C H I V E   O M E L E T

∎

THE KIND OF CAVIAR TO USE HERE is determined by your taste and budget. Choices are many: aside from the finest imported caviars (Beluga, Oestrova, Sevruga), several American producers are making excellent whitefish (golden) caviar, salmon caviar, and sturgeon (black) caviar. Do buy fresh or frozen caviar that has not been canned or pressed; this kind of processing alters the texture, one of the interesting things about caviar, and makes it too salty. Chives are the best allium to use with caviar, and oysters too, because they are less assertive than onions and shallots. If midnight suppers are in your scheme of things, this is one of the classic dishes, usually served with champagne. If not, it makes a fine Sunday morning breakfast.

SERVES 1

2 large eggs

1 tablespoon (15 ml) cold water

1/4 teaspoon (1 ml) salt

1 teaspoon (5 ml) fresh chopped basil or 1/4 teaspoon (1 ml) crushed dried basil

1½ teaspoons (8 ml) unsalted butter

1 tablespoon plus 1 teaspoon (15 ml plus 5 ml) snipped fresh chives

2½ tablespoons (38 ml) fresh caviar

1/2 teaspoon (2 ml) lime or lemon juice

1½ (22 ml) tablespoons sour cream

Beat the eggs, water, salt, and basil together well. Melt the butter in an omelet pan over moderate heat. Have all the remaining ingredients at hand.

When the butter sizzles, pour the eggs into the pan; keeping the pan on the burner, shake the omelet for 1 minute. Spoon 1 tablespoon (15 ml) chives and 1 tablespoon (15 ml) caviar in the center of the omelet and sprinkle the lime juice over the filling.

Continue to shake the pan until the eggs are barely set. Fold the omelet in half and remove to a warmed plate. Garnish with the sour cream and the remaining caviar and chives.

CAVIAR AND
CHIVE
OMELET

CRAB WITH CHIVE MOUSSELINE

■

ON THE EAST COAST, we use backfin or lump crab meat from the Chesapeake blue crab. Cooked crab of other kinds, such as Dungeness, may be used in place of the backfin crab, but the flavor will not be as sweet and fine. Though delicate in flavor, this dish is a rather rich treatment that we reserve for special dinners.

SERVES 6

1/2 cup (120 ml) unsalted butter

2 tablespoons (30 ml) lemon juice

5 tablespoons (75 ml) dry vermouth

1 tablespoon (15 ml) water

1/4 teaspoon (1 ml) freshly ground white pepper

1 tablespoon (15 ml) warm water

2 egg yolks, well beaten

Salt

2 pounds (900 g) lump or backfin crab meat or other cooked and shelled crab meat

3 tablespoons (45 ml) snipped chives

1/3 cup (80 ml) whipping cream (double cream), whipped

Melt the butter and set aside. In a small heavy-bottomed saucepan, simmer the lemon juice, 2 tablespoons (30 ml) of the vermouth, 1 tablespoon (15 ml) water, and white pepper until the mixture is reduced by one-third. Remove from the heat and rinse the sides of the pan with 1 tablespoon (15 ml) warm water.

Off the heat, whisk in the egg yolks. Return the sauce to low heat, stirring constantly until the mixture is barely steaming. Remove the sauce from the heat and mix in 2 teaspoons (10 ml) of the melted butter. Continue whisking butter into the sauce, about 2 teaspoons (10 ml) at a time, until all of it has been incorporated and the sauce has emulsified. Salt to taste. Cover and reserve while you prepare the crab.

Preheat the broiler with a rack about 6 inches (15 cm) from the heat.

Remove any bits of shell and cartilage from the crab meat and place it in a lightly buttered, heatproof gratin dish, individual gratin dishes, or scallop shells. Sprinkle the crab with the remaining vermouth. Blend the chives and whipped cream into the reserved sauce and spoon the mousseline over the crab meat.

Broil for 5 minutes or until the mousseline is puffed and browned. Serve immediately.

GRILLED TUNA WITH CHIVES

■

THE ENTHUSIASM OF AN AMERICAN FRIEND who had lived in Japan got us started experimenting with Japanese styles of cooking and ingredients. The Japanese are great herb lovers, though many of the ones they use are not well known in the United States. This dish reflects the absence of garlic and onions from Japanese cuisine, as they are considered too coarse and strong flavored. Green onions are used in many dishes, however, and chives, we think, are refined enough to fit the precepts of the cuisine. Grilled Tuna with Chives is especially handsome when cooked so that the grill marks show.

SERVES 4

1½ pounds (675 g) tuna steaks, each about 1/2 inch (1 cm) thick

3 tablespoons plus 2 teaspoons (45 ml plus 10 ml) tamari soy sauce

3 tablespoons (45 ml) mirin or dry sherry

Juice from a 1/2-inch (1-cm) piece of ginger

1 tablespoon (15 ml) plus 1 teaspoon (5 ml) sugar

1 small bunch chives

3 tablespoons (45 ml) rice vinegar

Mix 3 tablespoons (45 ml) of the tamari, the mirin or dry sherry, the ginger juice, and 1 teaspoon (5 ml) of sugar together, stirring to dissolve the sugar. Marinate the tuna in the mixture for about 30 minutes.

Prepare the sauce. Set aside a dozen chive leaves to garnish the plates and snip the remaining chives. Mix the rice vinegar, 1 tablespoon (15 ml) of sugar, and 2 teaspoons (10 ml) of tamari, stirring to dissolve the sugar. Stir the snipped chives into the sauce.

Grill the fish over a slow wood charcoal fire, on a range-top grill, or in the oven broiler. The tuna will take about 3 minutes to cook on each side.

Place the steaks on warm plates or a platter and pour the sauce over them. Arrange the chive leaves on top of each steak and serve immediately.

GARLIC CHIVE AND RICE SALAD

■

SECOND ONLY TO POTATO SALADS as summer dishes in our homes are rice salads. This variation is bright and sweet with vegetables and pleasantly pungent with garlic chives. We like either brown or white rice in this salad. It is best when made a few hours ahead, as the flavor develops on standing.

SERVES 6 TO 8

1 cup (240 ml) fresh or frozen peas

1 mint sprig

5 cups (1200 ml) cooked rice

1 large carrot

1 red or yellow bell pepper, roasted, seeded, and peeled

1 firm-ripe tomato

1/3 cup (80 ml) olive oil

1 tablespoon (15 ml) lemon or lime juice, or to taste

3 or 4 dashes Angostura bitters

1 garlic clove

Salt and freshly ground pepper

1/3 cup (80 ml) snipped garlic chives

2 tablespoons (30 ml) minced basil

2 tablespoons (30 ml) minced tarragon

Place the peas in a small saucepan with the mint sprig, barely cover with water, bring to a simmer, and cook for 1 minute. Drain, remove the mint, and cool.

Place the rice in a large bowl. Cut the carrot into quarters lengthwise and slice thin. Cut the pepper into 3/8-inch (8-mm) strips and cut the strips into 1-inch (2-cm) lengths. Cut the tomato into 1/2-inch (1-cm) dice. Add the vegetables to the rice.

Stir the olive oil, lemon juice, and bitters together with a fork to emulsify. Crush the garlic into the dressing and season with salt and pepper.

Add the dressing, garlic chives, basil, and tarragon to the rice and vegetables and toss well. Taste for seasoning. Refrigerate the salad for 1 to several hours. Let the salad come to cool room temperature before serving. Adjust the seasoning, if necessary.

M U S S E L   A N D   P O T A T O   S A L A D
W I T H   C H I V E   S A F F R O N
V I N A I G R E T T E

■

MOST MUSSELS AVAILABLE IN THE MARKET are raised in beds rather than harvested from rocks or beaches, which means they have little grit. You do need to remove their beards, the little clumps of fiber they put out to attach themselves. Mussels give off quite a bit of flavorful liquor when they are cooked; save it to use in the dish, whether it's soup, salad, or simple steamed mussels. Green-lipped mussels from New Zealand, if you can find them, are good in this dish.

Saffron has a particular affinity with shellfish, as with the alliums. This is a full-flavored salad, best with extra-virgin olive oil, and equally good as a first or main course.

SERVES 4 TO 6

4 dozen mussels	*1 tablespoon (15 ml) lemon juice*
3/4 cup (180 ml) dry white wine	*Salt and freshly ground black pepper*
2 garlic cloves, crushed	*2 pounds (900 g) new potatoes*
Pinch saffron threads	*1/2 cup (120 ml) snipped chives*
About 1/3 cup (80 ml) olive oil	*2 tablespoons (30 ml) chopped parsley*
2 tablespoons (30 ml) white wine vinegar	*Chive leaves and/or blossoms*

Debeard the mussels, then scrub and rinse them well. Put them in a very large pot or cook them in two batches. Add the wine and garlic to the pot. Cover the pot and cook the mussels over high heat until they just open, 2 to 5 minutes. Start checking for opened mussels after about 2 minutes, and remove them to a baking sheet to cool.

Discard any mussels which do not open. Shuck the mussels when they are cool enough to handle. Reserve some shells for garnish, if desired. Strain the pot liquor through a sieve lined with rinsed fine-weave cheesecloth. Check the mussels to see if they are sandy, and rinse them in the strained liquor to rid them of any sand.

If you have rinsed the mussels in the liquor, strain it again and toss about 2 tablespoons (30 ml) with the shucked mussels. Add a pinch of saffron threads to the remaining strained liquor and reduce it to about 1/2 cup (120 ml) in a small clean pan over high heat. Mix the reduced saffron mussel liquor with the olive oil, wine vinegar, and lemon juice. Season with salt and pepper.

Scrub the potatoes well and cut them in half. Steam them, cut side down, until they are just tender, about 15 minutes. Remove the steamer inset from the pan. Peel the potatoes if you like, using rubber gloves if your hands are sensitive to heat. Slice the potatoes about 1/4 inch (5 mm) thick.

Add the snipped chives and the parsley to the vinaigrette and toss it with the mussels and potatoes while the potatoes are still warm. Let the salad stand for about 30 minutes and adjust the seasoning. Arrange the salad on a platter and garnish with chive leaves, blossoms, or both.

CAULIFLOWER WITH BROWN BUTTER AND CHIVES

■

THIS SIMPLE CLASSIC IS BRIGHTENED by the combination of chives and tarragon vinegar. Try it with the beautifully baroque-looking chartreuse Italian cauliflower called Romanesco, sometimes sold as Romanesco broccoli.

SERVES 4 TO 6

1 small cauliflower, about 1 pound (450 g)	Salt and freshly ground pepper
4 tablespoons (60 ml) unsalted butter	1/4 cup (60 ml) snipped chives
2 tablespoons (30 ml) tarragon vinegar	1 to 2 tablespoons (15 to 30 ml) chopped Italian or curly parsley

Trim and wash the cauliflower and cut a cross in the stem about 1/2 inch (1 cm) deep. Cook the cauliflower whole in rapidly boiling salted water for 8 to 10 minutes, until it is just tender.

Melt the butter over medium-low heat until it turns nutty-golden brown. Remove from heat and let it cool to room temperature. Stir in the vinegar, and season lightly with salt and pepper.

Break the cauliflower into serving pieces and reshape the head in a serving bowl. Keep the bowl in a warm oven while you finish the sauce.

Stir the chives and parsley into the brown butter. Heat the butter over low heat for 1 or 2 minutes, then pour it over the cauliflower. Serve hot.

P O T A T O   A N D   T U R N I P   P U R E E
W I T H   S O U R   C R E A M   A N D   C H I V E S
■

HOW MANY MOTHERS HAVE MASHED turnips and potatoes together because every child knows turnips are to be despised? Ours did and we still like the combination; with chives it is especially good. This is fairly rich, and good served with braises or sautés that have a little acidity from wine or vinegar in their sauces.

SERVES 8

6 large russet potatoes

4 medium turnips

4 tablespoons (60 ml) unsalted butter

1/2 pint (240 ml) sour cream or
   yogurt

1/3 cup plus 1 tablespoon (80 ml plus
   15 ml) chopped chives

Salt and freshly ground pepper

Wash the potatoes and turnips and cut them in half. Steam them until fork-tender. Remove them from heat and peel. If your hands are sensitive to heat, wear rubber gloves.

Preheat the oven to 350° F (180° C). Mash the potatoes and turnips together with a potato masher, or put them through a ricer. Add the butter and sour cream. Blend well and stir in 1/3 cup (80 ml) of the chives. Season with salt and pepper.

Mound the puree in a baking dish and bake for 10 to 15 minutes, until the top is light golden brown. Garnish with the remaining chives and serve hot.

C O R I A N D E R

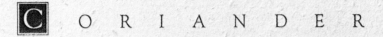

Cilantro *is the Spanish name,*

Chinese parsley is the same;

so coriander grows in fame,

and around the world makes pleasing dishes

with meats, vegetables, fruits, and fishes.

Our massed border of coriander (*Coriandrum sativum*) is the scene of one of our favorite summer stock productions. The drama begins when the bed is carpeted with the soft, tender green leaves of the young plants. This is the time for the first harvest. We gather the leaves gently, leaving some so the plants can grow back to flowering size. As the plants grow taller, the upper leaves become more fernlike and branching. The effect of the lacy hedge is at its height when the flowers open. The small white blossoms, borne in umbels, seem to float above the delicate foliage. Tiny, round green fruits gradually replace the flowers; they have a sweet, intense flavor, offering the gardener a refreshing tidbit. As the pageant draws to a close, the seeds mature to a pale golden brown. We cut the stalks and carefully dry the seeds, storing them with next year's garden props. When we have the space, we allow a few plants to take their final bow, sowing their own seeds for a return engagement.

Coriander has been highly regarded for many thousands of years around the Mediterranean basin, in India, and China. It is likened in the Bible to manna and probably grew in the Hanging Gardens of Babylon. The Chinese used coriander seed to flavor sweets and drinks; they believed it conferred immortality, perhaps because their knowledge was from the Egyptians, who placed packets of it and other spices in royal tombs. English and European herbalists, while disdaining the leaf, found the seed

THE SMALL WHITE BLOSSOMS, BORNE IN UMBELS, SEEM TO FLOAT ABOVE THE DELICATE FOLIAGE.

a pleasant sedative and calmative for both the nerves and stomach. Pliny and Dioscorides cautioned against excessive use of the seed, as it produces a narcotic stupor when taken in large amounts. Coriander seed is still an important ingredient of garam masalas, the complex spice blends of Indian cooking. It is used in pickling spices, sausages, and baked goods, and as the center of jawbreakers and confits.

Whereas the aroma of the seed is a fragile combination of orange, lemon, cumin, and anise, the aroma of the leaf is strong and pungent. We detect elements of fresh grass clippings, forest humus, and wild mushrooms. The taste is grassy and a bit oily, with an aftertaste which combines bitter and sweet to leave a faint citron flavor on the tongue. The coriander leaf's distinctive flavor and aroma become somewhat muted in cooking so that it gives a deeper, expansive flavor, rather than a sharp contrasting accent, to many types of food.

CORIANDER IS EASY

TO GROW IN CLIMATES

WHERE A MARCH

SOWING IS POSSIBLE.

Coriander is often used in dishes with many flavors and with spicy foods, though it combines harmoniously with fish and shellfish with few or no additions. It is used lavishly in curries; in Chinese cuisine, especially with seafood, chicken, and pork; in some Japanese dishes as a garnish; and in Arabic dishes of lamb and vegetables. Thai and Cambodian cooks are fond of the roots, which they use in curry pastes. A particularly tasty sauce from the Caucasus combines fresh coriander, walnuts, yogurt, red pepper, and garlic. In Portugal, the herb is featured in many meat and fish stews. In the New World, it is used throughout Mexico, Central America, and South America.

Coriander may be purchased almost year round in the United States in areas with large Latin, Indian, or Asian populations. It is commonly called Chinese or Mexican parsley or cilantro. As the leaves wilt easily, store bunches in the refrigerator in a glass or plastic jar with a little water, and covered loosely with plastic. Coriander sold with the roots attached lasts longer in storage than bunches that lack roots.

Coriander is an easy herb to grow in climates where a March sowing is possible; in cold climates, direct-sow seeds after all danger of frost, as seedlings do not take well to transplanting. Cover the seeds with about 1/2 inch (1 cm) of fine, fertile soil, then water regularly. Good drainage is important for coriander, as for most herbs. You may also grow coriander indoors in a flat or window planter of good potting mix. Here again, it requires full sun, water, and good drainage. Some herb growers, noting that insects stay away from coriander, consider it a good companion plant, indoors or out.

When days are long and hot, coriander goes to seed rapidly. To counter this natural tendency, growers have developed slow-bolting cultivars. Long Standing is available from several sources and Santo, from Johnny's Selected Seeds. These extend the harvest of leaves about 14 days, according to the producers, and may even provide all-season harvests, depending on local conditions. Whatever kind you grow, we recommend frequent cutting and staggered sowings to provide continued harvests.

The leaves may be harvested after the plants have reached about 5 inches (13 cm) tall. The aroma and flavor become more pronounced as the plant matures. Coriander leaves are best used fresh; however, they can be dried away from sun on a screen, individually frozen, or preserved in a light oil. When the seeds are golden brown (in about 90 days), harvest them or they will quickly reseed. As the aroma of coriander seed is very fragile, it is a distinct advantage to have a fresh stock. Store them in airtight containers and pulverize just before using.

WHATEVER KIND OF
CORIANDER YOU GROW,
WE RECOMMEND
FREQUENT CUTTING AND
STAGGERED SOWINGS.

HERB SAUCE WITH ROASTED CHILIS

■

AFTER AMERICAN COOKS had been introduced to pesto and the food processor, they began experimenting inventively with other herb combinations. This sauce is one of our inventions to combine Italian and Southwestern flavors. Though we like it best on homemade fettuccine or cheese ravioli, it is also good with grilled white-fleshed fish and any number of cooked vegetables, such as grilled tomatoes and eggplant and steamed or boiled summer squash and potatoes. Use fresh green chilis, adding an extra one, or a serrano or jalapeño pepper, if you like a spicier sauce.

MAKES ABOUT 2½ CUPS (600 ML), ENOUGH SAUCE FOR 1½ POUNDS (675 G) PASTA

1 cup (240 ml) packed cilantro leaves	3 large cloves garlic
About 2/3 cup (160 ml) packed basil leaves	1 large poblano and 1 large Anaheim chili, roasted, peeled, and seeded
1/3 cup (80 ml) packed Italian parsley leaves	3/4 cup (180 ml) freshly grated parmesan cheese
1 cup (240 ml) shelled pecans, lightly toasted	1/4 cup (60 ml) olive oil

Place the cilantro, basil, parsley, pecans, garlic, and chilis in a food processor bowl. Pulse until the ingredients are coarsely chopped. Add the cheese.

Start the processor, and pour the olive oil in a steady stream until it has been completely incorporated. The sauce should be quite thick, like pesto. Add a little more cheese or olive oil, if necessary.

TOMATO AND TOMATILLO SALSA WITH CILANTRO

■

THIS VERSATILE MILD SALSA can be served with Southwestern meals, as a dipping salsa, and as a relish with grilled chicken, pork, fish, and vegetables. It keeps well, tightly covered in the refrigerator, for as long as a week.

MAKES ABOUT 1 QUART (1 LITRE)

2 large tomatoes

1 pound (450 g) tomatillos

5 or 6 poblano or Anaheim chilis

1 medium onion, quartered

1 cup (240 ml) cilantro leaves

Lime juice

Salt

Roast the tomatoes, tomatillos, and chilis on a hot grill or under the oven broiler until their skins are charred.

Peel and core the tomatoes and cut them into quarters. Husk the tomatillos and put them in a processor with the tomatoes. Peel, stem, and seed the chilis and add them to the processor along with the onion and cilantro.

Process the vegetables until they are finely chopped. Add lime juice and salt to taste.

S A L M O N   I N   C H A M P A G N E   W I T H   C O R I A N D E R

■

WE'VE HAD MANY DISCUSSIONS about food and wine with our friend Joel Butler, a Master of Wine; he suggested this dish one spring during the California salmon season. Steaming the fish in this manner creates a wonderful perfume. The simple treatment is best with seasonal vegetables such as New Potatoes with Parsley, Garlic, and Lemon Peel (page 234), and perhaps asparagus or beets, warmed gently in a little crème fraîche and garnished with chervil.

SERVES 4 TO 6

2 pounds (900 g) salmon fillet, skinned and boned	24 coriander sprigs
	8 Italian parsley sprigs
Salt and freshly ground white pepper	1 cup (240 ml) champagne

Sprinkle the salmon lightly with salt and pepper on both sides. Cut an 18-by-30-inch (46-by-75-cm) piece of heavy foil. Put the foil on a baking sheet and fold up 3 inches (8 cm) along the lengths and 8 inches (20 cm) along the widths. Preheat the oven to 450° F (230° C).

Strew ten coriander sprigs and the parsley sprigs in the center of the foil. Place the salmon on the herbs. Pour the champagne over the fish and strew eight coriander sprigs on top. Fold the foil to make a package, sealing the ends tightly. Bake for 10 to 15 minutes, depending on the thickness of the fish.

Open the package, remove the cooked herbs, and place the salmon on a warm serving platter. Garnish with the remaining coriander sprigs and serve hot.

SNAPPER AND SHELLFISH SALAD WITH CORIANDER

■

CORIANDER, AS FRESH LEAVES OR DRIED SEEDS, is an excellent herb for fish and shellfish, as North Africans have known for centuries. Rinsing clams or mussels in their own liquor rids them of sand and grit without loss of flavor.

SERVES 4 TO 6

2 pounds (900 g) very small clams, such as Manila or cherrystone, scrubbed

1 cup (240 ml) dry white wine

4 Italian parsley sprigs

2 garlic cloves, mashed

1 pound (450 g) fresh snapper fillet or other firm-fleshed white fish fillet

1/2 pound (225 g) medium shrimp

1 lime

1/4 cup (60 ml) olive oil

2 tablespoons (30 ml) chopped coriander leaves

Salt

Coriander sprigs

Steam the clams open in a noncorrodible pan with the white wine, parsley, and garlic. As the clams open, remove them to a platter. When they have all opened, shuck them; discard any that do not open. Rinse the shucked clams gently in the pan juices to rid them of grit, then place them in a bowl. Strain the juices into a clean pan through a sieve lined with rinsed fine-weave cheesecloth. Save the cheesecloth.

Bring the juices to a simmer and poach the snapper for 3 to 4 minutes, until it is just done. Transfer the fish to a plate to cool.

Poach the shrimp in the same liquid until they are just done, about 2 minutes. Remove them to cool, then shell them. Strain the poaching liquid again through the cheesecloth.

Measure 1/4 cup (60 ml) of the poaching liquid into a small bowl. Add the lime juice, olive oil, and chopped coriander. Salt to taste.

Carefully flake the fish and remove any bones. Toss it gently with the clams, shrimp, and the vinaigrette. Cover and chill the salad for 2 hours. Remove from the refrigerator about 30 minutes before serving. Transfer the salad to a serving platter and garnish it with a few coriander sprigs.

CHEESE ENCHILADAS

■

QUESO COTIJO is a fresh, mildly tangy cheese available in Mexican food stores; it adds a real Southwestern touch to these enchiladas. For buffets or potluck suppers, this recipe and the following sauce recipe are easily doubled.

SERVES 6 TO 12

1 pound (450 g) cheddar, or monterey jack, or queso cotijo cheese

1/4 cup (60 ml) chopped coriander leaves

1/2 small red onion, diced

12 corn tortillas

1 recipe Green Chili Sauce with Cilantro (page 119)

Sour cream, optional

Grate the cheese and mix it with the chopped coriander and red onion.

Lightly oil a 9-by-12-inch (23-by-30-cm) baking dish. Preheat the oven to 350° F (180°C).

Warm the tortillas over a gas burner, or on a griddle on low heat for about 15 seconds on each side. Or wrap them in foil and warm them in an oven set at 300° F (150° C) for about 10 minutes. Be careful that the tortillas do not dry out during the warming.

Dip a tortilla in the Green Chili Sauce with Cilantro and place in the oiled dish.

Fill the tortilla with about 1/4 cup (60 ml) of the cheese mixture. Roll the tortilla, seam side down, in the oiled baking dish. Continue filling and rolling until the tortillas and filling have been used.

Cover the enchiladas with the remaining sauce and bake them for about 15 minutes. Serve immediately.

GREEN CHILI SAUCE WITH CILANTRO

■

THIS IS ONE OF OUR TWO FAVORITE sauces for enchiladas, huevos rancheros, and burritos; the other is a red chili sauce. The latter is spiced with cumin and coriander seed, and this one is flavored with cumin and coriander leaf. It can be made in advance and keeps well, refrigerated, for up to 5 days.

The amount of heat in green chilis depends on the variety of chili and growing conditions. If the chilis you have are mild, add a few jalapeños or serranos for heat. When the chilis are really hot, we sometimes add sour cream to temper the heat. We add it at the end of cooking, stirring it into the sauce and reheating gently just before serving.

MAKES ABOUT 3 CUPS (700 ML)

2 tablespoons (30 ml) corn or vegetable oil

1 cup (240 ml) diced onion

2 garlic cloves, chopped fine

2 cups (475 ml) green chilis, roasted, peeled, seeded, and chopped

1/2 teaspoon (2 ml) toasted and ground cumin seed

2 cups (475 ml) broth or water

Salt and freshly ground pepper

1/3 cup (80 ml) packed cilantro leaves, chopped coarsely

Sour cream, optional

Heat the oil in a frying pan over moderate heat. Add the onion and garlic, reduce heat to low, and sauté them slowly for about 10 minutes, stirring occasionally.

Add the chilis, cumin, and the broth and simmer gently for 10 minutes. Season with salt and pepper and add the cilantro, stir, and cook for 5 minutes more.

Puree half—or all of the sauce, if desired—in small batches in the blender. Return the sauce to the pan and taste for seasoning. Serve as desired. If the sauce seems very thick, it can be thinned with a little water.

PORK CHOPS WITH RED CABBAGE AND GREEN APPLES

■

FRYING-PAN SUPPERS ARE QUICK TO PREPARE, yet interesting in their medley of flavors. This one is naturally sweet and tart from the onions and apples. We usually serve it with just a crusty, country-style bread. Since the ingredients are those of German and Alsatian cooking, the dish is good served with beer or Gewürztraminer wine. The moisture of the vegetables and fruit is enough to cook the dish, but if you would like more pan juices, add a little beer or wine before the final cooking.

SERVES 6

6 loin pork chops, each about 1¼ inches (3 cm) thick and trimmed of excess fat

4 tablespoons (60 ml) clarified butter

1/2 pound (225 g) red cabbage, shredded

1 medium onion, sliced thin

4 medium Granny Smith or other tart green apples, cored and sliced thin

1 teaspoon (5 ml) ground coriander seed

2 tablespoons (30 ml) chopped coriander leaves

Salt and freshly ground black pepper

4 to 6 coriander sprigs

Use a large noncorrodible frying pan with a tight-fitting lid. Heat 1 tablespoon (15 ml) clarified butter over moderately high heat and sauté the pork chops on both sides, for about 5 minutes, until they are browned. Remove them to a platter and keep warm.

Heat the remaining 3 tablespoons (45 ml) of clarified butter over medium heat in the same frying pan. Sauté the cabbage, onion, and apples for about 5 minutes, tossing the pan to coat them evenly. Stir in the ground coriander seed and chopped coriander. Salt and pepper the vegetables and chops lightly.

Place the chops under the vegetables and fruit and cover the pan. Steam the chops for about 15 minutes, until they are just done. Transfer the vegetables and fruit to a warm serving platter and place the chops on top. Garnish the dish with coriander sprigs and serve hot.

CHICKEN MOLE WITH CORIANDER

∎

LATIN-AMERICAN FOOD STORES are the best places to find dried chilis, but some supermarkets carry an assortment of them, too. Mulato chilis give a rich, toasty, chocolate flavor to the mole; use a New Mexico or California dried chili if you can't find mulatos. As these chilis are usually hotter than mulatos, you will need only one. Chipotle chilis are smoke-dried jalapeños and are very hot. *Always* wear rubber gloves while working with chilis. Capsaicin, a compound concentrated in the pithy membranes and the seeds, can severely irritate the eyes, nose, lips, mouth, and even the skin of the fingers and hands. If you are unfamiliar with the taste of chilis, you should probably start with a third of the amount called for in this dish.

SERVES 4

3½- to 4-pound (1.6- to 1.8-g) frying chicken

3 tablespoons (45 ml) corn or vegetable oil

About 3 cups (700 ml) chicken stock

2 dried mulato chilis or 1 New Mexico or California dried chili

2 chipotle chilis or 2 small dried red chilis such as serranos or japones

1 cup (240 ml) boiling water

1 corn tortilla

3 garlic cloves, minced

2 tablespoons (30 ml) sesame seeds

1/3 cup (80 ml) unblanched almonds, chopped coarsely

1 tablespoon (15 ml) toasted and ground coriander seed

1/4 cup (60 ml) chopped coriander leaves

1 ounce (30 g) Mexican chocolate, or 1 ounce (30 g) semisweet chocolate and a pinch of cinnamon

Cut the chicken into serving pieces and reserve the giblets for another use. Sauté the chicken in a large frying pan in 2 tablespoons (30 ml) oil until it is browned, about 10 minutes. Pour in enough chicken stock to half cover the chicken. Cover the pan and simmer for 10 to 15 minutes.

Stem and seed the mulato and chipotle chilis. Soak them in the boiling water for about 15 minutes. Remove them from the water and chop them fine. Reserve the water.

Cut the corn tortilla into 1-inch (2-cm) strips. Sauté the chilis and tortilla strips in the remaining tablespoon (15 ml) of oil over low heat for 5 minutes. Add the minced garlic and sauté for another minute or two. Add the mixture to the chicken. Toast the sesame seeds and almonds in a small dry frying pan over low heat until they are pale golden brown, about 5 minutes. Shake the frying pan frequently for even browning.

Add the toasted seeds and almonds to the chicken along with the ground coriander seed. Add the reserved chili-soaking water. Simmer the chicken for another 10 minutes or so. Add the chopped coriander leaves and the chocolate (or chocolate and cinnamon) and stir until the chocolate dissolves, about 2 to 3 minutes. Serve the mole hot with corn tortillas.

SUMMER VEGETABLES SOUTHWESTERN-STYLE

■

IN THE SOUTHWESTERN UNITED STATES and northern Mexico, the combination of corn, squash, and chilis is called *calabacitas*. This version, which we have developed over the years, contains several additional ingredients that give the dish a very full flavor.

SERVES 6

2 tablespoons (30 ml) corn or vegetable oil

1 cup (240 ml) chopped onion

12 ounces (340 g) small summer squash; yellow, pattypan, or zucchini (courgettes)

1 garlic clove, minced

1 red bell pepper, roasted, peeled, seeded, and diced

2 poblano or Anaheim chilis, roasted, peeled, seeded, and diced

3 cups (710 ml) fresh or frozen and thawed corn kernels

2 medium tomatoes, chopped coarsely

About 1/2 cup (120 ml) cilantro leaves, coarsely chopped

Salt and freshly ground pepper

1 cup (240 ml) longhorn cheddar cheese, grated

Heat the oil in a heavy-bottomed saucepan and sauté the onion for about 2 minutes. Cut the squash into 1/4-inch (5-mm) slices and add them to the pan. Sauté for 2 or 3

SUMMER
VEGETABLES
SOUTHWESTERN
STYLE

minutes and add the garlic. Stir occasionally and cook for another minute or so.

Add the bell pepper and chilis to the pan, along with the corn and tomatoes. Stir well, cover, and lower the heat to moderate. Cook for another 5 minutes, stirring occasionally. If the pan is dry, add just a bit of water.

Add the cilantro, season with salt and pepper, and cook, covered, for another 2 or 3 minutes. Serve in a warm bowl or in individual bowls garnished with the grated cheese.

ORANGE, OLIVE, AND AVOCADO SALAD

∎

CORIANDER HAS AN AFFINITY with both avocados and oranges and is plentiful in the late winter and early spring when they are in season. This is a handsome salad that we like to serve with Latin-American and Middle Eastern dishes.

SERVES 4

1 small head escarole	1/3 cup (80 ml) oil-cured black olives
1 cup (240 ml) loosely packed coriander sprigs with tender stems	1/3 cup (80 ml) freshly squeezed orange juice
1 ripe Hass avocado	1/3 cup (80 ml) olive oil
1/2 lemon	1 garlic clove, minced
2 small oranges	Salt and freshly ground pepper

Remove the outer green leaves from the escarole and reserve for another use. Wash and dry the tender yellow-green inner leaves. Arrange them on a serving platter and scatter the coriander sprigs on top.

Cut the avocado lengthwise and peel it. Remove the seed and cut each half crosswise into 1/4-inch (5-mm) slices. Sprinkle a few drops of lemon juice on the avocado slices. Peel the oranges, removing the white pith, and cut them crosswise into 1/4-inch (5-mm) slices. Remove any seeds. Arrange the avocado and orange slices on the escarole and coriander. Pit the olives and scatter them over the salad.

Mix the orange juice, olive oil, and garlic together. Season with salt and pepper. Drizzle the dressing over the salad and let it stand 5 minutes before serving.

WINTER FRUIT SALAD WITH CORIANDER

■

THIS IS A REFRESHING END to a late winter meal and is especially good with several kinds of citrus, such as blood oranges, navel oranges, and honey or emerald tangerines. We like it as well without the dressing after a rich dinner or for brunch.

SERVES 8 TO 10

1½ pounds oranges and tangerines

1 medium-sized ripe pineapple, about 1½ pounds

2 firm-ripe bananas

1/2 cup (120 ml) loosely packed coriander leaves

1 recipe Coriander Coconut Dressing (recipe follows)

Peel the citrus fruit, removing the white pith, and cut into slices. Remove any seeds. Peel and core the pineapple and cut it into pieces. Peel and slice the bananas. Toss the fruit in a large serving dish with 1/4 cup (60 ml) of the coriander leaves. Garnish the salad with the remaining coriander leaves and serve with Coriander Coconut Dressing on the side.

CORIANDER COCONUT DRESSING

■

MAKES ABOUT 1¼ CUPS (300 ML)

1¼ cups (300 ml) unsweetened coconut milk

2 tablespoons (30 ml) honey

1 teaspoon (5 ml) ground coriander seed

Lemon juice to taste

Blend the coconut milk, honey, coriander seed, and lemon juice in the blender until the dressing is very smooth. Serve with fruit salad.

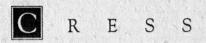RESS

WATERY cress, Queen of the stream,

in salads fine you have no peer;

poor man's bread, rich man's cream,

all men's delight for half the year.

We set out eagerly every year at the first signs of spring to inspect our favorite cress streams. The earth is still cold and moist underfoot as we follow the sound of the water to banks of fresh green growth. The tiny cress tendrils have their most subtle flavor now, a delicate balance of sweetness and spice. It is a special excitement to gather spring's first herbal bounty. Cress often naturalizes in wild and semiwild streams, but we must caution you not to gather any unless you are sure that the stream is free from human or animal contamination.

Spring abundance provides a welcome chance to prepare cress frequently and in different ways. Though the herb is not aromatic, its peppery flavor has added interest to salads and soups for centuries. Cress tingles the tongue so definitely that we like it best as a salad herb. It enlivens any green or vegetable salad and goes well with combination salads including grains, potatoes, pasta, fish, or chicken. Cress is a versatile and pretty garnish; its different forms and flavors and its availability stimulate the cook to use it freely.

Of the several varieties of cress, all members of the mustard family, watercress (*Nasturtium officinale*) is the best known and most commonly available, found in markets in fall and spring. This is the cress usually referred to in herb lore. Winter cress (*Barbarea verna*), which is cultivated commercially much more today than in the past, has a flavor and color very like those of watercress, but its leaves are

CRESS TINGLES THE

TONGUE SO DEFINITELY

THAT WE LIKE IT BEST AS

A SALAD HERB.

longer and more pointed. The pleasant bite of both winter and watercress disappears when they are cooked, replaced by a different but agreeable herbal vegetable taste with overtones of spinach, parsley, and mustard greens. Garden cress (*Lepidium sativum*) has paler and smaller leaves than watercress but a similar flavor. Heating destroys both color and flavor.

It should be eaten raw when the leaves are small and before it flowers.

When buying cress, look for shiny, deep green leaves in compact bunches; the small flowers, if any, should be closed. Store cress in the refrigerator, with the stems in water in an ample covered glass or plastic container and use within one or two days of purchase.

AN ATTRACTION OF WATERCRESS IS THE PLEASURE OF PICKING IT FREE AND WILD.

Cress takes its name from the Greek word *grastis*, meaning "green fodder", an indication of how long it has been valued as food. In fact, it contains goodly amounts of iron and vitamin C. Persians steeped cress in milk and gave it to their children to increase their growth. The Greek armies of Alexander's time ate it because they believed it imparted strength during battle. From the Middle Ages through the nineteenth century, English peasants ate cress in place of bread when they had no flour. The Romans, who knew all herbs, harvested wild cress for their salads.

Because winter and watercress require very rich marshy earth, running water, and protection from the cold, they are usually cultivated commercially. Unless you are lucky enough to have a stream running through your garden, growing watercress will be difficult. You may try sowing the seeds in flats of wet compost in the early summer or transplanting rooted stems to a trench. Either way, the soil must be kept constantly moist, but not soggy.

Garden cress, however, is easily grown. Indoors, spread seeds evenly on a piece of absorbent toweling in a tray, soak them thoroughly, and cover with waxed paper. Remove the paper when the seeds begin to germinate and keep the sprouts moist until they are from 4 to 6 inches (10 to 15 cm) tall. Trim them about 1/4 inch (5 mm) from the base and use in salads. In the garden, cover the seeds lightly with fine soil and keep it moist with a fine spray until the cress is ready to harvest. Mature garden cress may be eaten, though it has a definite bitterness.

One of the attractions of watercress is the pleasure of picking it free and wild. Another is the lush pageant of full-grown cress, its diadems of tiny white flowers suggesting one of its sobriquets, Queen of Herbs. In these recipes, cress contributes the crowning touch.

C R E S S   E G G   R O L L S

■

DEEP-FRIED FOODS are once-in-a-while specials for us. We prefer to start with fresh oil, which makes deep-frying rather expensive. To warrant the expense and the calories, a deep-fried dish has to be light-tasting, yet full of flavor. The cress in these egg rolls raises them to a new level of interest and makes them a worthwhile effort.

SERVES 8 TO 12 AS AN APPETIZER

2 cups plus 2 tablespoons (475 ml plus 30 ml) peanut oil

1/2 teaspoon (2 ml) black mustard seeds

1 garlic clove, minced

2 teaspoons (10 ml) freshly grated gingerroot

4 cups (950 ml) shredded green cabbage or Napa cabbage

1/2 pound (225 g) mushrooms, chopped

1 cup (240 ml) mung bean sprouts

1½ tablespoons (22 ml) soy sauce

2 cups (475 ml) packed cress leaves

2/3 cup (160 ml) shredded cooked chicken or bay shrimp, optional

1 egg

24 to 30 6-inch (15-cm) square egg-roll skins

3 or 4 cress sprigs

Heat 2 tablespoons (30 ml) oil in a wok or a large frying pan over moderate heat. Add the mustard seeds, garlic, and ginger. When the first mustard seed pops, add the cabbage and stir-fry for 3 minutes. Add the mushrooms and stir-fry for 3 minutes.

Add the mung bean sprouts and soy sauce and stir-fry for 2 minutes. Add the cress leaves and stir until they are barely wilted. Remove the wok or frying pan from the heat. Toss in the chicken or shrimp, if desired.

Lightly beat the egg. Fill each egg-roll skin with 2 tablespoons (30 ml) of the cooked mixture. Fold the corners over the center and seal the top flap of each egg roll with a dab of the beaten egg.

Heat the remaining 2 cups (475 ml) peanut oil in a wok or deep frying pan until the oil is very hot, almost smoking. Fry the egg rolls four at a time for 30 to 40 seconds on each side, or until both sides are golden brown. Remove with a slotted spoon and drain on paper towels. Keep cooked egg rolls hot on a warm serving platter while you fry the others, reheating the oil between batches.

Serve immediately with Chinese mustard and soy sauce for dipping. Garnish the platter with cress sprigs.

CRESS AND GOAT CHEESE SPREAD

THE TANGINESS OF GOAT CHEESE and the pepperiness of cress make a flavorful combination. This spread is best made ahead of time and allowed to mellow. It is good with cucumber slices, crackers, bagels, wheat or pumpernickel bread, or Oatmeal Bread with Thyme and Walnuts (page 323).

MAKES ABOUT 1½ CUPS (360 ML)

5 to 6 ounces (140 to 170 g) mild goat cheese, softened

2 to 3 tablespoons (30 to 45 ml) half-and-half (single cream)

2 to 3 tablespoons (30 to 45 ml) olive oil

3 tablespoons (45 ml) minced, oil-packed, sun-dried tomatoes

1 shallot, minced

1 packed cup (240 ml) cress leaves, chopped coarse

Salt and freshly ground pepper

Cress sprigs

Place the goat cheese in a bowl. With a fork, work in enough of the cream and olive oil to make a spreadable consistency. Add the sun-dried tomatoes, shallot, and cress and blend well. Season with salt and pepper.

Refrigerate for at least an hour before serving. Allow the spread to come to cool room temperature. Adjust the seasoning and add a bit more cream or olive oil, if necessary. Serve the spread in a bowl and garnish it with cress sprigs.

WATERCRESS CRÈME
FRAÎCHE SOUP

■

THIS IS A GOOD SPRING TONIC, which we like to drink as such when the first good market or wild cress comes in. As a first-course soup, it is light and brothy, and appropriate before a rich dinner such as filet mignon or salmon with Cress Béarnaise (page 132).

In addition to cress, crème fraîche takes particularly well to basil, chervil, chives, dill, sage, the savories, and tarragon. It is useful as a garnish for steamed or poached fish or chicken, and steamed or blanched vegetables. Directions for making crème fraîche are on page 308.

SERVES 4

1 quart (1 litre) defatted chicken stock or vegetable stock

3 cups (710 ml) packed watercress leaves

Small bunch chives, chopped

Salt and freshly ground white pepper

1 cup (240 ml) crème fraîche

Heat the stock over low heat until it barely simmers. Add the watercress and chives, and season with salt and pepper. Simmer for 5 minutes and stir in the crème fraîche.

Remove the soup from the heat and puree half of it in the blender in batches or in the food processor. Return to low heat for 2 to 3 minutes. Ladle the soup into warmed soup plates and serve immediately.

CRESS BÉARNAISE

■

THERE IS NO QUESTION that béarnaise and hollandaise sauces are indulgences, but they are so magical to make and so concentrated in flavor that only a little is necessary to gild the finished dish. Béarnaise is classic with the finest filet mignon and is excellent with any grilled red meat or fish, or with poached eggs. The shallots and cress give this one added texture that will also make a main course of a simple baked potato for all but the most insistent meat eaters. It is best to have all the ingredients ready and make the sauce just before serving; it takes only about 5 minutes. The sauce can be held for 10 minutes or so over, not in, hot water at 140° F (60° C). Whisk just before serving to lighten.

MAKES ABOUT 3/4 CUP (180 ML), SERVING 6 TO 8

1 large shallot, minced	*1 tablespoon (15 ml) hot water*
3 tablespoons (45 ml) white wine	*6 tablespoons (90 ml) cold unsalted*
3 tablespoons (45 ml) tarragon vinegar	*butter, cut into bits*
	Salt and freshly ground white pepper
1 egg yolk	*2 tablespoons (30 ml) minced cress leaves*

Place the shallot, white wine, and tarragon vinegar in a small, heavy saucepan. Reduce the liquid over moderately high heat to about 1 tablespoon (15 ml). Whisk the egg yolk with the hot water. Remove the pan from the heat and whisk in the yolk mixture.

Return the sauce to very low heat and add the butter, about one-quarter at a time, whisking vigorously and continually. When the sauce has emulsified to a glossy, medium-thick consistency, remove from heat and season with salt and white pepper. Stir in the minced cress leaves. Serve immediately.

SALMON AND PASTA SALAD WITH CRESS

■

A FULL-FLAVORED OLIVE OIL brings the elements of this salad together. Everything can be prepared up to a day ahead, but do not combine the ingredients until about 2½ hours before serving. For the best flavor and texture, add cold water to stop the pasta from cooking, then toss it with a little oil, rather than rinsing it.

SERVES 4

1 cup (240 ml) dry white wine

2 garlic cloves, 1 minced

1 bay leaf

6 peppercorns

6 parsley sprigs

1/2 teaspoon (2 ml) salt

1/2 pound (225 g) salmon steak or fillet

1/2 pound (225 g) baby carrots

6 ounces (170 g) tiny shell pasta

1/4 cup plus 1 teaspoon (60 ml plus 5 ml) olive oil

2 tablespoons (30 ml) Dijon-style mustard

Salt and freshly ground pepper

Lemon juice

1 cup (240 ml) packed cress leaves

1/2 cup (120 ml) Niçoise olives

Place the wine, the whole garlic clove, bay leaf, peppercorns, parsley sprigs, and 1/2 teaspoon (2 ml) salt in a small saucepan which is deep enough to allow the fish to be covered by the wine. Bring the liquid to a simmer and cook for 10 minutes.

Add the salmon and simmer it until just done, about 5 minutes. Remove the salmon from the pan and let it cool to room temperature. Meanwhile, strain the poaching liquid and reduce to 1/2 cup (120 ml).

Clean the carrots and pan-steam them in 1 cup (240 ml) water until they are barely tender. Drain them and rub off the skins under cold running water. Cut the carrots diagonally into 1/2-inch (1-cm) pieces and set aside.

Cook the pasta in boiling salted water al dente. Add about 2 cups (475 ml) cold water to the pot to stop the cooking. Drain the pasta and transfer it into a large bowl with the carrots. Toss with 1 teaspoon (5 ml) olive oil.

Mix the remaining olive oil, minced garlic, mustard, and reduced poaching liquid together. Season with salt, pepper, and lemon juice. Pour the vinaigrette over the pasta and carrots and toss well.

Flake the salmon carefully into the salad, removing bones and skin if necessary. Add the cress leaves and olives and toss everything together gently. Cover and chill for 2 hours. Let the salad stand at room temperature for about 30 minutes. Adjust the seasoning before serving in shell dishes or on salad plates.

BULGUR, CRESS, AND PINEAPPLE SALAD

■

BULGUR IS MADE OF HULLED WHOLE WHEAT BERRIES that are steamed and then ground; several grades of coarseness are available. Because it is partially cooked, it needs only steeping in hot liquid. This can be done ahead, and the bulgur kept in the refrigerator. The nutty flavor of bulgur plays off well here against the peppery cress and tangy pineapple.

SERVES 6 TO 8

2 cups (475 ml) coarse-grain bulgur wheat	1/2 cup (120 ml) olive oil, or to taste
4 cups (1 litre) hot chicken or vegetable stock	1 large clove garlic, minced
	1 cup (240 ml) packed cress leaves, coarse-chopped
1 small pineapple, about 1½ pounds (675 g)	Salt
	Several cress sprigs
1 lemon	Pineapple slices

Place the bulgur in a large bowl and pour the hot stock over it. Let it stand for 2 or 3 hours, then transfer to a fine sieve or a colander lined with rinsed fine-weave cheesecloth, and drain for at least 30 minutes.

Pare and core the pineapple. Cut enough of it into small pieces to equal about 1 cup (240 ml), with the juice. Juice the lemon and mix it with the olive oil and garlic.

Add the pineapple pieces and juice to the dressing. Stir in the cress leaves. Season with salt.

BULGAR,
CRESS, AND
PINEAPPLE
SALAD

Pour the dressing over the drained bulgur and toss well. Taste for seasoning. Marinate at room temperature for 2 hours. Slice the remaining pineapple about 3/8-inch (8 mm) thick. Transfer the salad to a serving dish and garnish with cress sprigs and pineapple.

AVOCADO CRESS SALAD WITH RADICCHIO

■

THE RICH, SUBTLE NUTTINESS OF AVOCADOS always calls for herbs; besides coriander, we like those with a little bite, such as cress and tarragon. Sometimes we substitute sherry or balsamic vinegar for the lemon juice in this salad. We especially like to serve it before simple baked, poached, or grilled fish dishes and for lunch with a bowl of soup.

SERVES 4

2 large ripe Hass avocados

1 lemon

Dash or two of Tabasco

2 or 3 tablespoons (30 to 45 ml) olive oil

2 small firm-ripe tomatoes, about 8 ounces (225 g), diced

1/2 cup (120 ml) diced mild onion such as Vidalia or Walla Walla

1/2 (120 ml) cup diced celery

1 cup (240 ml) packed cress leaves

Salt and freshly ground pepper

1 small head radicchio, about 6 ounces (170 g), or 1 small head red leaf lettuce such as red oak leaf

Cress sprigs

Halve the avocados and scoop out the meat, leaving about 1/4 inch (5 mm) next to the skin. Rub the avocado halves with half a cut lemon. Dice the avocado meat into 1/2-inch (1-cm) cubes and toss them with the lemon juice to taste, Tabasco, and 1 tablespoon (15 ml) olive oil.

Mix the tomatoes, onions, celery, and cress leaves with the diced avocados. Season with salt and pepper.

Fill the avocado shells with the vegetable mixture. Arrange the radicchio leaves and cress sprigs on four salad plates. Drizzle with olive oil and season with salt and pepper. Place the avocado halves on the salad leaves and serve at cool room temperature.

P O T A T O   P I E   W I T H   W I L T E D   C R E S S

∎

IN NORTHERN EUROPE, mashed potatoes are often combined with lightly cooked or shredded raw greens: cabbage, chicory, endive, escarole, or spinach. In this combination, rather than mixing the herb with the potatoes, we added a crowning wreath of cress. The rich and filling potato pie can stand as a main course, accompanied perhaps by Mushrooms with Thyme on Toast (page 320) and a green or vegetable salad. For the lightest texture, mash the potatoes while they're hot.

SERVES 6 TO 8

3 pounds (1.4 kg) russet potatoes	*2 large eggs*
1 medium white onion, diced fine	*1 cup (240 ml) milk*
About 5 tablespoons (75 ml) unsalted butter	*2 teaspoons (10 ml) salt, or to taste*
1½ cups (360 ml) coarsely grated gruyère or emmentaler cheese	*1 teaspoon (5 ml) freshly ground white pepper*
	3 cups (710 ml) packed cress leaves

Cut the potatoes in half and boil or steam them in their skins until they are fork-tender. Remove them from heat and peel. If your hands are sensitive to heat, wear rubber gloves while peeling. Mash or rice the potatoes in a large bowl.

Soften the onion over moderate heat in 4 tablespoons (60 ml) butter. Add the onions to the potatoes. Stir in the grated cheese and blend well. Preheat the oven to 375° F (190° C).

Beat the eggs with the milk and the salt and pepper. Add the milk mixture to the potatoes and combine well. Butter a 9½-inch (24-cm) glass or ceramic pie dish and transfer the potato mixture to it. Bake the pie for 45 minutes, or until the top is golden brown and crusty.

Barely wilt the cress leaves in a steamer over boiling water, about 30 seconds. Remove the pie from the oven and arrange the wilted cress leaves on top of it in a circle. Cut the pie into wedges and serve hot.

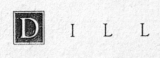ILL

Lullaby *dill, the baby calms to sleep;*

Fragrant dill, the cook bakes bread;

Fruitful dill, the gardener goes to reap.

This is the herb we rub shoulders with every summer, the tall golden brown flower heads as large as dinner plates and full of plump seeds waiting for us to pick, dry, and enter them in the county fair. It is stalwart and accommodating all year; we use the feathery fresh leaves freely in green salads and the seeds for heavier foods—breads and potatoes—or as an herb salt.

Throughout its history, dill (*Anethum graveolens*) has kept the mien of a cheerful, plain soul, ready to lighten everyday fare. Although many culinary and medicinal recipes list it, sacred, poetic, or fanciful imaginations have not found dill an inspiring herb. It has remained, for the diverse populations that have used it, a comforting, pleasant herb adapted to practical roles.

Its generic name, *Anethum*, is the Latin version of the Greek word for dill; the English word "dill" may be related to the Saxon *dillan*, "to lull or soothe", and with good reason. Dill water has soothed babies' colic for ages in England, Europe, and Turkey. Adults took dill wine as people today take bicarbonate preparations. It was probably for this calming effect on the stomach as much as for its complementary flavors that cooks began pickling cucumbers with dill. Every English household that cultivated herbs prepared dill vinegar for salads.

Although native to the Mediterranean area, dill is little used in the western part of that region. It is a daily herb, however, in Greece, Egypt, and the

DILL IS STALWART AND

ACCOMMODATING

ALL YEAR . . .

Middle East. It is popular in many Eastern European cuisines—in Rumania, Bulgaria, Poland, and Russia. It is used somewhat in France, Germany, and England, prolifically in the Scandinavian countries, especially Sweden.

The seeds, leaves, or both are found in baked goods of all descriptions, including breads, crackers, cookies, cakes, and pies. It commonly accompanies fish: the gravlax and marinated herring of Scandinavia, dill sauce for fresh trout in England, and fish grilled with dill in France and Russia. It appears in sauces for poultry and vegetables; with meats, particularly in Russian and Eastern European recipes; and to enliven simple egg or potato dishes. In small amounts, dill combines successfully with parsley or chervil to flavor the poaching liquid of chicken, fish, and early summer vegetables.

WHILE IT FLOURISHES IN

THE GARDEN . . . DILL

LANGUISHES IN

CONFINED AREAS.

The flavor of the leaves is a mixture of anise, parsley, and celery with a distinctive green bite on the sides of the tongue. The aroma is a clean combination of mint, citrus, and fennel with a touch of sea air. The seeds taste predominantly of caraway and anise.

Dill's aroma is fairly delicate and loses much in drying or cooking. We find dried dill weed to have limited uses; fortunately, fresh dill is available during most of the year in major produce areas of the United States. Stems and leaves of purchased or harvested dill should be green throughout.

Dill grows in most climates with the modest requirements of fairly friable soil, light fertilization, and sun. It is not easy to grow successfully indoors, as it needs about 18 inches (46 cm) of taproot space and much branching room. Some seed suppliers offer a dwarf cultivar, fernleaf dill, that grows only about two feet tall. While it flourishes in the garden and will conveniently reseed itself for years, it languishes in confined areas. It germinates and grows quickly and may be planted after danger of frost, or year round in mild climates.

The leaves are harvested before the plants set seed. If you want fresh dill weed into the late fall, sow seeds again in midsummer. You can begin plucking bits of leaf as soon as plants are 4 to 6 inches (15 cm) tall, but for maximum harvests, snip the leaves close to the stem about two months after planting. To harvest the seeds, allow flowers to form on some plants and the seeds to turn pale brown. Cut the tops with about a foot of stalk and hang upside down with the tops inside paper bags to catch the seeds. Be sure the seeds are completely dry before storing.

FRESH TOMATO SOUP WITH DILL

■

THIS REFRESHING SOUP is a good beginning to almost any summer meal. As the soup is chilled, the flavor of the tomatoes is especially important; they should be completely and perfectly ripe.

SERVES 6 TO 8

3 pounds (1.4 kg) ripe tomatoes	1 teaspoon (5 ml) paprika
1 medium cucumber	1/2 teaspoon (2 ml) salt
1/4 cup (60 ml) snipped dill	Dash Angostura bitters
1 garlic clove, minced	Dill sprigs
2 tablespoons (30 ml) grated onion	Sour cream

Blanch the tomatoes in boiling water for about 10 seconds. Cool under running water, then peel and seed them. Peel and seed the cucumber.

Puree the tomatoes and cucumber briefly, about 10 seconds, in the blender or food processor. Add the dill, garlic, onions, paprika, salt, and bitters and puree for a second or two.

Chill the soup for at least 2 hours. Adjust the seasoning and ladle into chilled soup bowls. Garnish with dill sprigs and sour cream.

DILLED RICOTTA TORTE

■

WE LIKE SERVING THIS SAVORY, rich torte for Sunday brunch or lunch as a change from more usual egg and cheese dishes. It can be baked ahead, then refrigerated for a day or so. It goes well with fruit and green salads as well as with sliced ham or smoked fish. We prefer to use natural cream cheese, without gums or chemicals, to processed cream cheese. The former is available in many markets, cheese stores, and delicatessens.

SERVES 8 TO 12

1 cup (240 ml) whole almonds, unblanched

1½ cups (360 ml) fine dry bread crumbs, preferably whole wheat

1/2 cup (120 ml) unsalted butter, softened

Salt

3/4 pound (340 g) natural cream cheese, softened

1 cup (240 ml) ricotta cheese

2 eggs

2 tablespoons (30 ml) half-and-half (single cream)

1/3 cup (80 ml) snipped dill leaves

1/2 teaspoon (2 ml) freshly grated nutmeg

1 teaspoon (5 ml) grated lemon peel

Dill sprigs

Make a medium-fine meal of the almonds in the blender or food processor. Transfer them to a bowl and blend in first the bread crumbs and then the softened butter. Season with about 1/4 teaspoon (1 ml) salt. Press the mixture on the bottom of a 9½-inch (24-cm) springform baking pan and about 1¼ inches up the sides.

Preheat the oven to 350° F (180° C). With an electric mixer on medium speed or with the food processor combine the cream cheese, ricotta, eggs, cream, dill, nutmeg, and grated lemon peel. Blend the mixture very well and season with salt.

Pour the mixture carefully into the prepared shell and bake for 1 hour and 10 minutes. Cool the torte to room temperature on a rack. Remove the springform ring and garnish the torte with dill sprigs. The torte may also be served chilled. If you make it in advance, remove it from the refrigerator about 30 minutes before serving, and remove the springform ring.

DILLED

RICOTTA

TORTE

DILL CORN STICKS

■

DILL AND CORN ARE A VERY GOOD, if not customary, combination. In winter, we like these with Baked Beans with Savory (page 280). They also complement any hearty legume or vegetable soup. In summer, if we don't feel like baking, we eat dill and corn in a simple sauté of fresh corn kernels, summer tomatoes, and shallots.

MAKES 14 STICKS

Corn oil

1 cup (240 ml) stone-ground cornmeal

1 cup (240 ml) unbleached white flour

1 tablespoon (15 ml) baking powder

1/2 teaspoon (2 ml) salt

2 eggs

1 cup (240 ml) cold water

1 cup (240 ml) fresh or frozen and thawed corn kernels

5 tablespoons melted butter (75 ml)

3 tablespoons (45 ml) snipped dill

Preheat the oven to 350° F (180° C). Generously oil two corn-stick molds and preheat the molds for 10 to 15 minutes.

Combine the cornmeal, flour, baking powder, and salt in a large bowl. In another bowl, lightly beat the eggs and combine them with the water, corn kernels, melted butter, and snipped dill.

Barely combine the liquid with the dry ingredients. Spoon the batter into the heated molds, filling each mold about three-quarters full. Bake for 25 to 30 minutes, until the sticks are golden brown. Serve hot.

POACHED MACKEREL WITH DILL AND CAPERS

■

MACKEREL IS AN UNDERAPPRECIATED and therefore inexpensive fish. It is nutritious and has a fine flavor, somewhat resembling that of other dark-fleshed fish such as bluefish. A similar dish is often served as an appetizer in France; we serve it that way and as a main course during the summer. Choose mackerel weighing about 12 ounces (340 g) each for this dish. Because mackerel has soft flesh, it is important to follow the recipe instructions carefully so as not to break up the fish.

SERVES 4 TO 6

2 cups (475 ml) dry white wine

1/4 cup (60 ml), plus 1 tablespoon (15 ml) white wine vinegar

3 cups (710 ml) water

1 carrot, sliced

1/2 onion, sliced

1 bay leaf

2 or 3 dill stems

1 teaspoon (5 ml) salt

3 cleaned mackerel, about 12 ounces (340 g) each

About 6 dill sprigs, enough to yield 1/4 cup (60 ml) chopped dill

2 tablespoons (30 ml) nonpareil capers

2 tablespoons (30 ml) olive oil

1/3 cup (80 ml) of the reserved cooking broth

Salt and freshly ground pepper to taste

Bring the white wine, 1/4 cup (60 ml) vinegar, water, carrot, onion, bay leaf, dill stems, and 1 teaspoon (5 ml) salt to a boil in a noncorrodible pan just large enough to hold the fish. Reduce the heat and simmer for 20 minutes.

Rinse the mackerel well. Slip them into the pan with the broth. The fish should be completely covered; if necessary, add more water, and a little more vinegar. Cook them for 10 minutes at a bare simmer.

Remove the pan from the heat and let the mackerel cool to room temperature in the broth, then remove them carefully with slotted spatulas. Strain the broth and reserve.

Fillet the mackerel carefully, discarding the skin and any small bones. Arrange the fillets on a serving dish.

Mix the chopped dill, capers, olive oil, remaining vinegar, and 1/3 cup (80 ml) of reserved broth together. Season with salt and pepper. Adjust the seasoning with broth or vinegar if necessary. Pour the vinaigrette over the mackerel. Serve immediately, or refrigerate until ready to serve. Let the dish stand about 10 minutes before serving if you have refrigerated it.

BAKED LEG OF LAMB WITH YOGURT DILL MARINADE

■

DILL AND YOGURT ARE USED TOGETHER frequently in Middle Eastern cooking, particularly in salads, salad dressings, and marinades. Yogurt as a marinade serves to tenderize as well as flavor meats. The baked lamb is meltingly tender, with a small amount of thick sauce formed of the yogurt and meat juices. Serve it surrounded with basmati rice or a rice pilaf.

SERVES 4 TO 6

3½- to 4-pound (1.6- to 1.8-kg) shank end leg of lamb

1 cup (240 ml) plain yogurt

3 tablespoons (45 ml) minced onion

2 garlic cloves, minced

6 Italian parsley sprigs, leaves minced

1/2 cup (120 ml) loosely packed chopped dill leaves

1/2 teaspoon (2 ml) cayenne pepper, or to taste

Salt and freshly ground black pepper

Bone and butterfly the leg of lamb or have the butcher do this. Remove as much fat and sinew as possible. Secure any small pieces or thin ends with wooden skewers.

Mix the yogurt with the onion, garlic, parsley, and dill, and season the mixture with cayenne pepper. Pat the marinade all over the lamb and place it in a shallow glass or ceramic casserole. Marinate the lamb at cool room temperature for 4 hours or, covered, in the refrigerator overnight.

Preheat the oven to 450° F (230° C). Salt and pepper the lamb lightly on both sides. Place it, cut side up, on a rack and roast it for 10 minutes. Reduce the heat to 350° F (180° C) and roast the lamb for 15 minutes. Turn it and roast it for 20 minutes longer.

The lamb will be rare, about 130° F (55°C) internal temperature.

Transfer the lamb to a cutting board and let it stand for about 5 minutes before cutting it into 3/8-inch (8-mm) slices. Transfer the lamb and the sauce to a platter and serve surrounded with basmati rice or rice pilaf.

D I L L E D   Y E L L O W   S Q U A S H

■

SUSAN'S GRANDMOTHER MADE THIS every summer at her Chesapeake Bay shore house when the squash came in season. We have added fresh dill to the recipe, but we cook it as she did, in a black iron frying pan.

SERVES 8

2½ pounds (1.1 kg) yellow summer squash

1 large sweet onion

4 tablespoons butter (60 ml)

1/3 cup (80 ml) chopped dill

Salt and freshly ground black pepper

Wash and trim the squash and cut it into rounds about 1/3 inch (8 mm) thick. Halve the onion lengthwise and cut it crosswise into thin rings.

Melt the butter in a heavy frying pan and sauté the vegetables over medium heat for about 10 minutes, until they are crisp-tender. Stir in the dill and season with salt and pepper. Lower the heat, cover and cook 5 minutes longer. Serve hot.

COLESLAW WITH DILL MAYONNAISE

∎

COLESLAW NEED NOT BE DULL and too sugar-sweet. It lends itself to herb variations, one of which follows. Sorrel, shredded fine, is an interesting and tangy addition to coleslaw.

SERVES 8

1 green cabbage, about 2 pounds (900 g), grated coarsely or shredded

2 carrots, grated fine

1 small red onion, diced fine

1/3 cup (80 ml) chopped dill

Lemon juice

Salt and freshly ground pepper

1 cup (240 ml) Dill Mayonnaise (recipe follows)

Combine the vegetables in a large bowl. Add the snipped dill and Dill Mayonnaise, and toss well. Season with lemon juice and salt and pepper.

DILL MAYONNAISE:

MAKES ABOUT 1 CUP (240 ML)

1 large egg yolk

Lemon juice

1/4 cup (60 ml) olive oil

1/2 cup (120 ml) vegetable oil

3 tablespoons (45 ml) snipped dill leaves

1 teaspoon (5 ml) ground mustard seed

1/2 teaspoon (2 ml) salt, or to taste

1/4 teaspoon (1 ml) paprika

Pinch cayenne pepper

2 teaspoons (10 ml) freshly grated horseradish, optional

Place the egg yolk in a bowl or a mortar. Stir in about a teaspoon (5 ml) of lemon juice. Mix the oils together and begin adding them drop by drop, stirring continually.

When half of the oil has been added, add the rest in a fine steady stream, stirring continually. When the mayonnaise has emulsified, stir in the dill, mustard seed, salt, and cayenne pepper. Adjust the seasoning with lemon juice. Stir in the grated horseradish, if desired.

To make the mayonnaise in a food processor or blender, place the yoke in the processor bowl or blender jar along with a little lemon juice. With the motor running, add the oils in a very fine stream, until the mixture emulsifies. Add the dill, mustard seed, salt, and cayenne pepper and pulse to blend. Add lemon juice to taste. Stir in the grated horseradish, if desired.

DILLED CUCUMBERS

■

THIS OLD-FASHIONED SIDE DISH is always welcome on our summer tables. It is especially good with English or Japanese cucumbers, which have tender skins and seeds. If you like sour cream, use it in place of the oil, and add just enough vinegar to your taste.

SERVES 6 TO 8

3 cucumbers, or 2 English or
    Japanese cucumbers

1 small red onion

3/4 cup (180 ml) loosely packed dill
    leaves

1/3 cup (80 ml) olive oil

1 1/2 tablespoons (22 ml) tarragon or
    white wine vinegar

Salt and freshly ground black pepper

Scrub the cucumbers and peel them if the skins are waxy or tough. If the skins are tasty, remove 4 or 5 strips lengthwise around the cucumbers to make a green-and-white design on the edges of the slices. Trim the ends and slice the cucumbers about 1/4 inch (5 mm) thick.

Halve the onion lengthwise, then cut it crosswise in thin slices. Chop the dill coarsely. Mix the oil and vinegar together and season with salt and pepper. Stir in the dill. Toss the vinaigrette with the vegetables and cover and marinate for at least 1 hour in the refrigerator before serving.

D I L L E D   B E E T   S A L A D

■

As eastern Europeans and Scandinavians know, beets and dill are a tasty combination. This dish uses the beetroot; try shredding the greens and stewing them gently for a few minutes with chopped garlic, olive oil, and balsamic vinegar.

Serves 4 to 6

2 pounds (900 g) small beets, about 2 inches (5 cm) in diameter

3 tablespoons (45 ml) lemon juice, or white wine vinegar

3/4 cup (180 ml) sour cream

Salt and freshly ground white pepper

1/4 cup (60 ml) snipped dill leaves

1 tablespoon (15 ml) freshly grated horseradish root, optional

Trim and scrub the beets and cook them in water to cover by 1 inch (2 cm) until they are just tender, about 15 minutes. Refresh them and peel under cold water when they are cool. Halve and cut them into thin slices, or grate them coarsely.

Mix the sour cream, dill, and lemon juice or vinegar together in a large bowl. Season with salt and white pepper. Add the horseradish for extra zest. Toss the beets with the mixture. Cover and chill for at least an hour. Remove the salad about 15 minutes before serving and arrange it on individual plates or on a serving platter.

BRAISED LEEKS WITH DILL AND PARSLEY

■

THIS IS A WONDERFUL DISH IN LATE SPRING when the new leeks are young, tender, and relatively inexpensive, and dill is at its flavor peak. Serve it at room temperature as an appetizer or salad course.

SERVES 4 TO 6

3 to 4 pounds (1.4 to 1.8 kg) young leeks, white parts no larger than about 3/4 inch (1.5 cm) in diameter: about 25 small leeks

2 tablespoons (30 ml) olive oil

1 cup (240 ml) water or broth

2 tablespoons (30 ml) tomato paste

4 or 5 dill sprigs

3 or 4 parsley sprigs

1 lemon

Salt and pepper to taste

Trim the leeks, leaving about 1 inch (2 cm) of the tender green on each leek. Wash well to remove all sand.

Place the leeks in a sauté pan with the olive oil and the water or broth. Cover and bring to a simmer. Stir in the tomato paste, and braise for about 12 minutes, until the leeks are tender.

Remove the leeks from the pan to cool. Mix the pan juices with lemon juice to taste, and season with salt and pepper. Chop the herbs coarsely. Pour the juices over the leeks. Scatter the herbs over the dish and serve.

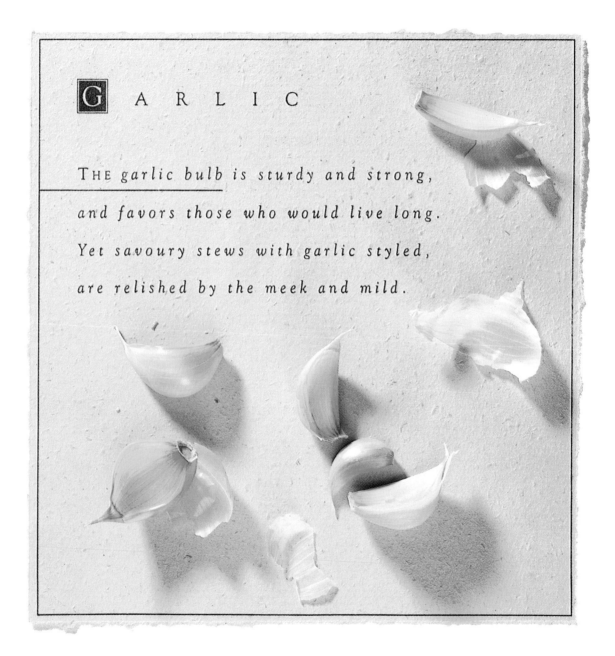

GARLIC

THE garlic bulb is sturdy and strong,

and favors those who would live long.

Yet savoury stews with garlic styled,

are relished by the meek and mild.

■ If we were faced with the unhappy predicament of banishing all herbs but one from our kitchens, we would have to choose garlic as indispensable. Clearly, we're not the only people who revel in the glories of garlic. The garlic harvest has been celebrated in Provence for centuries. Huge bowls of aïoli—garlic mayonnaise—in the centers of tables laden with bread, fresh vegetables, sausages, and plenty of young red wine are shared by the communities as they pay tribute to this season's bounty. Garlic films, festivals, books, and newsletters flourish, especially in California, where the bulk of the United States crop is grown. An annual garlic festival is held in Gilroy, a small northern California town that exudes a warm and powerful aroma in midsummer. There is a competition for the best garlic recipe of the year, a bulb topping contest, and of course a garlic queen.

Garlic is usually associated with Mediterranean cuisine, but it circles the temperate zone of the globe, featured in Mexican, Caribbean, South American, Middle Eastern, Indian, and Chinese cooking. It speaks of the hot sun even in the winter, adding pungency and warmth to the dishes prepared with it. The culinary use of garlic is ancient; recipes were recorded in Egypt, Babylonia, and China 2000 and 3000 years before Christ.

Allium sativum has inspired more magical, religious, and medicinal lore than any other herb. The Hebrews and Egyptians held it sacred; the Greeks

GARLIC . . . CIRCLES THE

TEMPERATE ZONE

OF THE GLOBE.

used it in temple purification ceremonies. In some Hebrew sects, the groom wore a clove in his wedding dress to symbolize a happy marriage. Roman charioteers ate garlic for strength. Even today Greek peasants find the strength for their hard lives on a basic diet of bread, garlic, and olives.

Garlic has long been used as a disinfectant and

as a folk remedy for colds and flus, as well as to ward off the plague and as an antidote for poison. Its antiseptic and digestive properties have been well documented in this century. It has sustained a reputation for conferring long life on its users, with the extra benefit of protecting them from evil.

GARLIC DEMANDS
CAREFUL HANDLING
AND STORAGE.

Much of the prejudice against garlic would surely vanish if more people sampled fresh, sweet, crisp-tender garlic, rather than the old, yellow, limp, or moldy bulbs packed in little boxes. Even further from the true taste are garlic salt, powder, flakes, chips, and chopped garlic preserved in oil. These preparations detract from otherwise successful dishes by leaving bitter, metallic, and other lingering off-flavors.

Paradoxically for such a strong-flavored herb, garlic demands careful handling and storage. Otherwise, the complex sulfur compound that gives garlic its distinctive flavor and odor is oxidized by exposure to air and to some metals and acids. The oxidation is what causes bitterness and harshness.

Hand-chopping with stainless steel tools is the best way to prepare garlic for most dishes, especially those in which the garlic is raw. Just the right amount of oil is released, and stainless steel does not discolor it as do carbon steel knives. Using the chopped garlic as soon as possible minimizes oxidation. If you have some extra chopped garlic, just cover it with oil, refrigerate it, and use it within a day or two.

The garlic press and food processor are handy for chopping garlic in some cases, generally marinades, long-simmered dishes, and those which contain other strong flavors. Pressing and processing smash the herb, releasing a good quantity of oil at once to the process of oxidation.

Store garlic bulbs in a cool, dry place, with good air circulation and out of direct sunlight. Do not store whole garlic in the refrigerator.

For some, garlic's odor is a deterrent to enjoying it, but there are many ways to render it inoffensive. The aroma is less noticeable when the meal is accompanied by salad greens—unless, of course, the salad dressing has garlic in it. Fresh parsley neutralizes garlic in the breath most effectively. In addition, roasting and poaching change the aroma and flavor, rendering them sweet, nutty, and much milder than those of raw garlic. Using whole cloves, peeled or unpeeled, in a sauté or stew makes the taste and odor less pungent than that of chopped garlic. The odor of garlic may be removed from the hands by rubbing them with salt and rinsing with cold water.

Garlic's essence, whether raw or cooked, has a wide appeal; it is popular with peasants and gourmets from Europe to Asia. Bean and game dishes seem to lack savor without it. The Chinese use it with fish and shellfish. French cooks use it in many ways, from brushing a wooden spoon with it and stirring a delicate sauce, to the whole cloves in aïoli.

Garlic is easy to grow outdoors. In cold climates, plant it after the first frost in well-mulched soil. In warmer climates, plant it in January or July/August, during a period when the soil is relatively dry. Garlic needs full sun and a soil that is well drained to prevent rotting. Buy bulbs for planting from a seed house or at the market; choose them as you would garlic for cooking: large, well-formed cloves; a bulb with the firmness of an apple; and no rotted cloves or mold on the paperlike skin.

Plant the individual cloves about 2 inches (5 cm) deep and 6 to 8 inches (15 to 20 cm) apart with the pointed end up. Do not overwater or fertilize during their last month in the ground (July or August, depending on the climate and when they were planted). Some garlic will not flower, though good, tasty bulbs can be harvested.

Harvest when the leaves are completely dry. Dig the bulbs and shake them free of excess soil. Lay them on a screen in a sunny place with good air circulation. Two or three days of full sun should be sufficient to dry the garlic. The outside skins should be moisture-free before storing. The tops can be cut off and the bulbs stored in mesh onion bags or in a box in a cool, dark place; or the tops can be left on and the garlic braided.

GARLIC NEEDS FULL SUN AND A SOIL THAT IS WELL DRAINED. . . .

Common white garlic is the variety we plant every year. Though we have grown elephant garlic, we find its flavor rather dull. Still, it's easy to grow, and rather interesting in salads. The red/purple-skinned garlic from Mexico is often the first new garlic available at the beginning of the season. It has the same simple cultivation requirements and the same flavor as common garlic.

One of the benefits of growing garlic is that you can harvest the young, tender green garlic plants before separate cloves form. They are delicate and fresh in flavor, resembling a very long scallion, with a white, tender bulb about 2 inches (5 cm) long and a medium green-yellow stalk 14 to 18 inches (36 to 46 cm) long. Green garlic may be used wherever garlic is called for, though more of it may be necessary because it is mild. The stalks are rather fibrous, but when sliced thin they are very good in salads and as a garnish.

ROASTED NUTS WITH GARLIC AND SOY SAUCE

■

WE USUALLY MAKE ROASTED NUTS in the fall and winter when fresh nuts are available. These are good hikers' and sports fans' snacks, equally tasty with cold water and cold beer. If your group doesn't like chili spiciness, use the paprika. Tamari soy sauce is aged longer than regular soy sauce and adds more flavor than salt.

MAKES ABOUT 5 CUPS (1200 ML)

5 cups (1200 ml) assorted raw nuts

1/3 cup (80 ml) tamari soy sauce

4 garlic cloves, crushed

1 teaspoon (5 ml) cayenne or ground red chili, or to taste

1 teaspoon (5 ml) paprika, optional

Preheat the oven to 350° F (180° C). Spread the nuts on a large baking sheet. Combine the soy sauce with the garlic and cayenne, stirring well. Sprinkle the soy sauce mixture over the nuts and toss them well. Shake the pan to spread the nuts into one layer.

Bake for a total of 20 minutes, removing the pan from the oven 2 or 3 times to stir the nuts.

Cut open a large brown paper bag. When the nuts are done, spread them to cool on the bag. When they are completely cool, pack them in an airtight container until ready to serve.

F E T T U N T A

■

WE WERE INTRODUCED TO FETTUNTA in a Tuscan farmhouse, around the large kitchen hearth. It was a revelation about simplicity in food: saltless whole wheat bread, garlic, olive oil, and coarse sea salt made one of the most satisfying dishes we had ever eaten. The other ingredients—mushrooms from an afternoon's hunting, homemade young Tuscan wine, and the sounds of Italian, German, and English—added to, but did not detract from, the absolute goodness of that garlic bread. We still like to toast the bread over an open fire and make a little hearth ceremony of rubbing it with garlic and anointing it with a really good Italian extra-virgin olive oil before serving it to friends.

Fettunta does not have to be made with Tuscan bread, but a crusty, country-style loaf is essential. This kind of bread is made with flour, water, yeast, and usually salt. The yeast, or other natural leavening such as sourdough starter, is kept to a minimum, and the dough is allowed to rise cool and slow, sometimes for as long as a day. The final loaves have a crisp crust and an airy, light interior crumb.

SERVES 6

4 garlic cloves

1/2 cup (120 ml) olive oil

1/2 teaspoon (2 ml) salt, or to taste

12 slices country bread, 1/2 inch (1 cm) thick

Peel the garlic and cut each clove in half. Mix the olive oil and salt in a small dish. Toast the bread until it is golden brown on both sides over an open flame or under the broiler. Rub the toast on both sides with the cut garlic, then dip one side of each slice briefly in the olive oil. Serve the fettunta immediately.

G A R L I C   P A R M E S A N   T W I S T S

■

THESE TWISTS ARE CRUNCHY OUTSIDE and bready inside, with a pleasant hint of garlic and cheese, making them perfect cocktail appetizers. They are good warm and at room temperature. If you make them ahead, cool them on baking racks, then store them in an airtight container.

MAKES ABOUT 2 DOZEN TWISTS

1/2 cup (120 ml) unsalted butter

3 cups (710 ml) unbleached white flour

1 teaspoon (5 ml) salt

1 tablespoon (15 ml) baking powder

1 cup (240 ml) freshly grated parmesan cheese

1 large egg, lightly beaten

1/2 cup (120 ml) lukewarm water

3 garlic cloves, minced

2 tablespoons poppy seeds

Melt the butter over low heat and set it aside to cool. Preheat the oven to 375° F (190° C).

Sift the flour with the salt and baking powder into a large mixing bowl. Stir in the cheese. Make a well in the flour mixture and add the egg, water, garlic, and butter. Stir with a wooden spoon until the liquids are incorporated. Knead the dough on a smooth surface for 5 minutes.

On a pastry cloth or a floured sheet of waxed paper, roll the dough into a 10-by-12-inch (25-by-30-cm) rectangle, 3/8 inch (8 mm) thick. Cut the dough into 1/2-inch (1-cm) strips and twist two strips together at a time. Cut these twists into 4-inch (10-cm) lengths and pinch the ends together.

Spread the poppy seeds on a sheet of waxed paper and roll the twists lightly in them. Place the twists on buttered and floured baking sheets about 1½ inches (4 cm) apart and bake for 25 minutes.

ROASTED EGGPLANT AND GARLIC SOUP

■

BOTH THE TAUPE COLOR AND THE MAIN INGREDIENTS are unusual for soup, but the flavor is full yet light, making it suitable for a first course. The smooth puree contrasts especially well with crunchy croutons.

SERVES 4 TO 6

2 pounds (900 g) eggplant

1 head roasted garlic (see following recipe)

1 quart (1 litre) chicken or vegetable stock

1½ tablespoons (22 ml) tarragon or white wine vinegar

4 tarragon sprigs, leaves minced

1 teaspoon (5 ml) cracked black pepper

Cut the eggplant in half lengthwise and place it, cut side down, on a jelly roll pan lined with aluminum foil. Add about 1/2 cup (120 ml) water to the pan. Bake the eggplant at 375° F (190° C) for about 30 minutes, until it is very tender. Let it stand until cool enough to handle.

Place the eggplant pulp in a blender or food processor. Squeeze the roasted garlic from its skins into the eggplant and puree them. Transfer the puree to a soup pot.

Stir in the stock and simmer the soup for 10 minutes or so. Add some of the garlic-flavored olive oil, if you like. Season the soup with salt and pepper.

Mix the vinegar, tarragon, and cracked pepper together in a small bowl. Ladle the soup into heated bowls and add about a teaspoon (5 ml) of the vinegar mixture to each bowl. Serve hot.

ROASTED GARLIC

■

ROASTED GARLIC CAN BE USED in an assortment of dishes. Mixed with a little of its roasting oil, it makes an intense garlic bread. It is a good soup base, as in the recipe above. Mixed with cream, it makes a lovely sauce for vegetables, pasta, and fish. With the addition of a little vinegar, it is a good sauce for grilled meats, fish, and vegetables.

Roasting changes garlic's flavor to a nutty, complex, sweet one, though it retains a slight pungency. The texture of roasted garlic is soft and tender; it can be easily squeezed from the cloves. If you want a lot of roasted garlic, double or triple the recipe. It is best used the day it is roasted, but leftover cloves can be squeezed into a small dish and just covered with olive oil, then stored, tightly covered, in the refrigerator for a day.

MAKES 1 HEAD OF ROASTED GARLIC

1 garlic head

1/2 cup (120 ml) olive oil

2 or 3 thyme sprigs

1 bay leaf

Salt and freshly ground pepper

Preheat the oven to 250° F (120° C). Break the garlic head into cloves; leave the inner skins on them. Place them in a small oven-proof dish and add the olive oil, thyme, and bay leaf. Season lightly with salt and pepper.

Bake the garlic until it is very tender, from 45 minutes to an hour, depending on the size of the cloves. Turn the cloves over from time to time. Remove from the oven and let the garlic cool to room temperature.

BURMESE-STYLE RICE AND NOODLES WITH ACCOMPANIMENTS

■

THE MANY TASTES AND TEXTURES IN THIS DISH, and the style of serving it with everything on the table, are typical of Southeast Asian cuisine. Though it is a one-course meal, the table looks abundant and interesting with the different condiments; most people enjoy choosing which to put on what. We like to accompany it with fresh cucumber pickles and/or Winter Fruit Salad with Coriander (page 125). Everything can be prepared ahead as the dish is served at room temperature. The authentic touches of crisp-fried garlic, dry fluffy rice, and deep-fried cellophane noodles are not at all difficult to do in an American kitchen. Crisp-fried garlic is used in several Southeast Asian cuisines; we use it also as a finishing touch to grilled or poached fish and stir-fried vegetables. When fresh chilis are not in season, use red pepper flakes instead.

ROASTED
EGGPLANT
AND GARLIC
SOUP

SERVES 6 TO 8

3 eggs

Salt and freshly ground black pepper

About 1/3 cup (80 ml) peanut or
vegetable oil

1 large onion, halved lengthwise and
sliced thin

1 head of garlic, cloves peeled and
minced

1 bunch green onions, trimmed with
about 4 inches (10 cm) of green

6 ounces (170 g) bean sprouts, rinsed
in boiling water and drained

2 to 4 fresh small hot red or green
chilis, according to heat and your
taste, seeded and sliced thin

8 or 10 coriander sprigs, chopped
coarse, including stems

1/2 cup (120 ml) dry-roasted peanuts

2 or 3 limes or lemons, cut in wedges

Vietnamese or Thai fish sauce

2 ounces (60 g) dried shrimp, optional

3 cups (710 ml) cooked rice

1 pound (450 g) new potatoes,
steamed, peeled, and sliced

8 ounces (225 g) vermicelli noodles,
cooked al dente, drained, and
tossed with a little oil

2 ounces (60 ml) cellophane noodles,
deep-fried and coarsely crumbled

Beat the eggs with salt and pepper and about a tablespoon (15 ml) of water. Lightly
oil a frying pan, or cook the omelets in a nonstick pan. Pour half of the egg mixture in
the heated omelet pan over medium heat and cook until set on one side, about 30
seconds.

Turn the omelet and cook the other side until done, about 30 seconds. Place the
omelet on a plate and cook the other omelet.

Cool the omelets to room temperature, then roll them and cut them in thin strips.
Place on a serving dish.

Fry the onion slices in 2 tablespoons (30 ml) of oil over medium-high heat, until they
crisp and brown slightly around the edges. Transfer to a serving dish.

Rinse about half the garlic under cold water, then squeeze it very dry in paper towels.
Place the remaining garlic in a small serving bowl and just cover with oil. Heat about
1/2 tablespoon (8 ml) oil in a small sauté pan over medium-low heat. Add the rinsed
garlic and reduce the heat to low. Cook the garlic, stirring occasionally until pale golden
and crisp, about 4 minutes. Cool and crumble, then place in a small serving bowl.

Cut the green onions diagonally into 1-inch (2-cm) lengths. Place them in a serving

dish. Pat the bean sprouts dry and place them in another serving dish. Place in separate serving dishes the peanuts, lime wedges, and optional dried shrimp. Fill a small cruet with the fish sauce.

Arrange the rice, potatoes, vermicelli noodles, and cellophane noodles on a serving platter, or in individual dishes. Serve at room temperature.

GARLIC CHICKEN WITH INDONESIAN PEANUT BUTTER SAUCE

■

INDONESIAN CUISINE USES GARLIC IN GREAT QUANTITY. We were introduced to it in Holland, where it is very popular. This dish will appeal to garlic lovers but has enough different flavors to find favor with others, too. *Sambal oeulek*, available in specialty stores, is an Indonesian red hot pepper paste. If you can't find it, use hot red pepper flakes to taste. Rinsing the minced garlic removes most of the oils that turn acrid in cooking; still, watch it carefully so that it does not burn. We serve this dish with rice and steamed or stir-fried vegetables such as cabbage, broccoli, or green beans.

SERVES 4 TO 6

3- to 4-pound (1.4- to 1.8-kg) frying chicken

Salt and freshly ground pepper

3 tablespoons (45 ml) peanut oil

6 garlic cloves, minced

2 tablespoons (30 ml) dried onion flakes

1 tablespoon (15 ml) soy sauce

Juice of 1/2 lemon

2 teaspoons (10 ml) sambal oeulek

1 cup (240 ml) warm water

1/2 cup (120 ml) smooth natural peanut butter

Pinch of sugar

1/2 cup (120 ml) dry unsweetened shredded coconut

Rinse the chicken well and pat it dry. Cut it into serving pieces and salt and pepper them lightly. Sauté the chicken in a large frying pan in 2 tablespoons (30 ml) of the peanut oil over moderately high heat for 15 minutes, turning frequently. Remove the skillet from the heat and transfer the chicken to a platter.

Rinse the garlic in a sieve and pat it very dry. Cook it until crisp in 1/2 tablespoon (8 ml) of peanut oil in a small pan over low heat. Stir frequently until the garlic is crisp and golden, about 5 minutes. Cook the dried onion flakes in 1/2 tablespoon (8 ml) peanut oil over low heat until they are crisp and golden, about 3 minutes.

Drain all the fat from the chicken skillet. Add half of the crisp garlic and onion, the soy sauce, lemon juice, and sambal to the skillet. Reserve the remaining crisp garlic and onion for garnish. Stir well to combine and cook for 5 minutes. Stir in the water and peanut butter to make a smooth sauce. Add the chicken and cook, covered, over moderately low heat for about 25 minutes, stirring occasionally to prevent the sauce from sticking.

While the chicken is cooking, toast the coconut in a small skillet over low heat until it is golden, about 5 minutes, tossing frequently. When the chicken is done, transfer it and the sauce to a heated serving platter. Sprinkle with the reserved crisp garlic and onion and the toasted coconut. Serve immediately.

CREAMY MUSHROOM GARLIC SAUCE

∎

THOUGH WE USUALLY SERVE THIS sauce with pasta, it is also good with vegetables, especially cabbage, cauliflower, and broccoli, and a pleasant change in scalloped potatoes or potato gratin.

MAKES ABOUT 2 CUPS (475 ML), ENOUGH FOR 4 SERVINGS OF PASTA

1/4 pound (115 g) sliced mushrooms

3 garlic cloves, crushed

4 tablespoons (60 ml) unsalted butter

1 cup (240 ml) whipping cream (double cream)

1/2 cup (120 ml) parsley, minced

1 cup (240 ml) freshly grated parmesan cheese

Salt and freshly ground black pepper

Sauté the mushrooms and garlic in the butter over low heat for about 5 minutes. Add the cream and parsley and bring the sauce to a simmer, then stir in the cheese. Season with salt and pepper.

GARLIC AND
HERB CHEESE

■

THIS CHEESE IS SIMPLE TO MAKE, less expensive than the prepackaged herb cheeses, and better tasting. The touch of vinegar makes it less cloying. Herb lovers will find the spread good for experimentation since the cheese is a neutral base that flavors well. Tarragon, dill, and basil are good candidates, but others could be tried. A few minced, oil-packed, sun-dried tomatoes are another possibility.

MAKES ABOUT 2½ CUPS (600 ML)

1 pound (450 g) natural cream cheese at room temperature

2 to 3 tablespoons (30 to 45 ml) half-and-half (single cream) or milk

10 parsley sprigs, leaves minced

4 or 5 marjoram sprigs, leaves minced

4 or 5 summer savory sprigs, leaves minced

2 garlic cloves, crushed

About 1/4 teaspoon (1 ml) salt

Pinch of cayenne pepper

1 teaspoon (5 ml) herb or white wine vinegar, optional

Cream the cheese, moistening it with cream or milk if it is dry. Add the herbs, garlic, salt, a pinch of cayenne, and the vinegar if desired. Blend the mixture well, cover tightly and refrigerate for at least 2 hours before serving.

Adjust the seasoning with more garlic or herbs, salt or cayenne pepper. The cheese improves in flavor after a day and may be kept for 2 to 3 days tightly covered and refrigerated.

T O M A T O   C R E A M   P A S T A   S A U C E

∎

THIS IS ONE OF OUR WINTER BUSY-DAY SAUCES that utilize preserved basil. It is good with all ribbon noodles, as well as delicatessen ravioli and tortellini. Whether you use half-and-half (single cream) or whipping cream (double cream) will depend on how rich a sauce you like. Tomato paste in tubes, usually imported, has the best tomato flavor.

MAKES ABOUT 2¼ CUPS (540 ML), ENOUGH FOR 4 OR 5 SERVINGS OF PASTA

1/4 cup (60 ml) tomato paste

2 tablespoons (30 ml) chopped fresh or preserved basil, or 1 scant teaspoon (5 ml) dried crumbled basil

1 or 2 garlic cloves, minced

Salt and freshly ground pepper to taste

2 cups (475 ml) half-and-half or whipping cream

1/2 cup (120 ml) freshly grated parmesan cheese

Thoroughly mix all of the ingredients except the cheese in a saucepan. Barely simmer over very low heat for 8 to 10 minutes. Serve over hot pasta and sprinkle with grated parmesan.

ASPARAGUS WITH
GARLIC SAUCE

■

WHEN TOM DEBAGGIO TOLD US about this preparation several years ago, it struck a chord in our thrifty hearts. We use it faithfully every spring and have passed it on to many others because it is so good and uses the thick ends of the asparagus that we hate to throw away. Tom searched his files for the source of the recipe: in his 1984 spring catalog, under "Asparagus", he had printed Ann Crutcher's Asparagus Butter recipe from *The Washington Post*. Our recipe is different, but we thank her for the concept and so will you. Frequently, we use olive oil rather than butter and serve the resulting palest of green sauces over pasta, poached salmon, or other fish.

SERVES 6

2 pounds (900 g) fresh asparagus	*4 tablespoons (60 ml) unsalted butter*
3 to 4 cloves garlic, peeled	*Salt and freshly ground pepper*

Rinse the asparagus; do not break off the tough ends. Using a vegetable peeler or a sharp paring knife, peel the asparagus from about halfway down the stalk to the thick end. Break or cut the asparagus at the weak point where the thick end starts and the tender one stops.

Place the thick ends and the garlic cloves in a small noncorrodible saucepan and barely cover them with water. Bring them to a boil over moderate heat and simmer them for 15 to 20 minutes, until they are tender.

Meanwhile, rinse the tender parts of the asparagus. Place them in a pan with a tight-fitting lid, and barely cover them with water.

When the simmering stalks are tender, start to cook the tender asparagus tips. They should be cooked al dente, about 3 to 5 minutes, depending on their size.

In the blender, puree the stalks, garlic, and liquid with the butter. Add salt and pepper to taste.

Drain the asparagus tips, place them in a warmed serving dish, and pour the warm sauce over them. Serve immediately.

MOROCCAN LENTILS

■

WHEN SUSAN LIVED IN MOROCCO, she became friends with the manager of the little hotel where she stayed for a winter. Abdelkader, who had worked as a cook on a Spanish ship, taught her how to make many Moroccan and Spanish dishes; this is one of which we are particularly fond. It is spicy, so you may want to use less cayenne than the amount called for. Lentils make a good main course with just crusty bread and a salad to accompany them; they are also good partners to grilled sausage.

SERVES 6

2 cups (475 ml) brown lentils

1 large onion, chopped

4 cups (1 litre) water

1 teaspoon (5 ml) salt

3 tablespoons (45 ml) olive oil

2 cups (475 ml) chopped tomatoes

1/4 cup (60 ml) olive oil

1 large bay leaf

4 garlic cloves, minced

1/2 cup (120 ml) chopped parsley

1 teaspoon (5 ml) cayenne pepper, or
to taste

Wash and pick over the lentils and put them in a heavy 3-quart (3-litre) saucepan with a tight fitting lid. Add the onion and add it to the saucepan with the water, salt, and 3 tablespoons (45 ml) olive oil. Bring to a boil, reduce heat and simmer for 30 minutes or until most of the liquid has been absorbed.

Add the tomatoes, olive oil, bay leaf, garlic, parsley, and cayenne pepper. Simmer for 20 minutes, stirring occasionally. Transfer to a heated serving dish and serve hot.

CABBAGE, MUSHROOM, AND WALNUT GRATIN

■

THIS HEARTY CASSEROLE is a good cold-weather supper. Making it with rye or pumpernickel bread gives it an Eastern European flavor that we like. Serve it with crusty rye bread and mustard (or mustard mixed with a little butter), pickled onions or pickled beets, and garlic dill pickles or cornichons.

SERVES 6 TO 8

1 small green cabbage, about 1 pound (450 g)

1/2 pound (225 g) mushrooms, sliced

1 small onion, diced small

4 tablespoons (60 ml) unsalted butter

3 garlic cloves, minced

3 tablespoons (45 ml) all-purpose flour

2 cups (475 ml) half-and-half (single cream) or milk, at room temperature

1 tablespoon (15 ml) soy sauce

1/4 cup (60 ml) parsley leaves, chopped

1 tablespoon (15 ml) thyme leaves, minced

Pinch of cayenne pepper

Freshly grated nutmeg to taste

1/2 cup (120 ml) freshly grated parmesan cheese

1 cup (240 ml) chopped walnuts or pecans

1 cup (240 ml) soft whole-grain bread crumbs

Wash the cabbage and slice it into thin wedges. Steam it until barely tender, about 7 minutes. Spread half the cabbage in a lightly oiled 2-quart (2-litre) gratin or soufflé dish.

Soften the mushrooms and onion in the butter over moderately low heat. Add the garlic, cook for about 3 minutes, then increase the heat to medium.

Add the flour all at once, stirring constantly. When the flour and butter begin to bubble, stir in 1 cup (240 ml) of the cream or milk. Combine well and stir in the rest of the cream or milk and the soy sauce.

Preheat the oven to 350° F (180° C). Add the parsley, thyme, cayenne, and nutmeg to the sauce. Gradually stir in the parmesan cheese. Cook the sauce over low heat for 5 minutes, then add the chopped nuts.

Pour half the sauce over the cabbage in the dish, then add the rest of the cabbage and cover it with the remaining sauce. Sprinkle the bread crumbs over the gratin and bake it for 25 to 30 minutes, until the crumbs are lightly browned. Serve hot.

L EMON B ALM

BALMY summer days will bring
quiet cheer to gardens all
and fragrant kitchens will recall
Melissa's promise of the spring.

Lemon balm (*Melissa officinalis*) evokes high summer memories: the soft hum of bees in still air, the sun at the height of its languor-producing power, and balm's sweet scent reviving heat-weary palates and spirits. The fragrances of the most perfect lemon and the sweetest honey mingle in its leaves in a way that soothes and excites the sense of smell as no other herb does. When we want a quiet reflection on summer evenings, we take a rosy, refreshing Balmy Sunset (see recipe) into the garden.

Balm's perfume, however, is not its only important feature; its generic name, *Melissa*, the Greek word for bee, proclaims its extreme attractiveness to this insect. Our balm patch is abuzz all summer, especially when the plants are in bloom in July and August.

Balm has always been associated with longevity. Tea with balm and honey was a popular drink in ages when long life might be accompanied by wisdom and the calm reflective joys. Balm wine or tea was also recommended to scholars for sharp memories and clearheadedness and, somewhat contradictorily, to insomniacs for its sleep-inducing properties.

The culinary uses of lemon balm center around light foods: green salads, fruit salads, and macerated fruits. The crushed fresh leaves steeped with Ceylon or Assam tea and then iced make a refreshing hot-weather beverage. It is worth drying balm (though it will lose some of its aroma) to be able to serve this tea hot in winter.

LIKE GARLIC, BALM HAS ALWAYS BEEN ASSOCIATED WITH LONGEVITY.

Balm is seldom used in cooked dishes, but we find that it contributes a subtly sweet, grassy flavor and a hint of lemon to a variety of foods. We like it especially with vegetables, light grains, baked fish and chicken, and in desserts. Lemon balm should be added very near the end of cooking, as its volatile oils are dissipated by heat. Its fragrance is preserved fairly well in baked goods because it is captured in the surrounding dough.

Lemon balm is unfussy to grow, especially in the garden. It can be grown from seed, rooted cuttings, or by root division. Like many other herbs, this herb prefers light soil to heavy clay, but it will adapt if some amendments are worked in. The soil should be fairly fertile, well balanced, and well drained. Balm thrives in full sun but can be grown in partial shade as well. The hardy root system will survive the coldest winters if the plants are well mulched.

Balm is a member of the mint family (*Mentha* spp.) and looks and grows much like them, though it does not send runners, like many of the mints. Still, it likes some space and is best planted next to other vigorous perennials or in a spot of its own. Balm grows from 2 to 2½ feet (60 to 75 cm) tall, bushing out laterally, so that each plant should be given 2 feet (60 cm) all around. Trim it occasionally to maintain its handsome bushiness. Grown indoors, it needs at least four hours of sun daily, good drainage, and plenty of water.

LEMON BALM AND CHIVE BUTTER

■

THIS, LIKE OTHER HERB BUTTERS, keeps in the refrigerator for a week when tightly covered, and up to 2 months in the freezer. It is good with virtually any steamed or blanched vegetable and with poached or grilled white-fleshed fish and salmon.

MAKES ABOUT 1 CUP (240 ML)

1/2 cup (120 ml) unsalted butter

2 tablespoons (30 ml) minced lemon balm

1 tablespoon (15 ml) minced parsley

1 tablespoon (15) snipped chives

Salt to taste

Soften the butter and combine with the minced herbs. Salt to taste and cover and chill overnight to ripen the flavors.

CRAB SOUP WITH LEMON BALM AND COCONUT MILK

■

AS MUCH AS WE LIKE Thai and Cambodian food, we often have difficulty finding the herbs for it. By experimenting with temperate zone herbs, here using lemon balm rather than lemongrass, we can still enjoy these cuisines when tropical herbs are out of season. If you cook the Dungeness or blue crabs yourself, steam them over plain water and do not sprinkle with any seasoning. Though the crab flavor will not be as pronounced, a pound of fresh steamed and picked crab meat may be used. In this case, make the broth with chicken stock. You will need only half of the unsweetened coconut milk for this recipe. The remainder will keep very well in the freezer for up to 6 months.

SERVES 6 TO 8

1 large steamed crab, such as Dungeness, 3½ to 4 pounds (1.6 to 1.8 kg), or the same amount of steamed blue crabs

1/2-inch (1-cm) piece ginger, peeled

12 large lemon balm sprigs

3 shallots, 2 chopped

2 garlic cloves, chopped

2 tablespoons (30 ml) Thai or Vietnamese fish sauce

1 teaspoon (5 ml) dried shrimp paste, or 1/2 teaspoon (2 ml) anchovy paste

1 14-ounce (400-ml) can unsweetened coconut milk

1 green Thai or serrano chili

1 red Thai or serrano chili

Zest of 1/2 lime

Juice of 1 lime, or to taste

Scrub the crab well, then crack the shells and remove the meat, keeping it in large pieces. Set the meat aside.

Break the shells into small pieces with a mallet or the blunt side of a chef's knife. Place the broken shells in a food processor with 1 cup (240 ml) water and process for about a minute. Scrape the shells and liquid into a noncorrodible pan and add 4 cups (1 litre) water.

If you are using pre-shelled crab meat, place 4 cups (1 litre) chicken stock in a noncorrodible pan.

Slice the ginger about 1/8 inch (3 mm) thick and add to the shells and water or to the stock. Bruise six lemon balm sprigs and add them to the pan along with the chopped shallots and garlic. Simmer the broth for 15 minutes, skimming occasionally. Strain the broth into a clean noncorrodible pan.

Stir the coconut milk very well and add half of it to the broth. Remove the leaves from the remaining lemon balm and shred them. Cut the remaining shallot in a fine dice. Stem the chilis and slice them in thin diagonal pieces. Remove the seeds if desired. Add the lemon balm, shallot, chilis, and lime zest to the broth and simmer for 5 minutes. Add the crab meat and lime juice and heat through. Serve hot.

BAKED SNAPPER WITH ONIONS AND BALM

∎

THOUGH WE USUALLY MAKE THIS with the fish listed below, any mild white-fleshed fish would do. It takes little time to prepare, and is good with chard or spinach wilted with a little olive oil and garlic. For a nice presentation, surround the fish with the chard or spinach and garnish the platter with lemon wedges.

SERVES 4 TO 6

2 medium yellow onions, sliced thin

2 tablespoons (30 ml) unsalted butter

1½ pounds (675 g) fillet of snapper, rock cod, or sea bass

1 teaspoon (5 g) sea salt

1/2 teaspoon (2 ml) freshly ground white pepper

12 large lemon balm sprigs

1/2 cup (120 ml) medium-dry white wine

Lemon balm leaves

Sauté the onions in the butter over medium heat for 5 minutes and set them aside. Mix the salt and pepper together and rub the fillets on both sides with the mixture.

Preheat the oven to 450° F (230° C). Lightly butter a 9-by-12-inch (23-by-30-cm) baking dish and line it with six sprigs of lemon balm. Lay the fish on the balm and spread the onions over it. Cover the onions with the remaining six sprigs of lemon balm. Pour the wine into the dish and bake for 7 to 9 minutes, until the fish just flakes. Remove the cooked lemon balm . Arrange the fish and onions on a serving platter and garnish with fresh lemon balm leaves.

HERBED RISOTTO

∎

RISOTTO IS ONE OF MANY ITALIAN DISHES that has found favor with Americans during the past decade. It is quite versatile, as it accommodates ingredients and flavors from earthy to delicate. Arborio is a short-grained rice that must be simmered and stirred to allow the grain to absorb the liquid and keep its firmness. We have not seen any American Arborio, but the Italian import is widely available. This risotto reminds us of those we have eaten in Venice, where a delicate version flavored with vegetables, and occasionally seafood, is preferred. It is a good first course before almost any spring or summer dinner.

SERVES 4

1¼ cups (300 ml) Italian Arborio rice

1 tablespoon (15 ml) unsalted butter

1 tablespoon (15 ml) olive oil

1½ quarts (1½ litres) hot chicken or vegetable stock

Salt and freshly ground pepper

1 bunch green onions with some green, sliced thin

3 tablespoons (45 ml) minced lemon balm

1 tablespoon (15 ml) minced parsley

1 tablespoon (15 ml) minced fennel or dill

1/2 cup (120 ml) freshly grated parmesan cheese

Sauté the rice in the butter and olive oil over medium heat for 5 minutes, stirring constantly. Reduce the heat to low and add 1 cup (240 ml) stock, stirring well. Salt and pepper lightly.

Cook the rice uncovered over low heat for 18 to 20 minutes, adding 1/2 cup (120 ml) stock at a time and stirring well after each addition. The rice should be al dente and slightly creamy when it is done. It may not be necessary to add all of the stock. When the rice is almost done, stir in the spring onions.

When the rice is done, remove it from the heat and stir in the minced herbs and parmesan cheese. Serve immediately.

PINEAPPLE BALM SORBET

■

WE HAVE EXPERIMENTED WITH HERB and flower sorbets from rosemary to lavender, and this remains one of our favorites. The tanginess of pineapple and the honeyed sweetness of lemon balm are unusually palatable together. This is a good finish to a spicy meal.

MAKES ABOUT 1½ QUARTS (1.5 LITRES)

1/2 cup (120 ml) sugar (castor sugar)

1 cup (240 ml) boiling water

1 large, ripe pineapple, about 2½ pounds (1 kg)

1/2 cup (240 ml) packed balm leaves

Dissolve the sugar in the boiling water and set aside to cool. Pare and core the pineapple. Cut it into chunks and measure 5 cups (1200 ml) of chunks. Puree them with the balm leaves in a food processor, or by batches in a blender. Stir the sugar syrup into the puree and blend well.

To make the sorbet in an ice cream machine, follow the manufacturer's instructions. To make the sorbet in the freezer, pour the mixture into a stainless steel bowl and freeze for 40 minutes to 1 hour, until very firm. Remove from the freezer and break the sorbet into 1-inch (2-cm) chunks with a spoon and stir well. Return to freezer for 1 hour or as long as desired.

Ten minutes before serving, break up the sorbet and blend or process to a smooth consistency. If you have made the sorbet in an ice cream machine, this step will not be necessary. Transfer the sorbet to chilled serving glasses and return to freezer for 5 minutes.

L E M O N   C A K E

■

THIS CAKE IS LIGHT AND LEMONY, delicious served plain with tea. We like it as well for dessert with the custard sauce below.

SERVES 8 TO 10

7 tablespoons (105 ml) unsalted butter	1 cup (240 ml) flour
	1/4 teaspoon (1 ml) salt
3 large eggs	Grated rind of 1 lemon
1 egg yolk	Handful of small lemon balm leaves
2/3 cup (160 ml) sugar (castor sugar)	

Preheat the oven to 375° F (190° C). Butter and flour an 8-inch (20-cm) square cake pan. Melt the butter over low heat and set aside to cool. Beat the eggs and egg yolk with the sugar until the mixture becomes pale yellow, thick, and fluffy, about 5 minutes.

Sift the flour three times with the salt. Very slowly fold the flour, one-third at a time, into the egg mixture. Carefully fold in the melted butter, one-third at a time. When the batter is thoroughly blended, fold in the lemon rind.

Scatter the lemon balm leaves in the bottom of the prepared pan. Pour the batter carefully into the pan, spreading it evenly. Bake for 20 minutes. The cake is done when the top is pale golden brown, the edges pull away slightly, and a cake tester comes out clean. Cool on a rack to room temperature before turning out of the pan.

C U S T A R D   S A U C E :

MAKES ABOUT 1½ CUPS (360 ML)

3/4 cup (180 ml) milk	1/2 cup (120 ml) sugar (castor sugar)
5 lemon balm sprigs	2 egg yolks
1½ teaspoons (8 ml) cornstarch (cornflour)	1 teaspoon (5 ml) rum

Scald the milk with the lemon balm in a small pan. Remove the pan from the heat and bruise the balm against the side of the pan with a wooden spoon. Steep the mixture for 1 hour.

Remove the balm from the pan and whisk in the cornstarch. Add the sugar and cook the mixture over low heat, stirring occasionally, until the sugar is dissolved.

Beat the egg yolks lightly in a small bowl and whisk in about 1/2 cup (120 ml) of the hot milk. Pour the egg yolk mixture back into the pan and cook the custard over low heat, stirring constantly, until it is thick enough to coat a wooden spoon.

Remove the custard from the heat and stir in the rum. Serve warm or cover and cool to room temperature.

BALMY SUNSET

■

MOUNT GAY, CRUZAN, AND PUSSERS RUM are dark Caribbean rums that give this punch a tropical touch. The longer the punch steeps, the more rich and mellow the flavor. With a splash of sparkling water, it is a welcome refreshment after a hot weed-wrestling session.

SERVES 4

1½ cups (360 ml) unsweetened pineapple juice	Few dashes of Angostura bitters, optional
1 cup (240 ml) freshly squeezed orange juice	4 or 5 lemon balm sprigs
	Lemon balm leaves
3/4 (180 ml) cup dark rum	
1½ teaspoons (8 ml) Grenadine	Splash of sparkling or seltzer water, optional

Mix the pineapple juice, orange juice, rum, grenadine, and optional bitters in a glass pitcher. Add the lemon balm sprigs, bruising them slightly. Steep the punch in the refrigerator at least 3 hours, preferably all day.

Remove the lemon balm sprigs from the punch. Rub the rims of four chilled glasses with a lemon balm leaf. Serve the punch on the rocks or over crushed ice. Garnish with lemon balm leaves, and add a splash of sparkling water if desired.

BALMY

SUNSET

LIME BALM TART

■

BALM'S SWEETNESS PLAYS OFF the tartness of citrus so well and its aroma echoes that of citrus so well that they are natural partners. We find this tart lighter and the flavor more subtle than most curd tarts or meringue pies, though it is made with eggs and butter. The pastry shell may be made ahead and kept in the freezer, tightly wrapped, for as long as a month. The custard can also be made ahead and refrigerated for a day. Let it come to cool room temperature before assembling the tart and baking the meringue.

SERVES 8

PASTRY:

1/2 cup (120 ml) unsalted butter, well-chilled

1¼ cups (300 ml) unbleached white flour

1 tablespoon (15 ml) sugar

Pinch of salt

1½ to 2 tablespoons (22 to 30 ml) cold water

Cut the butter into bits. Mix the flour, sugar, and salt. Cut the butter into the flour by hand, or in a food processor with the steel blade, to make a medium meal. Add just enough water to bind the dough, and gather the pastry to form a flattened round about 3/4 inch (2 cm) thick. Cover the dough with plastic wrap and refrigerate for at least 30 minutes.

Preheat the oven to 375° F (190° C). With your fingers, press the dough into a 9-inch (23-cm) tart pan with a removable bottom. Cover and chill at least 30 minutes.

Bake the shell for 10 minutes and prick it lightly with a fork. Bake another 10 to 15 minutes, until golden brown. Cool to room temperature on a rack.

F I L L I N G :

1/2 cup (120 ml) milk

2 tablespoons (30 ml) cornstarch (cornflour)

1/2 cup (120 ml) sugar (castor sugar)

Pinch of salt

4 lemon balm sprigs

4 extra-large eggs, separated

1/4 cup (60 ml) lime juice

4 tablespoons (60 ml) unsalted butter, cut into bits

Grated zest of 1 lime

1/4 cup (60 ml) minced lemon balm leaves

3 tablespoons (45 ml) sugar

Pinch of cream of tartar

1 lime, halved and sliced thin

Small lemon balm leaves

Dissolve the cornstarch in the milk in a heavy-bottomed saucepan. Place over low heat and add the sugar and balm sprigs. Bruise the balm against the side of the pan with a wooden spoon. Stir until the mixture is hot.

Beat the egg yolks lightly in a small bowl. Pour a few tablespoons of the hot milk into the yolks and stir well. Pour the yolk mixture back into the hot milk and blend well. Cook for a minute or two, then stir in the lime juice and zest.

Stir continually until the mixture begins to thicken. Add the butter to the custard, a few pieces at a time, blending well. Remove the custard from the heat when it starts to bubble. It should be thick.

Let the custard cool a bit and then remove the balm sprigs. Cover and cool to room temperature.

When ready to assemble the tart, preheat the oven to 400° F (200° C).

Beat the egg whites together with the sugar and cream of tartar until they are glossy and form peaks.

Stir the minced balm leaves into the custard and blend well. Spread the custard into the pastry shell evenly and cover it with the beaten egg whites.

Bake for 5 minutes, or until the meringue is golden brown. Cool the tart to room temperature. Garnish the tart with the lime slices and small balm leaves and serve.

ARJORAM AND OREGANO

MARJORAM *sings of sweet earth's flowers,*

while oregano summons the spicy powers.

Delightful myths and lovely uses surround sweet marjoram, while herbal remedies and hearty dishes are associated with oregano, its close cousin. Marjoram has long been one of the most popular culinary herbs. Its cultivation in the Mediterranean has been recorded for twelve centuries, spreading from its native Northern Africa and Southwest Asia. Recipes dating from the Renaissance call for marjoram in salads, in egg dishes, with rice, and with every variety of meat and fish. It was used to flavor beer before people started using hops, and as a tea in England before Eastern teas were imported.

Sweet marjoram has almost as much mythology linking it with love as basil does. The Romans began circulating the story that it had been touched by Venus, who left its perfume to remind mortals of her beauty. Marjoram was used in love potions and bridal bouquets in France, Italy, Greece, Spain, Portugal, and England from the Renaissance until the nineteenth century, a period when herbs were known and used by peasants, witches, and royalty. Italians gave nosegays of marjoram to banish sadness. Indians knew it well, though they did not use it in cooking as it was a plant sacred to Vishnu.

Oregano was named by the Greeks from *oros*, "mountain", and *ganos*, "joy". Its history, 1300 years longer than marjoram's, is mainly medicinal, with the relief of ailments from toothaches to opium addiction claimed by a long list of herbalists. The

MARJORAM'S

FRAGRANCE IS STILL

PRIZED BY PERFUME AND

SOAP MAKERS AS WELL

AS BY COOKS.

Spanish and Italians began recording its use for cooking during the fourteenth century, especially in meat and vegetable stews and with shellfish. Since World War II, when spice merchants began promoting and importing it in quantities, oregano has moved from obscurity to its position as one of the most popular dried herbs in the United States.

Marjoram's fragrance is still prized by perfume and soap makers as well as by cooks. We share with the bees the enjoyment of marjoram's blossoms in late summer. While we are drying the clusters of small purple flowers, we anticipate the further pleasure of our herb and flower potpourri. The Romans, who recognized and chronicled the sensual delights of many plants, made sachets of marjoram, oregano, rosemary, and lavender to perfume linens and baths. The sweetness of marjoram's aroma and the spiciness of oregano's complement one another equally well in the kitchen.

THE SWEETNESS OF MARJORAM'S AROMA COMPLEMENTS THE SPICINESS OF OREGANO'S.

Their use together and the similarity of their appearance and growing habits have caused problems with identification for cooks and herbalists alike. It is worthwhile to sort through the subspecies and cultivars, as flavor, aroma, and cold-hardiness vary greatly.

The following are culinary varieties. Sweet marjoram is classified as *Origanum majorana*. *O.* × *majoricum* is a hybrid of sweet marjoram and *O. vulgare* subspecies *virens*, and is sold as Italian oregano, oregano, or hardy marjoram. *O. v.* subspecies *hirtum* (formerly *O. v.* subspecies *heracleoticum)* is sometimes sold as Greek oregano or mountain oregano. All the plants above grow in clumps and do not spread.

The sprawling *O. vulgare* may be called practically anything, including wild marjoram, winter marjoram, and wild oregano, but it is not a culinary herb. We urge you again, especially with this group, to buy plants from competent and reliable growers. Most oregano seed is either the tasteless *O. vulgare* or a mixture of varieties. True-to-type culinary marjoram and oregano are grown mostly from cuttings; marjoram has pale purple-violet flowers, and most oreganos have white flowers. We made the mistake of buying and planting *O. vulgare* as a border for a small perennial bed. Two years later, it had taken over, and we spent a day digging it out. At least, the violet flowers could be used in dried arrangements.

Mexican oregano, *Lippia graveolens*, belongs to the verbena family. It has similar flavor and aroma to common oregano, though sharper and earthier. Another variety worth mentioning is Greek oregano (*O. onites*), called *rigani* in Greece. This oregano has a distinctive sharp aroma that is preferred for most Greek dishes. It, like marjoram, is not winter-hardy in cold climates.

The characteristics which identify fresh marjoram are a perfume reminiscent of sweet broom and mint, pale green leaves with faint silvery shadows, and a slightly bitter, resinous flavor. When dried, marjoram retains its sweet aroma and its color becomes a pale grayish-green. Fresh oregano has a spicier fragrance than marjoram, with hints of clove and balsam. O.v. subspecies *hirtum*, which is used in its native Greece as well as in Italy and France, has a sharper aroma and more bitter flavor than O. × *majoricum*, which is commonly cultivated in the United States, Italy, and Spain. The fresh leaves of both of these oreganos are green with a yellowish tinge. They dry to a lighter color, and their flavor is very pungent, rather like a blend of peppermint, pine, and clove oils. They are more oval, pointed, and larger than those of marjoram.

As cut fresh oregano and marjoram are not common in American markets, it is worth the small effort to cultivate them yourself. O. × *majoricum* is a hardy perennial which will survive northern winters if well mulched. O. *v.* subspecies *hirtum* is somewhat hardy; O. *onites* and sweet marjoram are perennials only in mild Mediterranean climates, but they do well in pots indoors during the winter.

The origanums like good drainage, weed-free soil, and enough room around them for their fine-branching lateral roots. We fertilize our oreganos about once a month with a 10-10-10 liquid fertilizer diluted to half the recommended strength. Indoors, oregano and marjoram are easily grown, especially in a well-drained container. They are fairly unfussy plants, but should be pinched back before they flower for maximum leaf harvest. They may be trimmed severely and will profit from this usage, giving handsome, bushy little plants and many savory dishes. Both oregano and marjoram dry well if the stems are cut and laid on screens, or tied in bunches and hung upside down in a warm dry place.

FRESH OREGANO HAS
A SPICIER FRAGRANCE
THAN MARJORAM . . .

S T U F F E D   M U S H R O O M S   W I T H   O R E G A N O

■

THIS DISH CAPITALIZES on the absorbent property of mushrooms; here, they are cooked in a little wine. These popular appetizers lend themselves to several variations: you may cook them in broth rather than wine, use marjoram instead of oregano, or add a few tiny imported canned clams to the stuffing and cook the mushrooms in the clam juice. The recipe is easily doubled.

SERVES 6 TO 12

12 large mushrooms

3 tablespoons (45 ml) olive oil

1 garlic clove, minced

1/3 cup (80 ml) chopped parsley

1 tablespoon (15 ml) chopped fresh oregano or 1 scant teaspoon crumbled dried oregano

1/3 cup (80 ml) fine dry bread crumbs

1/4 cup (60 ml) freshly grated parmesan cheese

Salt and freshly ground pepper

1/2 cup (120 ml) dry white wine

Carefully wipe the mushrooms clean. Remove the stems and mince them. Heat the olive oil in a small frying pan and sauté the stems with the garlic over moderate heat for about 3 minutes.

Preheat the oven to 350° F (180° C).

Remove the mixture from the heat and add the parsley, oregano, bread crumbs, and parmesan cheese. Season well with salt and pepper, and blend the mixture well.

Divide the stuffing among the mushroom caps, packing and mounding it. Arrange the mushrooms in a lightly buttered 11-by-8-inch (28-by-20-cm) gratin dish. Add the wine to the dish and bake the mushrooms for 10 minutes.

Place the dish under a preheated broiler about 2 inches (5 cm) from the heat for about 1 minute, or until the tops are golden brown. Transfer the mushrooms with a slotted spatula to a warm platter. Serve hot or warm.

SUMMER SQUASH STUFFED WITH PORCINI

■

DRIED PORCINI MUSHROOMS (*Boletus edulis*) are a staple in many Italian kitchens; though they are expensive, a small amount provides a woodsy, rich flavor. Fresh boletes are one of the world's great gustatory experiences, especially when they are brushed with fine olive oil, studded with tiny slivers of garlic, and roasted. In specialty food stores, choose porcini with slices intact and a good proportion of cap to stem; avoid crumbled and dusty-looking pieces. The stuffed squash are a good accompaniment to roasts of meat or poultry or can serve as a first course.

SERVES 6

1/2 ounce (15 g) dried porcini mushrooms

1 cup (240 ml) soft bread crumbs

3 small zucchini (courgettes), about 1¼ pounds (560 g)

1 tablespoon (15 ml) chopped marjoram, or a combination of marjoram and oregano

1 egg, lightly beaten

1 garlic clove, minced

1/4 cup (60 ml) freshly grated parmesan cheese

Salt and freshly ground pepper

Olive oil

Soak the porcini in about 1/2 cup (120 ml) boiling water for 15 or 20 minutes. Trim them and rinse them very carefully to rid them of sand. Chop them medium fine. Strain the soaking liquor through rinsed fine-weave cheesecloth into a clean bowl. Soak the bread crumbs in the porcini liquor for 10 minutes, then squeeze them dry.

Wash and trim the zucchini. Cut them in half lengthwise and steam for 5 minutes. Remove them to cool. Scoop out the pulp, leaving walls about 1/4 inch (5 mm) thick, and chop it.

Combine the zucchini pulp with the porcini, bread crumbs, egg, marjoram, garlic, and cheese. Season with salt and pepper. Preheat the oven to 375° F (190° C).

Lightly oil the zucchini cases. Fill them with the stuffing. Place them in a lightly oiled baking dish and bake for about 25 minutes, until the tops are light golden brown. Serve hot or at room temperature.

SPANAKOPITA

■

IF YOU DON'T HAVE GREEK OREGANO, use a little more common oregano. Fresh phyllo (also spelled filo and fillo) is easier to work with than frozen but may be harder to find. Frozen phyllo, available in many supermarkets, should be kept covered with a well-wrung-out damp tea towel. Work with one piece at a time; when phyllo dries out, it cracks very easily, just the quality that makes the baked phyllo so appetizing. Spanakopita is good as an appetizer, its usual place in Greek cuisine, or as a main course.

SERVES 6 TO 10

1 pound (450 g) fresh spinach

1 medium onion, diced fine

3 tablespoons (45 ml) unsalted butter

1 tablespoon (15 ml) fresh Greek oregano leaves, minced, or 1 scant teaspoon (5 ml) crumbled dried Greek oregano

10 ounces (280 g) feta cheese

Freshly grated nutmeg

Salt and freshly ground pepper

1/2 pound (225 g) fresh phyllo

1/2 cup (120 ml) melted unsalted butter

Clean and stem the spinach. Cook it with the water that clings to the leaves in a covered pot over moderate heat until it wilts, about 2 minutes. Drain the spinach in a colander, then chop it coarsely and transfer it to a large bowl.

Sauté the onion in 3 tablespoons (45 ml) butter over moderate heat for about 10 minutes. Add the onion to the spinach along with the oregano.

Crumble the cheese, add it to the spinach, and stir the mixture well. Season with nutmeg, salt, and pepper. Preheat the oven to 375° F (190° C).

Have the phyllo ready and the melted butter warm. Working carefully with three phyllo sheets, brush each sheet on one side with the butter. Place the sheets in a buttered 9-by-12-inch (23-by-30-cm) shallow baking dish. Spread about one-fifth of the filling over the phyllo. Continue buttering three sheets at a time and spread each layer with filling. The last layer will be phyllo.

Bake for 30 minutes or until the spanakopita is golden brown. Cut into triangles or diamonds and serve hot.

SIMPLE TOMATO SAUCE

■

MARJORAM TEMPERS THE BRASSINESS of oregano in this all-purpose sauce. Aside from the usual pasta and pizza applications, it is good with polenta, under or over baked or grilled summer vegetables such as squash and eggplant (aubergines), and many kinds of fish, from swordfish, bluefish, and tuna to snapper and sea bass. It is an excellent base for fish stews such as cioppino. Really flavorful tomatoes, either fresh or canned, are essential. Fresh plum tomatoes give the sauce the right medium-thick density. Other varieties can be used; just reduce the sauce a bit if the tomatoes are watery.

MAKES ABOUT 1 QUART (1 LITRE)

2 pounds (900 g) tomatoes, peeled, seeded, and diced, or a 28-ounce (800-g) can tomatoes, most seeds removed, and flesh diced

1 tablespoon (15 ml) and 1 teaspoon (5 ml) chopped fresh oregano or 1 teaspoon (5 ml) crumbled dried oregano

2 teaspoons (10 ml) chopped fresh marjoram or 1/2 teaspoon (2 ml) crumbled dried marjoram

1 medium red onion, diced fine

1 garlic clove, minced

2 tablespoons (30 ml) olive oil

1 teaspoon (5 ml) salt, or to taste

In a noncorrodible saucepan, combine the tomatoes, oregano, marjoram, onion, garlic, olive oil, and salt. Bring to a boil and simmer the mixture over moderate heat for 20 minutes, stirring occasionally.

HEARTY MINESTRONE

∎

A MINESTRONE SHOULD BE individual and variable. Use vegetables which are fresh and appealing; every season's version of minestrone has a different character. Onions, carrots, garlic, and some greens are necessary, but try minestrone without tomato, add sausage, use rice instead of pasta, and experiment with basil. Since we can find imported Italian and French beans (cannellini and haricots), we usually use those. Any kind of white beans, as well as chick peas and kidney beans, are good in minestrone.

SERVES 8 TO 10

2 celery stalks, chopped

2 large carrots, chopped

1 large potato, chopped

1 large red onion, chopped

1/4 cup (60 ml) olive oil

14-ounce (400-g) can Italian
     tomatoes

1½ quarts (1½ litres) chicken or
     vegetable stock

3 garlic cloves, chopped

1 medium zucchini (courgette), sliced

1/4 pound (115 g) green beans, cut
     in 1-inch (2-cm) lengths

1 pound (450 g) chard, stems cut in
     1-inch (2-cm) lengths, leaves
     shredded

1 cup (240 ml) cooked beans

1 cup (240 ml) small dried pasta,
     such as shells or butterflies

1 tablespoon (15 ml) fresh chopped
     marjoram or 1 teaspoon (5 ml)
     crumbled dried marjoram

1 tablespoon (15 ml) fresh chopped
     oregano or 1 teaspoon (5 ml)
     crumbled dried oregano

Salt and freshly ground pepper

3/4 cup (180 ml) freshly grated
     parmesan cheese

Sauté the celery, carrots, potato, and onion in the olive oil in a large soup pot over medium heat for about 7 minutes. Add the tomatoes, stock, and garlic and cook for about 20 minutes. Add the zucchini, green beans, and chard stems and cook for another 5 minutes. Add the chard leaves, beans, pasta, and marjoram and oregano to the soup. Season with salt and pepper. Cook for 10 minutes. Adjust the seasoning and let the soup stand, covered, for 10 minutes off the heat. Serve hot, and pass the parmesan cheese.

HEARTY
MINESTRONE

MARJORAM CORN BREAD

■

THIS IS A TOOTHSOME CORN BREAD, enriched with whole grains. For a lighter version, use all or part unbleached white flour for the whole wheat flour. Marjoram lends a nice touch of sweetness without adding sugar. Other herbs we like in corn bread are chives and dill. Use 1/4 to 1/3 cup (60 to 80 ml) chives, or 2 tablespoons (30 ml) dill instead of the marjoram.

SERVES 8

1½ cups (360 ml) cornmeal,
   preferably stone-ground

1½ cups (360 ml) whole wheat flour

1 teaspoon (5 ml) baking powder

1 teaspoon (5 ml) baking soda

3/4 teaspoon (4 ml) salt

1/2 cup (120 ml) wheat germ or oat
   bran

2 tablespoons (30 ml) chopped fresh
   marjoram or 1½ teaspoons (8 ml)
   crumbled dried marjoram

2 cups (475 ml) milk

2 eggs

1/4 cup (60 ml) vegetable oil or
   melted butter

Preheat the oven to 350° F (180° C).

Sift the cornmeal, whole wheat flour, baking powder, baking soda, and salt into a large bowl. Add the wheat germ or oat bran and marjoram and mix the ingredients lightly.

Combine the liquid ingredients in a small bowl, and whisk them for 1 minute.

Add the liquid ingredients to the dry ingredients and blend well. Pour the batter into a buttered 12-inch (30-cm) pie plate and bake for 30 minutes or until a cake tester inserted in the center comes out clean. Let the corn bread cool in the plate on a rack for 10 minutes before cutting.

JALAPEÑO AND OREGANO SALSA

■

FRESH SALSAS ARE QUICK TO MAKE and superior to any commercial canned versions we have tried. In addition, they have no preservatives, and the amount of salt can be controlled. To make the salsa in a food processor, add the stemmed and seeded peppers, the tomatoes, onions, and garlic, all rough-chopped, to the work bowl with the oregano. Pulse until the vegetables are in small pieces. Do not process to a puree. Serve the salsa with white-fleshed fish, any Southwestern meal, or corn chips. Mixed with sour cream, it makes a quick enchilada sauce; added to diced or mashed avocado, it is a good guacamole. For a flavor variation, use cilantro instead of oregano.

MAKES ABOUT 2 CUPS (475 ML)

4 jalapeño or 6 serrano peppers

2 pounds (900 g) ripe tomatoes, peeled and diced fine

1 small white onion, diced fine

2 garlic cloves, minced

1 tablespoon (15 ml) fresh oregano leaves, chopped

Salt to taste

Few drops lime juice or white wine vinegar, optional

Wearing rubber gloves, remove and discard the stems, seeds and ribs from the peppers. Dice them fine.

Combine the peppers, tomatoes, onion, and oregano in a bowl. Season with salt. Add lime juice or vinegar, if desired. The salsa is best if allowed to stand at room temperature for 1 hour before serving.

CHILIS RELLENOS

■

THIS IS A VARIATION OF Southwestern-style rellenos, which have a very fluffy egg batter. The cornmeal and whole wheat flour batter here adds substance and flavor. We like these better with salsas than cooked sauces; try Jalapeño and Oregano Salsa (page 195) or Tomato and Tomatillo Salsa with Cilantro (page 115).

SERVES 4 TO 8

8 poblano or Anaheim chili peppers, roasted and peeled

1/2 pound (225 g) monterey jack cheese

2 large eggs

2 tablespoons (30 ml) water

1 tablespoon (15 ml) minced fresh oregano or 1 teaspoon (5 ml) crumbled dried oregano

1/3 cup (80 ml) cornmeal, preferably stone-ground

1/3 cup (80 ml) whole wheat pastry flour

Salt and freshly ground pepper

Vegetable oil

Make a lengthwise slit in the peppers. Remove the seeds and ribs carefully but leave the stems intact. Do not rinse the peppers but pat them dry.

Cut the cheese into eight pieces to fit the peppers and stuff each pepper with a piece of cheese.

Beat the eggs, water, and oregano together in a flat bowl. Stir in the cornmeal and flour. Season lightly with salt and pepper. Thin the batter if necessary to a coating consistency with 1 to 2 tablespoons (15 to 30 ml) more water.

In a deep frying pan heat 3/4 inch (2 cm) of oil to 375° F (190° C). Dip the stuffed peppers into the batter to coat them on all sides. Add four battered peppers at a time to the hot oil. Fry them for about 1 minute on each side, or until they are golden, then transfer them with a slotted spoon to paper towels to drain. Serve hot.

GENOVESE-STYLE STUFFED BREAST OF VEAL

■

THIS CIMA ALLA GENOVESE is a classic Ligurian dish whose tastiness and handsome appearance more than compensate for the work of sewing it together. It is elegant, impressive summer buffet or party fare, with a full, but more refined, flavor than most pâtés. Sew it with a large needle and unwaxed dental floss. This works well, and no special needle is required. Unsliced, the cima keeps well for 5 to 6 days in the refrigerator. After it has been cut, it will keep 3 to 4 days refrigerated.

SERVES 12 TO 14 AS AN APPETIZER,
OR 6 TO 8 AS A MAIN COURSE

4½- to 5-pound (2-kg) breast of veal

2 carrots, chopped

1 onion, chopped

1 large celery stalk, chopped

1 bay leaf

2 teaspoons (10 ml) coarse salt

6 eggs

1 large bunch spinach, stemmed and leaves cleaned

2 tablespoons (30 ml) chopped fresh marjoram, or 1 tablespoon (15 ml) crumbled dried marjoram

6 ounces (170 g) ground pork

6 ounces (170 g) ground veal

1/2 cup (120 ml) freshly grated parmesan cheese

1/2 cup (120 ml) shelled pistachios

About 1½ teaspoons (8 ml) salt

Freshly ground black pepper

Freshly grated nutmeg

Carefully bone the breast of veal, leaving the meat in one piece. Trim the veal of extra fat. Place the boned veal on a board, skin side up, and pound it to an evenly shaped rectangle. Cover the meat while you prepare the stock and filling.

Divide the bones into pairs and put them in a stockpot large enough to hold the rolled breast. Add the carrots, onion, and celery to the stockpot with the bay leaf and coarse salt.

Hard-cook four of the eggs, then cool and shell them.

Chop the spinach fine. Place the spinach, marjoram, ground pork and veal, cheese, pistachios, and the remaining eggs in a large bowl. Add the salt, pepper, and nutmeg, and mix everything together well with your hands. Season the mixture well or it will be too bland. To test the seasoning, fry about a tablespoon (15 ml) of the mixture until it is done, then taste it; add more seasoning, if necessary.

Spread the stuffing lengthwise along the breast and bury the hard-cooked eggs in the stuffing, spacing them evenly. Beginning at one end, wrap the meat around the stuffing, and sew the meat carefully with a blanket or overhand stitch.

Wrap the cima in a 30-by-12-inch (75-by-30-cm) piece of muslin or fine-weave cheesecloth. Tuck the ends of cloth under and tie it securely with kitchen twine or unwaxed dental floss.

Place the cima in the stockpot, cover with 1 inch (2 cm) of water and bring to a boil. Reduce heat and simmer the cima, uncovered, for 1 hour, skimming occasionally. Cover the pot and simmer 1½ hours longer.

Remove the pot from the heat and let it cool for an hour. Remove the cima from the stock and place it in a shallow baking dish or deep platter. Place a baking sheet on top and add a weight, such as a heavy pan or three or four 2-pound (1-kg) cans.

Strain the stock and reserve for another use. Let the cima stand at room temperature for 3 or 4 hours, then remove the weight and refrigerate for at least 24 hours before serving.

To serve, unwrap the cloth and remove the thread. Let the cima stand at room temperature for 1 hour. Slice into 3/8-inch (8-mm) slices on a slight diagonal.

L A S A G N A   C A S A L I N G A

■

CASALINGA IS A TERM OF APPROBATION on Italian restaurant menus. It literally means "housewife", and connotes a dish made honestly, with no shortcuts, and a little rustic in feeling or presentation. When we were living and working in Italy, we liked making this lasagna with our own chickens and eggs and good local olive oil. The chicken can be poached ahead, cooled, and refrigerated. The next day, the entire lasagna can be assembled a day before serving, and refrigerated.

SERVES 8 TO 10

1 recipe Egg Pasta (page 71)

2½- to 3-pound (1.1- to 1.4-kg) chicken, poached and cooled

1 medium onion, diced

3 tablespoons (45 ml) olive oil

28-ounce (800-g) can plum tomatoes

4 garlic cloves, minced

2 tablespoons (30 ml) chopped fresh marjoram

1 tablespoon (15 ml) chopped fresh oregano or 1 teaspoon (5 ml) crumbled dried oregano

1/4 teaspoon (1 ml) cayenne pepper

Salt and freshly ground pepper

1 pound (450 g) ricotta cheese

2 large eggs

1/3 cup (80 ml) chopped Italian parsley

1 cup (240 ml) freshly grated parmesan cheese

Freshly grated nutmeg

Follow the directions for making, resting, and rolling the pasta on pages 71–72. Cut the pasta into 5-inch (12.5-cm) lengths and set aside so that the pieces do not touch.

Skin and bone the poached chicken and cut the meat into about 1/2-inch (1-cm) dice.

Soften the onion in the olive oil over medium-low heat. Add the plum tomatoes and break them up with a wooden spoon. Stir in the garlic, 1 tablespoon (15 ml) of the marjoram, the oregano, and cayenne pepper. Season with salt and pepper. Simmer the sauce for about 20 minutes, then stir in the diced chicken. Let the sauce cool to room temperature and make the cheese filling.

Mix the ricotta cheese with the eggs, parsley, remaining marjoram, and parmesan cheese in a bowl. Season with salt, pepper, and nutmeg.

Bring 6 to 8 quarts (6 to 8 litres) of salted water to a boil. Add a tablespoon or two (15 to 30 ml) of oil to a bowl filled with about 3 quarts (3 litres) of cold water.

When the water is rapidly boiling, drop in four pasta pieces and cook for 15 seconds. Do not overcook. Remove the pasta to the cold water with a large strainer or slotted spoon. Repeat until all the pasta has been parcooked.

Preheat the oven to 375° F (190° C). Butter a 13-by-9-by-2-inch (33-by-23-by-5-cm) lasagna pan.

Blot excess water gently from each piece of pasta with a tea towel or paper towel as you use it.

Drape pasta barely overlapping pieces, about 1½ inches (4 cm) over the outside edge of the pan on all sides. Cover the bottom of the pan with one or two pieces of pasta. Spoon about 2/3 cup (160 ml) of chicken filling over the pasta. Cover with pasta squares and spread about 2/3 cup (160 ml) of cheese filling over the pasta. Repeat the layering until all the fillings have been used up. Cover the last layer of filling with pasta and fold the edges over the top. Drizzle the top with a little olive oil.

The lasagna may be prepared ahead to this point. Cover tightly and refrigerate for as long as 24 hours. Remove the lasagna from the refrigerator about 30 minutes before baking.

Bake the lasagna for about 25 minutes. The edges and top should be light golden brown and crunchy. Let the lasagna stand for about 10 minutes before cutting and serving.

S T E W E D   S W E E T   P E P P E R S

■

THERE ARE MANY VARIATIONS of this stew, called peperonata and usually served as an appetizer in Italy. Sometimes it is made without any herbs, including garlic, and sometimes basil replaces marjoram or oregano; often it does not have tomato. For another Italian version, try adding a few tablespoons (20 to 50 ml) of dry white wine and stewing it a few minutes longer. It is a versatile late summer dish: colorful, always tasty, easily doubled, and good hot or at room temperature. Like many stews, it tastes even better when made ahead of time. We like to serve it with crusty bread and cheese for lunch.

SERVES 4 TO 6

3 large sweet bell peppers; 1 red, 1 yellow, and 1 green

3 to 4 tablespoons (45 to 60 ml) olive oil

1 small onion, sliced lengthwise in 1/4-inch (5-mm) slivers

2 garlic cloves, slivered

1 large tomato, diced, optional

Leaves from 1 or 2 oregano and/or marjoram sprigs

Salt and freshly ground pepper

Wash the peppers, stem and seed them, and remove any large ribs. Cut them lengthwise into 3/8-inch (8-mm) strips.

Heat the olive oil in a skillet. Sauté the peppers over medium heat, stirring occasionally, for about 5 minutes. Add the onion and garlic to the pan and cook for about 5 minutes.

If you are using the tomato, add it to the pan. Cook for about 3 minutes, stirring occasionally.

Add the oregano and/or marjoram and season with salt and pepper. Lower the heat, stir the ingredients, cover the pan and cook for 10 to 15 minutes. Serve hot or at room temperature.

ROASTED RED PEPPER AND FENNEL VINAIGRETTE

■

GARDEN PEPPERS AND FENNEL make a special end-of-harvest salad or appetizer, but market vegetables are a good substitute. Marjoram shows its sweet, harmonious nature to advantage in this dish.

SERVES 4 AS A SALAD, 6 AS AN APPETIZER

2 large red bell peppers, roasted and peeled

2 Florence fennel bulbs, about 1¼ pounds (560 g)

2 to 3 tablespoons (30 to 45 ml) balsamic or red wine vinegar

1/3 cup (80 ml) olive oil

1 garlic clove, minced

1 tablespoon (15 ml) fresh marjoram leaves, coarsely chopped

1 tablespoon (15 ml) fresh Italian parsley, coarsely chopped

Salt and freshly ground black pepper to taste

Marjoram blossoms, optional

Cut the peppers in half and remove the seeds. Slice them into 3/4-inch (2-cm) slices.

Trim and clean the fennel and cut it lengthwise into 1/4-inch (5-mm) slices. Blanch for about a minute in lightly salted boiling water. Drain, cool to room temperature, and pat dry.

Arrange the peppers and fennel on a serving platter.

Place the vinegar in a small bowl. Whisk in the olive oil to form an emulsion. Stir in the garlic, marjoram, and parsley. Season with salt and pepper.

Drizzle the vinaigrette over the vegetables. Marinate for an hour or so at room temperature before serving. Garnish the salad with marjoram blossoms.

CHILIS EN ESCABECHE WITH OREGANO

■

A BIG PLATTER OF COLORFUL, taste-tingling chilis and peppers is a very Southwestern way to brighten and lighten a meal of meat and masa dishes, such as adovados (red chili stews), chorizo, grilled meats, tamales, burritos, and enchiladas. This is a fresh, light escabeche, with less vinegar and more herb than usual. It may be prepared ahead and kept refrigerated for 2 or 3 days. It will change in character but will still be good. If red hot cherry peppers are not available, add an extra serrano and jalapeño.

SERVES 4 TO 6

3/4 cup (180 ml) white wine vinegar	3 or 4 jalapeño peppers
2 cups (475 ml) water	2 hot red cherry peppers
1 teaspoon (5 ml) salt	1 large sweet onion
1/2 teaspoon (2 ml) sugar	2 tablespoons (30 ml) olive oil
4 medium-sized bell peppers: red, green, yellow, and purple, if possible	2 tablespoons (30 ml) coarse-chopped fresh oregano leaves

Bring the vinegar, water, salt, and sugar to boil in a noncorrodible saucepan. When the sugar and salt are dissolved, remove the pan from the heat.

Stem and seed the bell peppers and chilis. Cut the bell peppers into lengthwise strips about 1/4 inch (5 mm) thick. Cut the chilis into lengthwise slivers. Peel the onion and cut it into lengthwise slivers.

Place the vegetables in a glass or stainless steel bowl and pour the pickling liquid over them. Toss in the olive oil and oregano. Cover the bowl and marinate in the refrigerator for 3 hours before serving. Drain the liquid from the escabeche before serving or storing. Serve at cool room temperature.

THE MINTS

Balsam and pepper, apple and ginger,
many tastes their names have lent,
while spear describes the leafy finger.
In such a bunch of jolly herbs
why is none named merriment?

■ **P**rofusion, infusion, and confusion characterize the mint genus, *Mentha*. Its growing habits and many members explain the first attribute; its long history as a medicinal and social tea, the second; and its large number of varieties, the third. We have carefully rooted through our mint beds to offer some clarification of the kinds of mints, and some inspiration for their uses.

The many species of mints, and their tendencies to crossbreed, makes marketing and buying capricious. Even experts do not always describe the same species in the same way. Of course, the advantage of such a large and various group is that there are mints to whet the appetite of almost everyone.

The mints in this chapter are the ones that we have grown and used. When choosing mints, look for flavor and appearance which appeal to you. Sniff, and if possible, taste the leaves. Remember, leaves from a greenhouse plant will be milder than those from a garden mint. Growing mint from seed is notoriously variable; we advise against it. Cultivars and sterile hybrids such as peppermint are propagated by cuttings or root divisions.

In the garden, plant different varieties away from one another to retain individuality. Especially for small gardens, we strongly advise confining mint in tubs or pots, either buried in beds or left to stand as handsome container plants. Mints spread rapidly by runners, and can change from a pleasurable little bed to a nuisance in one season. Rather than bemoan

IN THE GARDEN, PLANT

DIFFERENT VARIETIES OF

MINT AWAY FROM ONE

ANOTHER . . .

their habits, plan for them. Water, good drainage, and a well-fertilized soil are their only growing requirements. They prefer sun in most climates, but will grow in partial shade and thrive there in very hot climates. ✦

Mint can be snipped freely for kitchen use throughout the season. Larger plantings intended for drying can be cut back three times. Early and mid-summer cuttings should be taken 2 to 3 inches (5 to 8 cm) above the ground. The late harvest should take place just before flowering or when the lower leaves yellow, whichever comes first. Cut the plants back to the ground at this time. Hang mint in bunches upside down or strip the leaves from the stems and dry on a screen in a shady, dry, and warm place.

... MINT ACCOMMODATES ITSELF TO A WIDE RANGE OF CLIMATES.

Peppermints have the strongest flavor and offer great versatility for those who love mint. One of the small pleasures of growing herbs is to work in the garden with a tingly peppermint leaf under the tongue. Blue Balsam (*Mentha* × *piperita* 'Mitcham') has the most intense, in fact, balsamic, taste. It is excellent for cooked dishes and refreshing in summer drinks. Blue Balsam's stem and leaves have a deep purple-blue cast. The leaves are somewhat larger and rounder than those of regular peppermint. It tends to branch lower and grows about 2½ feet (75 cm) tall.

Peppermint (M. × *piperita*) does have a hint of pepper and is good in cooked dishes, especially in jellies and mint sauces. The plant will grow erect to about 3 feet (90 cm), and the leaves may be slightly fuzzy. Both of these peppermints have medicinal and stomach-soothing uses and make wonderful teas. They are therefore good herbs to grow in abundance and to dry.

Spearmints (*Mentha spicata*) are milder and sweeter than peppermints and are good in salads or wherever a lighter flavor is desired. These are the mints which people associate with mint juleps, fresh mint teas, sauces, and jellies. Sipping a glassful of hot, sweet spearmint tea always weaves the fabric of memory so that we are once again sitting at an outdoor cafe in Morocco. The scent of garden mint just after a rain entwines yet another thread and we are children in Arizona, playing in the shady mint patch that flourishes under the outdoor water cooler. At home in desert places or northern latitudes, mint accommodates itself to a wide range of climates. Forms and variations in this group are great. We have grown rounded, fuzzy-leaved spearmints and pointed, sharply serrated-leaved varieties, the plants being from 1½ to 3½ feet (46 to 107 cm) tall.

Yerba buena (M. *cordifolia*) has pale green

leaves that are used often in Latin American, Southwestern, and Mexican cooking. Its flavor is a bit coarser than that of spearmint.

Pineapple mint (M. *suaveolens* 'Variegata') is a sweetly citrus flavored mint which we like to use in confections, for candying, and for punches because of its aroma and small leaves. There are two varieties: one has green leaves with slight irregular variegations in the spring, and the other has green leaves with beautiful variegation all year long. It grows to about 2½ feet (75 cm) tall.

Orange mint (M. *piperata* var. *citrata,* sometimes classified as M. *aquatica*) is also called bergamot mint, but should not be confused with bee balm (*Monarda didyma*), also known as bergamot, nor with bergamot orange (*Citrus aurantium* subspecies *bergamia*), the source of oil of bergamot. Orange mint is highly perfumed with a strong citrus flavor that we enjoy in iced drinks. The delightful fragrance is exceptional in fruit preserves and butters or as part of a bouquet. We grow a lot of it to use in tea blends.

The long and colorful history of mint has been recorded in Greek mythology, the Bible, and herbals of all times. Romans used it to flavor many kinds of food and drinks and adorned their halls with it in preparation for feasts so that the smell would stimulate the guests. As Pliny observed, "The smell of mint stirs up the mind and appetite to a greedy desire for food." The herb symbolized strength to the Greeks, who used it in their athletic ceremonies. Whether or not they brought it with them when they colonized Sicily in pre-Roman times is not known, but mint is still an important flavor in Sicilian cooking.

"THE SMELL OF MINT STIRS UP THE MIND AND APPETITE TO A GREEDY DESIRE FOR FOOD."

The Elizabethans used mint not only as a strewing herb, but in the bath, to strengthen the nerves and stomach, and to whiten the teeth. Mint is used in many of these ways today—from air fresheners and bath oils to toothpastes and stomach preparations. Nicholas Culpeper, writing in the mid-seventeenth century, listed 40 ailments for which mint is a cure.

As an herb which is still esteemed throughout the world both culinarily and medicinally, mint is an important part of our kitchens and gardens. In the following recipes, the suggested mints may be replaced with any you prefer.

MOROCCAN MINT TEA

■

TO PREPARE THE TRADITIONAL MOROCCAN TEA, the tea must be green, with a mild flavor; the mint *must* be fresh; and it must be spearmint. The tea is very sweet; there is always sugar in the bottom of the glass in Morocco. It should be served in small glasses with several fresh sprigs in each, and sipped slowly, the better to inhale the mildly invigorating aroma.

MAKES 6 SMALL GLASSES

1 heaping tablespoon (15 ml) green tea, such as Dragonwell or Gunpowder

About 20 spearmint sprigs

1/4 to 1/2 cup (60 to 120 ml) sugar (castor sugar)

Boiling water

Rinse a teapot with boiling water and pour the water out. Add the green tea and enough spearmint to loosely fill the pot about three-quarters full. Add at least 1/4 cup (60 ml) sugar and fill the pot with boiling water. Steep for 5 minutes. Add two or three mint sprigs to each glass and pour the tea.

MINT DAIQUIRI

■

WITHOUT GETTING INTO PARTISAN DEBATES about mint juleps (kind of mint, type of sugar, to muddle or not, etc.), we'd like to suggest this alternative. Peppermint stands up to the alcohol, and Blue Balsam is the one we always choose.

MAKES 8 DRINKS

6 limes

1/2 cup (120 ml) sugar

4 cups (950 ml) water

5 large peppermint sprigs

3/4 cup plus 2 tablespoons (210 ml) light rum

2 tablespoons (30 ml) clear crème de menthe

Squeeze enough limes to make 1/2 cup (120 ml) lime juice. Dissolve the sugar in the lime juice and add the water. Adjust the taste with more lime juice or sugar. Soak the large mint sprigs in the limeade, bruising the leaves a bit against the side of the pitcher. Add the rum and crème de menthe.

Chill the mixture for at least 30 minutes. Serve the daiquiris on the rocks with a small sprig of fresh mint for garnish.

M I N T E D   P E A   S O U P

■

PEAS AND MINT HAVE A LONG HISTORY together in English cookery. Some other simple combinations are peas stewed in heavy cream (double cream) with chopped mint, or sweated in a little butter until they are tender, then flavored with mint and pepper. The soup, one of our spring herb staples, is a handy recipe when the peas are of uneven size. Because it is pureed, it doesn't matter if the small peas cook a little longer so that the large ones are done.

SERVES 6

1½ pounds (675 g) fresh peas, shelled	2 shallots, diced fine
3 tablespoons (45 ml) chopped spearmint leaves	1½ cups (360 ml) half-and-half (single cream)
2 tablespoons (30 ml) unsalted butter	Salt and freshly ground white pepper

Put the peas and chopped mint in a pan and barely cover with water. Cover and cook over low heat until the peas are just tender, about 5 minutes.

Sauté the shallots in butter in a small pan over moderate heat until they are soft and golden.

Puree the peas and shallots together. Return them to the pan and add the cream, season with salt and freshly ground white pepper. Heat over low heat until the soup is very hot, but do not allow it to boil.

MINTED LAMB, MIDDLE EASTERN STYLE

■

MINT IS ONE OF THE BEST-LOVED HERBS in the cooking of the Middle East; Egyptians, Tunisians, Cypriots, and many other peoples use it frequently. This is our version of a pan–Middle Eastern dish, incorporating elements we have enjoyed in different places. Save the bone to make a little lamb stock with half an onion, half a bay leaf, a pinch of thyme, and some mushroom stems, if you have them. This will deepen the flavor of the dish. For a Middle Eastern presentation, place the stew in a copper or brass serving dish, surround it with couscous or rice, and garnish with mint sprigs.

SERVES 6

3-pound (1.4-kg) boned leg of lamb, preferably the shank end

2 large onions, about 1 pound (450 g), halved and sliced thin

3 tablespoons (45 ml) unsalted butter

1 cup (240 ml) lamb stock or water

4 tablespoons (60 ml) honey

2 garlic cloves, minced

2 teaspoons (10 ml) fresh thyme leaves or 1 teaspoon (5 ml) dried thyme

1 teaspoon (5 ml) toasted and ground cumin seed

1/2 teaspoon (2 ml) ground allspice

Salt and freshly ground pepper

1/4 cup (60 ml) chopped mint

1 tablespoon (15 ml) minced marjoram

Trim the lamb of extra fat and connective tissue and cut it into 1½-inch (4-cm) pieces.

Sauté the onions in the butter over low heat for 10 minutes. Push the onions to the side of the pan and increase the heat to medium.

Add the lamb to the pan and brown it lightly all over. Add the stock or water, honey, garlic, thyme, cumin, and allspice. Season with salt and pepper. Cover and cook over low heat for about 45 minutes.

Remove from the heat and stir in the mint and the marjoram. Cover for 10 minutes. Serve hot.

SICILIAN-STYLE FISH WITH MINT SAUCE

■

IN SICILY, THIS IS MADE WITH SMALL, whole fish that have been gutted and scaled. Since these are not readily available in American markets, we thought to try swordfish, which is a popular fish in Sicily. This is quite tasty, as is shark, which has a similar texture but is less expensive. If you can get fresh sand dabs or fresh sardines, try the recipe with them. This is a summer dish, an appetizer or main course to be served at cool room temperature. It is excellent with plain boiled or steamed new potatoes. To our taste, spearmint is the best flavor choice.

SERVES 4 TO 6

2 pounds (900 g) swordfish or shark	1/2 cup (120 ml) water
About 1/2 cup (120 ml) all-purpose flour	1/2 cup (120 ml) fresh mint leaves, coarse-chopped
1/3 cup (80 ml) olive oil	3 tablespoons (45 ml) capers
3 garlic cloves, minced	Salt and freshly ground pepper
1/2 cup (120 ml) white wine vinegar	

Trim any skin from the fish. Dice the flesh in about 3/4-inch (2-cm) pieces. Season the fish lightly with salt and pepper and dredge in the flour to coat well. Shake off excess flour. Heat the olive oil over medium-high heat in a pan large enough to hold the fish in one layer, or cook it in two pans.

Brown the fish all over, tossing it or shaking the pan, until it is light golden brown, about 3 minutes. Add the garlic and cook for a minute. Add the vinegar, water, mint, and capers. Season with salt and pepper, cover, and simmer for 5 minutes, or until the fish is just cooked.

Turn the fish and sauce onto a serving platter to cool to room temperature before serving.

ROAST DUCK WITH
GOOSEBERRY MINT SAUCE

■

ROASTING DUCK INITIALLY at a high temperature produces a crisp skin. Pricking the skin well is important so that most of the fat melts out. Mint sauce is coupled in many minds with lamb, but it is just as good with the richness of duck and the wild taste of venison and elk. While the classic sauce for lamb is made with only water, vinegar, sugar, and fresh mint, gooseberry or currant jelly has the fruity tartness and sweetness that goes well with duck, goose, and game.

SERVES 4

4- to 5-pound (1.8- to 2.3-g) duck	Large bunch Blue Balsam mint or other peppermint
Salt and freshly ground pepper	
1 celery rib, diced	1/2 cup (120 ml) gooseberry jam or jelly, or currant jelly
1 carrot, diced	1/4 cup (60 ml) shredded mint leaves
1 onion, diced	Mint sprigs

Preheat the oven to 450° F (230° C).

Wash the duck and pat it dry. Prick the skin all over, especially over the fatty deposits on the legs. Salt and pepper it lightly inside and out. Place the duck, breast up, on a rack set in a roaster pan or on a baking sheet. Roast for 20 minutes.

Remove the duck from the oven and fill the cavity with the vegetables and as many mint sprigs as will fit loosely. Pour the accumulated fat from the pan and reduce the oven temperature to 350° F (180° C).

Roast the duck for 45 minutes to 1 hour, depending on the doneness desired.

Remove the duck to a heatproof serving platter. Carefully pour the fat from the pan and pour the cooking juices into a small saucepan. Stir in the gooseberry jam and the shredded mint. Simmer the sauce for 1 or 2 minutes over low heat.

Set the oven temperature to 450° F (230° C). Brush the duck lightly with the sauce and return to the oven for 3 to 4 minutes, until the skin is glazed. Remove the duck and let it stand for 5 minutes before carving. Mix the accumulated juices with the remaining sauce and serve separately. Garnish the platter with mint sprigs, if desired.

ROAST DUCK

WITH

GOOSEBERRY

MINT SAUCE

MINTED TOMATOES GRATINÉ

■

FRIED TOMATOES WERE A SUMMER TREAT that Carolyn's father, Robert Dille, used to prepare for the family when the children were small. He used only a touch of salt and served the tomatoes and their pan juices on toast. We have added mint and put the bread, in the form of crumbs, on top. The melting-sweet flavor still means summer to us, whether the tomatoes are served with roasted or grilled meat or poultry, or as a quick supper with scrambled eggs.

SERVES 3 OR 4

3 firm-ripe tomatoes, about 1½ pounds (675 g)

3 tablespoons (45 ml) unsalted butter

2 tablespoons (30 ml) rough-chopped fresh spearmint leaves

5 tablespoons (75 ml) fine dry bread crumbs

3 tablespoons (45 ml) freshly grated parmesan cheese

2 tablespoons (30 ml) fine-chopped fresh spearmint leaves

Salt and freshly ground pepper, optional

Slice the tomatoes into 1/2-inch (1-cm) slices. Melt the butter with the rough-chopped spearmint over medium-low heat. Sauté the tomatoes in the butter for about 1 minute on each side.

Preheat the oven broiler. Place the tomatoes in a heatproof serving dish or on a baking sheet. Combine the butter and mint from the pan with the bread crumbs, cheese, and fine-chopped mint. Divide the mixture evenly on top of the tomato slices.

Grill the tomatoes, about 5 inches (13 cm) from the heat, until the gratin is golden brown. Serve the tomatoes and their juices in a warmed dish.

CUCUMBER MINT RAITA

■

CUCUMBERS AND YOGURT are a frequent combination in the Indian relishes called raitas, as they are both cooling. Herbs and spices vary, according to the region, and the cucumbers may be grated. Serve the raita with curries, or other spicy dishes, and as the

Indians do, for lunch with flatbread.

MAKES ABOUT 4 CUPS (1 LITRE)

1 pound (450 g) cucumbers

2 cups (475 ml) plain yogurt

2 tablespoons (30 ml) minced onion

3 tablespoons (45 ml) minced mint

Scant 1/2 teaspoon (2 ml) salt

1/2 teaspoon (2 ml) ground cardamom

Peel the cucumbers if the skins are bitter or waxed. Seed them and dice them medium-fine. You should have about 1½ cups (360 ml) diced cucumber. Combine the cucumber with the other ingredients. Cover the raita and chill for at least an hour before serving.

N E W   P O T A T O E S   W I T H   M I N T

■

POTATOES HAVE MANY HERB PARTNERS, including mint; their earthiness is accented, yet somehow subdued, by mint's sweetness. If the potatoes are from the garden or are really fresh, there is no need to peel them. The skins have a subtle flavor of their own.

SERVES 6 TO 8

2½ pounds (1.1 kg) new potatoes, preferably about 1½ inches (4 cm) in diameter

3 tablespoons (45 ml) unsalted butter

1 tablespoon (15 ml) chopped mint leaves

Salt and freshly ground pepper

Scrub the potatoes and peel, if desired. Steam small potatoes whole for 5 minutes. If you are using larger potatoes, halve or quarter them and steam them for 3 minutes.

Heat the butter in a large frying pan over moderate heat and add the potatoes and mint. Cook for 5 to 7 minutes over medium-high heat, until the potatoes are just done. Shake the pan continuously while the potatoes are cooking. Transfer the potatoes to a hot platter, sprinkle lightly with salt and plenty of pepper, and serve immediately.

BUTTERMINT COOKIES

∎

THESE ARE CRISP, MINTY, AND BUTTERY refrigerator cookies that are particularly good with herb or black tea and with fresh fruit and fruit compote desserts. They make us think of our grandmothers' tins of oval pastel buttermint candies, though they are not as sweet. The dough will keep in the freezer for a month or so. Store the cookies in airtight containers after they have cooled.

MAKES ABOUT 4 DOZEN COOKIES

12 tablespoons (180 ml) unsalted
  butter, softened

2/3 cup (160 ml) sugar (castor sugar)

1 large egg

1/2 teaspoon (2 ml) vanilla extract

1/2 teaspoon (2 ml) peppermint
  extract, optional

2 cups (475 ml) unbleached white
  flour, sifted

2 tablespoons (30 ml) minced
  peppermint or orange mint leaves

Pinch of salt

Cream the butter and sugar. Beat in the egg and the extracts. Gradually mix in the flour, and stir in the minced peppermint and a pinch of salt. The dough will be soft.

Divide the dough into three parts. Using plastic wrap to shape the dough, roll each part into a cylinder about 1¼ inches (3 cm) in diameter. Chill the rolls for an hour, or place in the freezer for 20 minutes.

Preheat the oven to 350° F (180° C). Remove the plastic wrap and slice the dough 1/4 inch thick. Place the slices on ungreased baking sheets and bake for about 10 minutes, until they are a light golden brown. Immediately transfer the cookies to racks to cool.

G R A P E   M I N T   J E L L Y

■

ANY PURPLE GRAPES WITH SEEDS are good for jelly. We usually use Concord, but there are many local varieties, such as Ribier and Mystic. We find that seedless varieties do not have enough grapiness to yield flavorful jelly. This recipe relies on the old method of extracting pectin from the grape skins and seeds so that powdered pectin is unnecessary. We don't think squeezing the bag matters here because the jelly is so dark that cloudiness is not detectable. The fragrant mint-grape combination was a fortuitous one that occurred to us while we were picking Susan's Concord grapes, underplanted with mint. Smelling the trodden mint while popping grapes into our mouths propelled us right into the kitchen. We've tried several mints in this recipe, and like the tealike flavor and aroma of bergamot mint best.

MAKES ABOUT 6 HALF-PINT (240-ML) JARS

2½ pounds (1.1 kg) purple grapes	*1 cup (240 ml) light honey*
28 fresh mint leaves	*2 large mint sprigs*
2 cups (475 ml) sugar (castor sugar)	*6 small mint sprigs*

Wash the grapes and layer them in a large noncorrodible pan, mashing each layer as it is added. Add 20 of the fresh mint leaves and stir. Bring the grapes to a simmer on low heat and cook for 20 minutes.

Pour the hot mixture into a jelly bag or a large sieve lined with dampened fine-weave cheesecloth, straining it into a bowl. Squeeze the cloth to obtain all the juice. Return the pulp to a saucepan and just cover it with water. Add eight more mint leaves and bring to a simmer. Cook 15 minutes and strain again, squeezing to get all the juice. There should be 4 cups (950 ml) of juice; if necessary, add a little water to equal this amount.

Reheat the juice in a clean noncorrodible pan with the sugar and honey. Add two large mint sprigs and stir well. Simmer and continue stirring until the jelly just sheets from a metal spoon or reaches 220° F (104° C) on a jelly thermometer. Or use the saucer jell test described on page 61. Remove the mint sprigs.

Have ready six sterilized hot half-pint (240-ml) jelly jars with a small, clean sprig of mint in each jar. Ladle the hot jelly into the jars immediately and seal according to the manufacturer's instructions. If any jars do not seal, refrigerate them and use the contents within 2 weeks.

M I N T   I C E   C R E A M   I N
C H O C O L A T E   M I N T   C U P S

■

BOTH SPEARMINT AND PEPPERMINT are good in ice cream and with chocolate. As this ice cream is fairly rich, it holds well in the freezer. The cup presentation makes it suitable for a buffet party, with an assortment of other confections. Informally, the ice cream is good served in scoops, with a chocolate sauce poured over.

MAKES 1 GENEROUS QUART (ABOUT 1 LITRE)

2 cups (475 ml) whipping cream (double cream)	*4 large peppermint or spearmint sprigs, leaves removed*
1 cup (240 ml) milk	*3 extra-large egg yolks*
2/3 cup (160 ml) sugar (castor sugar)	*2 tablespoons (30 ml) crème de menthe*

Rinse the mint leaves and pat them dry. Combine the cream, milk, sugar, and mint in a heavy-bottomed noncorrodible saucepan. Bruise the mint against the side of the pan with the back of a wooden spoon. Bring the mixture to a simmer, remove from heat, and let steep for about 20 minutes.

Whisk the egg yolks in a small bowl. Slowly pour about 1/2 cup (120 ml) of the warm cream mixture into the yolks and blend well. Pour the yolk mixture into the saucepan, stir well, and gently reheat the mixture over medium-low heat. Stir constantly until the custard coats a spoon, 5 to 7 minutes.

Strain the custard into a bowl, pressing on the mint to release all of the flavor. Chill the custard well. Add the crème de menthe and process in an ice cream maker according to the manufacturer's directions. Allow the ice cream to ripen in the freezer for a few hours before serving.

CHOCOLATE MINT CUPS
■

THE CUPS CAN BE PREPARED a day ahead of time, then placed in an airtight container and kept in the freezer until ready to serve. Use 1¾-inch (4-cm) muffin tins lined with 1¾-inch (4-cm) fluted paper cups. If you don't have small muffin tins, serve the ice cream in commercially made chocolate shells; just follow the instructions for adding the mint leaves and crème de menthe.

MAKES 18 TO 20 CUPS

8 ounces (225 g) bittersweet or semisweet chocolate

1½ teaspoons (8 ml) vegetable oil

20 1¾-inch (4 cm) fluted baking papers

18 to 20 small mint leaves

About 1 tablespoon (15 ml) crème de menthe

Small mint leaves

Break the chocolate into small pieces and melt it with the vegetable oil in the top of a double boiler over gently simmering water. Using a pastry brush, quickly and evenly spread the melted chocolate in the fluted baking papers.

Place the chocolate cups in muffin tins as you make them to keep their shape. Place the finished cups in the freezer for 15 minutes.

After the cups have hardened a bit, remove them from the freezer and place a small mint leaf in each one. Sprinkle each leaf with a few drops of crème de menthe. Return to the freezer for a few minutes, then remove papers and keep the cups covered in the freezer until ready for assembly.

When ready to serve, carefully spoon the ice cream into the cups, making small mounds. Arrange the ice cream cups on a platter, garnish them with mint leaves, and serve the dessert immediately. Or place the filled cups in a freezer-proof dish, cover well, and keep frozen for as long as 24 hours. Remove the cups about 10 minutes before serving. Arrange them on a serving dish, garnish with mint leaves, and serve.

PARSLEY

THE last to leave, yet rises early,

it floats in pots, and lies on plates.

Whether its shape is flat or curly,

it's a character with pleasing traits.

A good theater production has one understudy who can play any part. Parsley fills this role in the kitchen with ease and versatility. The cook can direct it with confidence to star or support as needed. It requires little prompting, and its fresh green taste does not quarrel with those of other cast members.

A bite of fresh parsley reveals its faint peppery tang and green apple aftertaste. The brilliance of its emerald leaves and its mild yet piquant flavor have made it a standard garnish; it is a pleasant counterpoint to most vegetables, fish, and meats. Parsley is the sine qua non of bouquets garnis and fines herbes; for soups and stews, it is the herb which is difficult to overuse. So familiar that it seems plain, it adorns all manner of dishes from fresh salads to long-simmered ragouts. Parsley's reputation is as a companionable herb, lending subtlety to many of the stronger herbs and enhancing the milder ones.

Parsley's clean and delicate taste has a long history of being appreciated. To cleanse and refresh the palate, the Romans served it at feasts. They were the first people recorded as eating parsley, but the Greeks, a thousand years before, made wreaths of it for weddings and athletic games and fed it to their horses before battle to ensure valor. The word parsley comes from the Greek *petros*, "rock", referring to its rocky wild habitat. As its cultivation spread throughout Europe and Asia Minor, parsley became one of the most popular culinary herbs. The Renaissance

ITALIAN PARSLEY

HAS BROAD,

FLAT LEAVES.

herbalists of England had a wealth of medicinal uses for it, as well as advice on when and how to plant it.

Curly parsley (*Petroselinum crispum* var. *crispum*), is the one fresh herb that is a staple in U.S. markets. Parsley is as rich in vitamins and minerals as its sprightly leaves suggest, chiefly vitamins A and C and iron. Italian parsley (*P. crispum* var.

neapolitanum) has much broader, flat leaves. The Italian parsley we prefer is the Catalogna strain, for its dark, handsome, celerylike foliage and fuller flavor. We grow it from seed, as it is rarely available as plants or in bunches in the market.

Parsley's slow germination has stimulated some fanciful theories: that it goes to the devil nine times and back before it sprouts and that a pregnant woman planting it speeds germination. We used to soak the seeds in warm water for a day or two before sowing in the belief that this would promote germination. However, we've found that this doesn't really make a difference; sprouting is still quite variable, taking anywhere from a week to 24 days, usually about 14. Parsley, especially the curly type, is very hardy and may be used well into winter, even when the leaves have frozen. In the summer too, when other herbs are blooming or have gone to seed, parsley is in the wings, a seasoned standby. Although it is a biennial and will reseed itself, we sow parsley every year to have a plentiful and fine-tasting crop. Second-year plants seem to have more

... WHEN OTHER HERBS ARE BLOOMING OR HAVE GONE TO SEED, PARSLEY IS IN THE WINGS ...

finely divided leaves and a grassier flavor. The herb will grow well in full sun but some shade helps to develop a deeper green color. It is a heavy feeder, requiring plenty of water and fertilizer.

Harvest parsley by cutting stems about an inch (2 cm) above ground level, and taking the outer ones first. The stems of tender parsley may be used as well as the leaves. We follow the practice of many cooks of saving the stems for stocks. So little of the real flavor is in the dried or frozen leaves, and parsley is so easy to grow or buy, that we do not preserve it.

P A R S L E Y   C H I C K   P E A   P Â T É

■

WE SERVE THIS PÂTÉ WITH PITA BREAD or toast points, though crackers or sourdough bread will work, too. It is similar to hummus but thicker and spreadable, as well as more flavorful. Tahini is a rich and delicious sesame seed paste, about the consistency of peanut butter. It is sold in many supermarkets and at Middle Eastern and health food stores.

SERVES 8 TO 12 AS AN APPETIZER

1 cup (240 ml) dried chick peas

1/2 cup (120 ml) tahini

Juice of 1 lemon

1/4 cup (60 ml) olive oil

1/4 cup (60 ml) reserved chick pea stock

1 cup (240 ml) packed parsley leaves, chopped fine

3 garlic cloves, minced

1/2 teaspoon (2 ml) toasted and ground cumin seed

1/2 to 1 teaspoon (2 to 5 ml) cayenne pepper

Salt and freshly ground pepper

Red sweet pepper strips

Black oil-cured olives

Parsley sprigs

Wash and pick over the chick peas. Cover them with 4 cups (1 litre) cold water in a large pan and soak overnight, or cover them with the water, bring them to boil, simmer 5 minutes, and soak for an hour.

Drain the chick peas and rinse them. Add fresh water to cover them by an inch (2 cm) and cook them for about an hour, or until they are tender. Drain the chick peas and reserve 1/4 cup (60 ml) of the cooking liquid.

Puree the cooked chick peas in a food processor or food mill. Combine the puree, tahini, lemon juice, and olive oil in a bowl, blending well. Add the parsley and garlic to the mixture. Add the cumin seed, cayenne pepper, and season with salt and pepper. The mixture should be thick; if it crumbles and does not hold together, add the reserved cooking liquid, a little at a time.

Shape the pâté into a dome on a serving dish, or pack it into a 1-quart (1-litre) terrine or bowl. Chill covered for at least 1 hour. If refrigerated for longer than an hour, remove about 20 minutes before serving. Garnish with red pepper strips, black olives, and parsley.

GREEN GOODNESS DRESSING
■

MOST SALAD DRESSINGS ARE BEST MADE FRESH, since they become dull and flat under refrigeration; this is an exception. It is the kind of tangy, herby dressing that goes well with many salads: grain, potato, pasta, blanched vegetable, and green. A little added basil, tarragon, or dill makes good variations. The kind of olive oil to use depends on how much olive flavor you like.

MAKES ABOUT 1½ CUPS (360 ML)

2 cups (475 ml) packed parsley leaves	2 garlic cloves, crushed
Juice of 1 lime or lemon	1 teaspoon (5 ml) Dijon-style mustard
1 tablespoon (15 ml) white wine vinegar	1/2 teaspoon (2 ml) salt
	1 cup (240 ml) olive oil

Blend all of the ingredients at low speed in a blender for 1 minute and at high speed for 30 seconds, or until the mixture is bright green. Adjust the seasoning with lemon juice, vinegar, or salt if necessary. The dressing keeps, covered and chilled, for 1 week. Stir it before using.

SALSA VERDE
■

WE CAN'T SAY ENOUGH about the green herb sauces so much a part of Spanish, French, and Italian cuisine. They are easy to prepare and infinitely versatile. The quantity of fresh green herbs they require reminds us of summer, when the herb garden is at its peak, even when we make them in winter. This sauce is good with artichokes, asparagus, beets, carrots, cauliflower, eggplant, fennel, green beans, leeks, sweet peppers of any color, potatoes, and tomatoes. Prepare the vegetables by steaming, blanching, braising, roasting, or grilling, or serve them raw, according to the vegetable and season. Salsa verde also goes with any simply prepared meat, variety meat, most white-fleshed fish, and chicken. Poaching or roasting are the techniques that best complement salsa verde's liveliness. Experiment with using tarragon, summer savory, or a few fennel leaves instead of, or in addition to, the marjoram. A green sauce featuring basil may be found on page 50.

MAKES ABOUT 2½ CUPS (600 ML)

2 cups (475 ml) packed Italian parsley leaves

1/4 cup (60 ml) loosely packed marjoram or oregano leaves, or a mixture

1/4 cup (60 ml) loosely packed rocket leaves, optional

1 1-inch (2-cm) slice country bread, crusts removed

1/2 cup (120 ml) olive oil

1/4 cup (60 ml) minced sweet onion such as Vidalia

2 or 3 garlic cloves, minced

2 tablespoons (30 ml) white wine vinegar

1 tablespoon (15 ml) nonpareil capers

Salt and freshly ground pepper

2 or 3 anchovy fillets, chopped fine, optional

1/4 cup (60 ml) fine-diced ripe tomato, optional

1/4 cup (60 ml) fine-diced red bell pepper, optional

1 hard-cooked egg, chopped fine or sieved, optional

Pound the parsley and marjoram, and the optional rocket, in a mortar and pestle or chop in a food processor. Soak the bread in a little water for 10 minutes, then squeeze out most of the liquid. Add the bread to the mortar or food processor and mix it with the herbs.

Add the olive oil to the herbs as if making a mayonnaise, a few drops at a time, blending or pulsing to incorporate.

When all the olive oil has been added, blend in the onion, garlic, vinegar, and capers. Season the sauce with salt and pepper. Add other ingredients, if you like.

Let the sauce stand at least 30 minutes before serving. Adjust the seasoning and serve at room temperature. The olive oil will not emulsify completely; a little will remain on top of the sauce. Store any leftover sauce in a tightly covered glass container in the refrigerator for as long as a week.

CREAM OF PARSLEY SOUP

■

SOME PEOPLE EAT SWEET ONIONS LIKE APPLES; we like parsley by the bunch. We save the stems for stocks and broths, and in this recipe we have chopped quantities of the leaves for a clean-tasting green soup. Either curly or Italian parsley may be used here. The *mezzaluna*, an Italian half-moon-shaped knife, is an excellent tool for chopping herbs, especially large amounts. It reduces a board full of leaves to minced herbs quickly and cleanly, without mashing them—thereby causing them to lose their juices, as a food processor does.

SERVES 6

2 bunches parsley, enough for about 3 cups (700 ml) chopped leaves

4 tablespoons (60 ml) unsalted butter

4 tablespoons (60 ml) flour

1 quart (1 litre) hot chicken or vegetable stock

2 teaspoons (10 ml) minced fresh summer savory or 1 scant teaspoon (5 ml) crumbled dried summer savory

2 cups (475 ml) half-and-half (single cream)

Salt and freshly ground pepper

Freshly grated nutmeg

1/2 cup (120 ml) freshly grated imported pecorino or romano cheese

6 slices country bread, toasted and rubbed with a cut clove of garlic

Remove the leaves from the parsley. Add a small handful of the stems to the stock. Chop the parsley leaves fine and set aside.

Melt the butter over low heat in a soup pot. Stir in the flour and cook for 5 minutes to make a roux. Remove the parsley stems from the stock. Take the pan with the roux off the heat and add the hot stock in a stream, whisking vigorously. Continue to whisk until it is thickened and smooth. Add the savory and simmer the mixture, stirring occasionally, for 10 minutes.

Add the cream and chopped parsley, and season with salt, pepper, and nutmeg. Heat the soup through over low heat; do not let it boil.

Ladle the soup into heated bowls. Divide the cheese over the bread slices. Garnish each serving with a cheese crouton and serve hot.

P A R S L E Y   B A T T E R   B R E A D

■

BECAUSE THIS IS A BATTER BREAD, it can be made in two or three hours from start to finish, depending on how warm a place you put it to rise. It is a homey, whole-grain loaf that satisfies the hunger for hot-from-the-oven bread with melting butter. The recipe can be doubled.

MAKES 1 LOAF

1 tablespoon (15 ml) honey	2 tablespoons (30 ml) vegetable oil
1/2 cup (120 ml) lukewarm water	1½ teaspoons (8 ml) salt
2 tablespoons (30 ml) dry yeast	3 cups (710 ml) whole wheat flour
1½ cups (360 ml) very hot water	1 cup (240 ml) unbleached white flour
1 cup (240 ml) stone-ground cornmeal	1 cup (240 ml) minced parsley

Combine the honey, lukewarm water, and yeast in a small bowl. Let the mixture stand until the yeast becomes foamy.

Combine the hot water, cornmeal, oil, and salt in a large bowl. When the mixture has cooled to warm, add the yeast mixture, then the flours, 1 cup (240 ml) at a time, stirring well after each addition. Stir the parsley into the batter.

Set the bowl, covered with a damp towel, in a warm place until the dough has tripled in bulk. Beat the batter down with a wooden spoon and turn it into a standard-size oiled loaf pan.

Let the batter rise for 15 minutes. Preheat the oven to 450° F (230° C).

Bake the loaf for 10 minutes. Reduce the oven to 350° F (180° C) and bake for 50 minutes or until the top is a rich brown.

SPAGHETTI WITH PARSLEY, GARLIC, OIL, AND RED PEPPER FLAKES

■

VARIATIONS ON THE SPAGHETTI-AND-OIL THEME are common in southern Italy, where the dish is a workday mainstay, preceded perhaps by some mozzarella and tomatoes, and followed by a green salad. It is quick, as the sauce is made while the pasta is cooking. Best-quality ingredients can elevate this beyond an everyday dish: fresh garlic, extra-virgin olive oil, just-picked Italian parsley, imported parmesan, and good dried hot peppers. For a change, leave out the red pepper flakes, and use an Italian romano or asiago in place of the parmesan.

SERVES 4 TO 6

1 pound (450 g) spaghetti

1/3 to 1/2 cup (80 to 120 ml) olive oil

3 to 4 cloves garlic, minced

Red pepper flakes to taste

1/4 cup (60 ml) minced parsley

Salt and freshly ground pepper

Freshly grated parmesan cheese

Bring abundant water to a rolling boil. Salt the water and add the spaghetti. Make the sauce while the pasta is cooking.

Add the olive oil, garlic, and pepper flakes to a frying pan. Warm the ingredients over low heat. The garlic should not cook.

Cook the pasta al dente and drain it. Add the pasta to the frying pan with the olive oil, add half the parsley, and toss well. Season with salt and pepper.

Transfer the pasta to a warm platter or to pasta bowls, and garnish with the remaining parsley. Serve immediately. Pass the parmesan and extra red pepper flakes separately.

FETTUCCINE WITH SCALLOPS AND PARSLEY SAUCE

■

THE RICHNESS OF THIS DISH is lightened by the goodly amount of parsley. It is a good first course before a baked or grilled fish entree.

SERVES 4 TO 6

1 pound (450 g) sea scallops

4 tablespoons (60 ml) unsalted butter

1 shallot, minced

1/2 cup (120 ml) minced parsley

1/2 cup (120 ml) dry white wine

1/2 cup (120 ml) whipping cream (double cream)

1 cup (240 ml) half-and-half (single cream)

1 cup (240 ml) freshly grated parmesan cheese

Salt and freshly ground pepper

Freshly grated nutmeg

Lemon juice

1 recipe spinach or egg fettuccine (pages 71–72), or 1 pound (450 g) fresh pasta, cooked al dente

Rinse the scallops and trim them of tough connective tissue. Cut the scallops into bite-sized pieces.

Melt the butter in a large frying pan over medium-low heat. When it foams, add the shallot and 1/4 cup (60 ml) of the minced parsley. Sauté gently for 5 minutes.

Add the white wine, increase the heat, and reduce the liquid to about 6 tablespoons (90 ml). Reduce heat, add the scallops, and cook gently for a minute. Add the creams and heat for 2 minutes. Add the parmesan and the rest of the parsley.

Remove the sauce from the heat and season with salt, pepper, nutmeg, and lemon juice. Serve immediately over hot, drained fettuccine on a heated platter.

FILLET OF SOLE
WITH PARSLEY

∎

THE HERB IS USED HERE in a classic egg batter for delicate sautéed fish, giving the dish extra flavor and an attractive appearance echoed by the green and gold garnishes.

SERVES 4 TO 6

2 eggs

1/2 teaspoon (2 ml) salt

Leaves from 6 or 8 Italian parsley sprigs, chopped fine

4 tablespoons (60 ml) unsalted butter

2 pounds (900 g) sole fillets

1 cup (240 ml) flour

Parsley sprigs

Lemon wedges

Beat the eggs with the salt in a flat-bottomed bowl until they are homogeneous. Stir in the chopped parsley. Melt the butter, over low heat, in a frying pan large enough to hold the fish in one layer.

Dredge the sole in the flour, shaking off the excess. Leave the fillets on a lightly floured surface and adjust the heat under the butter to medium.

Dip the sole fillets into the egg and parsley mixture, covering both sides, then place them in the frying pan and sauté 2 minutes or until pale golden brown on one side. Turn the fillets and cook for 2 more minutes. Serve on a heated platter garnished with parsley sprigs and lemon wedges.

HERBED BROWN RICE CASSEROLE

■

CASSEROLES ARE THE KIND OF COMFORT FOOD that we have relied on since our student days. We like ones such as this that have a number of flavors yet are simple to make. We've found that children (ours and others') love casseroles when they are not too spicy. This one is a satisfying vegetarian main course, or a good side dish with chicken fricassee or roast or braised pork or veal. Leftovers may be shaped into patties and sautéed.

SERVES 4 AS A MAIN COURSE, OR 8 AS A SIDE DISH

4 cups (950 ml) cooked brown rice

1¼ cups (300 ml) soft whole-grain bread crumbs

1 cup (240 ml) chopped parsley

2 eggs, lightly beaten

1½ cups (360 ml) chopped pecans or other nuts

3 tablespoons (45 ml) olive oil

1 onion, diced

1 cup (240 ml) sliced mushrooms

3/4 cup (180 ml) freshly grated parmesan cheese

2 garlic cloves, minced

1/4 cup (60 ml) vegetable stock or water

1/2 teaspoon (2 ml) chopped fresh marjoram

1/2 teaspoon (2 ml) chopped fresh thyme

1/4 teaspoon (1 ml) cayenne pepper

Salt

Combine the brown rice, 1 cup (240 ml) of bread crumbs, the parsley, eggs, and nuts in a large bowl. Soften the onion in the olive oil over medium-low heat for about 5 minutes. Add the mushrooms and cook 2 minutes longer. Mix the vegetables into the rice. Stir in 1/2 cup (120 ml) parmesan cheese and the garlic.

Toss the mixture with the stock or water, herbs, and cayenne pepper. Salt lightly and turn the mixture into an oiled 1½-quart (1½-litre) casserole. Preheat the oven to 350° F (180° C).

Mix the remaining bread crumbs and cheese and spread over the casserole. Bake for 35 to 40 minutes, until the casserole is a rich golden brown.

SWEET POTATO AND PARSLEY SALAD

■

PEOPLE WHO DON'T LIKE the usual sugary concoctions will appreciate the way sweet potatoes are prepared in this recipe. Both the dark orange ones—often sold as yams—and the light yellow sweet potatoes may be used. Bake or steam them in their jackets, as you prefer, but do not overcook them. A fruity, full-flavored olive oil does make a difference in this salad.

SERVES 6

6 cooked sweet potatoes, about 2½ pounds (1 kg)

1 small onion, diced fine

1 medium celery rib, diced fine

1/3 cup (80 ml) olive oil

1 lemon

2 teaspoons (10 ml) soy sauce

1/2 cup (120 ml) coarse-chopped parsley

Leaves from 4 or 5 marjoram sprigs, chopped, or 1 teaspoon (5 ml) crumbled dried marjoram

Salt and freshly ground pepper

1/2 cup (120 ml) freshly toasted cashew nuts, optional

Peel the sweet potatoes, then cut them into 1/2-inch (1-cm) dice. Place them in a large bowl with the onion and celery.

Mix the olive oil, lemon juice, and soy sauce in a small bowl. Stir in the parsley and marjoram. Season the dressing with salt and pepper. Toss it with the sweet potatoes and adjust the seasoning.

Just before serving, sprinkle the salad with the toasted cashew nuts. The salad may be served warm or at room temperature.

SWEET
POTATO AND
PARSLEY
SALAD

NEW POTATOES WITH PARSLEY, GARLIC, AND LEMON PEEL

■

THIS IS A GARDENER'S DISH: simple, direct, and best when the potatoes are fresh from the ground and marble-sized. As long as you can find tiny potatoes, no larger than an inch (2 cm) in diameter, the dish can still be made, but the cooking time may increase to twice as long, depending on how long the potatoes have been stored. Since the potatoes are cooked at a low temperature, we use a full-flavored extra-virgin olive oil. The finishing parsley mixture, gremolata in Italian, is an important part of the dish osso buco. It is similar to the French persillade, which does not usually contain lemon peel, and is used similarly to garnish roasted and grilled meats, and occasionally vegetables.

SERVES 4 TO 6

2 pounds (900 g) tiny new potatoes, red, white, or gold

4 tablespoons (60 ml) olive oil

1/4 cup (60 ml) chopped Italian parsley leaves

2 or 3 garlic cloves, minced

Grated zest of 1 lemon

Salt and freshly ground pepper

Clean the potatoes well, but do not scrub off the tender skins. Heat the olive oil over medium heat in a heavy-bottomed pot large enough to hold the potatoes in one layer and equipped with a tight-fitting lid.

Add the potatoes to the pan, salt lightly, reduce the heat to low, and cover the pot. Cook for about 15 minutes, shaking the pot several times so that the potatoes cook evenly. Meanwhile, mix the parsley, garlic, and lemon zest together.

When the potatoes are tender and the skins are slightly crisped, season lightly with salt and pepper. Remove the potatoes to a warm serving platter with a slotted spoon. Toss them immediately with the parsley mixture and serve hot.

BRAISED ARTICHOKES WITH PARSLEY

■

ONE OF OUR STUDENTS TOLD US about removing the chokes from artichokes with a melon baller, practically confirming again that to teach is to learn. The technique is neat and quick. Medium-sized artichokes usually have better flavor and texture than large ones and are less expensive, too. These may be served hot as a vegetable course or at room temperature as an appetizer. This is a very Italian treatment; no dipping sauce is necessary.

SERVES 6

6 medium-sized artichokes	3 garlic cloves, minced
1 lemon	1 teaspoon (5 ml) salt
1 cup (240 ml) parsley leaves, chopped	1/4 cup (60 ml) dry white wine
	1/2 cup (120 ml) water
1/4 cup (60 ml) mint leaves, chopped	1/4 cup (60 ml) olive oil

Cut the stem ends of the artichokes flush with the bases. Rub all cut surfaces with a cut lemon half as you work. Snap off the lower outer leaves and cut the center thorny tips about 1½ inches (4 cm) from the tops. Trim the thorns from the remaining leaves with scissors. Remove some center leaves with a small sharp knife. Remove the chokes with a melon baller.

Mix the parsley, mint, and garlic with the salt. Gently spread the artichoke leaves from the center out and stuff the parsley mixture between the leaves. Loosely pack some of the herb mixture in the centers.

Choose a heavy noncorrodible pan large enough to hold the artichokes loosely. The lid must fit tightly. Pour the wine and water into the pan and add half of the cut lemon. Place the artichokes in the pan and drizzle the olive oil over them.

Cover the pan and bring the liquid to a simmer over medium heat. Reduce the heat slightly and cook the artichokes for 20 to 30 minutes or until an inside leaf detaches easily.

Transfer the artichokes to a serving dish and pour some pan juices over each one. Serve hot or at room temperature.

R O S E M A R Y

IN *the rocky cliffs,*

Hanging o'er the sea,

Forgotten not by sun and dew,

Blooms sweet rosemary.

■ We cannot claim positively that any herb lightens doldrums or depression, but we are always cheered when we brush rosemary leaves through our fingers to release its refreshing scent. Its quintessential fragrance of seacoast with pines affects us like an offshore breeze at early evening. The drears and dulls are blown away, even if we are miles from the sea and enduring the freezing days of February.

Rosemary is an herb of diverse and strong symbols, the great majority of which are beneficent. Popularized in Ophelia's plea "There's rosemary. That's for remembrance, pray love, remember," it was also the emblem of loyalty and friendship. Where basil symbolized the quickening of love, rosemary betokened its lastingness and was woven into bridal wreaths as early as the Roman republic. It was put under nuptial mattresses to encourage faithfulness as well as to keep away insects and mildew.

The plant's beautiful form and flowers gave rise to some legends full of symbolic meaning. One of the oldest is that a beautiful young woman from Sicily was changed into a rosemary bush. At the time of this transformation, Sicily was under the domination of Circe, who caused violent volcanoes to erupt and plants to wither and die. She also enchanted the inhabitants so that they would throw themselves into the sea. The blue-eyed woman who had become rosemary held to the cliffs to remind men of the ever-renewing power of good in the world.

The Romans transplanted rosemary to England where the sea-saturated climate of the south was mild enough to favor it. The name is from the Latin *ros marinus,* dew of the sea. It flourished under cultivation during the Middle Ages and Renaissance, every garden having its single or several bushes, often pruned in fanciful or symmetrical shapes. Some favorite uses of the essential oil, or the

ROSEMARY IS AN HERB

OF DIVERSE AND STRONG

SYMBOLS, THE GREAT

MAJORITY OF WHICH ARE

BENEFICENT.

leaves and flowers, were in refreshing baths, as an insect and moth repellent, as a mouthwash, and in liniments.

Incensier, a French term for rosemary, comes from its use as incense in church ceremonies. Its pleasing scent was not the only reason for this tradition; rosemary's reputation against evil was well established. It was put in sachets under pillows to prevent nightmares and carried to funerals to be placed on graves in the belief that dark spirits would not disturb departing souls under the protection of light-loving rosemary.

ROSEMARY'S AROMA

COMBINES FIR,

BALSAM, AND

OCEAN AIR.

Rosemary seems to have gone somewhat out of favor as a culinary herb except in Italy, where it is still much loved. A sprig of rosemary (and sometimes a branch of sage as well) are commonly included with purchases at butcher shops in northern Italy. Italians consider it excellent with roast meats, poultry, and fish. Branches of the herb are usually put on the coals when lamb and kid are roasted. It is also used in bean dishes, with potatoes, and in certain sweets. Chopped fine and strewn over pecorino cheese anointed with fine Tuscan olive oil, it appears with the cheese course in lieu of dessert.

Rosemary's aroma combines fir, balsam, and ocean air. Its tannin and camphor components give it a moderate bitterness and pepperiness, which are especially good with foods rich in fat or with bland foods such as potatoes or legumes. Some find the flavor of rosemary very strong, but its champions like the warmth and richness it gives to hearty dishes and its spiciness with more delicate fare. Dried rosemary may be generally substituted for fresh except with cheeses. Rosemary leaves must be dried whole to preserve their oils, but they should be ground or tied in cheesecloth to prevent the sensation of chewing on pine needles. The strength of dried rosemary varies greatly, but a general rule is to use one-quarter the amount of the fresh herb.

Although rosemary is a true Mediterranean plant and will not survive extremely cold winters, it can be grown indoors with the following care. Keep the plants in appropriate-sized containers, transplanting as necessary. When transplanting, allow plenty of room for the roots. Use a mix of perlite or large-grained sterile sand, humus, and potting soil for good drainage and aeration. Set the plants outdoors in the summer, taking care to water them well. About one month before the first frost is expected, bring the plants to a protected area near the house. Move them into the house in two weeks, before the heat is turned on, so that they have time to adjust to the temperature difference. Rosemary loves light and this need must be met in the house or garden.

Rosemary is best started from cuttings, as seed germination is slow. Rooted cuttings and larger plants are available from herb or nursery suppliers. *Rosmarinus officinalis* is the herb to buy for culinary use, and the easiest to grow. There are a large number of varieties of this species, and from the cook's point of view, all can be used successfully. They have different aromas, slightly different flavors, and quite different physical characteristics, such as plant and leaf size, variegation, flower color, and cold-hardiness. We urge you to discover which ones you like. Growth can be slow, but when rosemary does take hold, it is a plant for generations. It may be trimmed to make a fine dwarf plant or for fanciful topiaries.

Water and mist rosemary regularly, and fertilize with a 10-10-10 liquid fertilizer at half the recommended strength at least once a month, both outdoors and in. Reduced sunlight and lower daytime temperatures in the house lessen the need for water; let the plants dry between waterings.

A fairly recent introduction is worth mentioning for cold climates: Hill Hardy, *R. officinalis* 'Madalene Hill'. We have good reports on this variety's hardiness to –10° F (–23° C). Of course, the plant should be well mulched for the winter. Hill Hardy has well-balanced aroma and flavor for culinary use.

In mild climates, rosemary does very well against brick or stone. We have seen some magnificent plants growing against walls and barns in Italy, where the plant apparently spread by self-layering. It grows well as a freestanding shrub, too. It is a popular hedge in the coastal areas of northern California where Italian families settled. A low-growing tender variety, *R. officinalis* var. *prostratus*, makes a fine ground cover, growing from 10 to 12 inches (25 to 30 cm) tall and spreading easily.

ROSMARINUS OFFICINALIS

IS THE HERB TO BUY

FOR CULINARY USE, AND

THE EASIEST TO GROW.

MULLED ROSEMARY WINE AND BLACK TEA

■

WHEN WE FIRST TASTED A SIMILAR PUNCH at a German friend's Christmas party, we turned to one another and said "Rosemary!" It is just the herb to banish any suggestion of cloying at the back of the palate. This beverage has become a tradition for our holiday festivities, partly because the aroma is so inviting. With practically no effort and little expense, the house has a more wonderful fragrance than a dozen potpourris can achieve. The punch can be kept warm over very low heat for a few hours. If you have a wood stove, you might do as Susan does: place a batch on the back of the stove before cross-country skiing. Or keep the punch warm on the stove or in a crockpot and transfer it to a punch bowl as needed. For large parties, the recipe is easily doubled and tripled. If any punch is left over, remove the oranges and rosemary, let it cool to room temperature, then refrigerate. Reheat gently with fresh oranges and rosemary; the punch will be a bit stronger but still quite enjoyable.

MAKES ABOUT 2 QUARTS (2 LITRES)

1 bottle claret or other full-bodied red wine

1 quart (1 litre) black tea, preferably Assam or Darjeeling

1/4 cup (60 ml) mild honey

1/3 cup (80 ml) sugar (castor sugar), or to taste

2 oranges, sliced thin and seeded

2 3-inch (8-cm) cinnamon sticks

6 whole cloves

3 rosemary sprigs

Mix the wine and the tea together in a noncorrodible saucepan. Add the honey, sugar, oranges, spices, and rosemary. Heat over low heat until barely steaming. Stir until the honey is dissolved.

Remove the pan from the heat, cover, and let stand for at least 30 minutes. When ready to serve, heat to just steaming and serve hot.

DOLMADES WITH ROSEMARY

■

THIS VERSION OF DOLMADES is more lavish than some lemon-soaked dabs of rice heavily wrapped in grape leaves that we have encountered. Dolmades are wonderful al fresco food, whether at a picnic or on the patio. Try heating them on the grill the next time you are grilling Mediterranean-style lamb, chicken, fish, or vegetables.

MAKES ABOUT 40 DOLMADES

2 cups (475 ml) short-grain white rice

3 cups (710 ml) water

1½ teaspoons (8 ml) salt

2 shallots, diced

6 tablespoons (90 ml) olive oil

1/2 cup (120 ml) currants

1/2 cup (120 ml) pine nuts, lightly toasted

2 tablespoons (30 ml) minced fresh rosemary or 2 teaspoons (10 ml) crumbled dried rosemary

1/4 cup (60 ml) chopped parsley

2 tablespoons (30 ml) lemon juice, or to taste

1 8-ounce (225-g) jar grape leaves

In a saucepan, combine the rice, water, and 1 teaspoon (5 ml) of salt. Cover, bring to a boil and reduce heat. Cook the rice until tender, about 20 minutes.

Soften the shallots and sauté them in 3 tablespoons (45 ml) of the olive oil in a small frying pan for about 5 minutes. Add them to the cooked rice along with the currants, pine nuts, rosemary, and parsley.

Dissolve the remaining salt in the lemon juice and add to the rice mixture. Toss in the remaining olive oil to mix well.

Remove the grape leaves from the jar and trim the stems. Blanch the leaves in unsalted boiling water for 2 minutes. Refresh them under cold water and pat dry.

Use 1 heaping tablespoon (20 to 25 ml) of rice mixture for the large leaves and 1 level tablespoon (15 ml) of mixture for the smaller leaves. Roll the leaves and place them on a lightly oiled tray. The dolmades can be made ahead to this point, and stored, covered, in the refrigerator for as long as 24 hours.

Stack the dolmades carefully in a steamer or spaghetti cooker. Add water to the pan so that it is just below the inset. Weight the dolmades with a small plate.

Cover the pan and steam for 20 minutes. If the dolmades have been refrigerated cook them about 5 minutes longer. Serve hot or at room temperature.

CALZONE WITH PROSCIUTTO AND ROSEMARY

■

THE AROMAS OF ROSEMARY, olive oil, and bread dough never fail to conjure good food memories from the years we spent in Umbria and Tuscany, where the three are often combined. Though you may not have those memories, your kitchen will have that mouth-watering aroma when you make these baked calzone. If you are new to calzone, which look like turnovers, make six the first time, as larger portions of dough are easier to work with. Stretch the dough to a uniform thickness without thin spots or holes. Follow the instructions carefully for mounding the filling and crimping the calzone closed. If Italian fontina is not available, use mozzerella instead. Some domestic and Scandinavian cheese are labeled fontina, but they have none of the flavor or melting properties of the true fontina.

MAKES 6 TO 8 CALZONE

1 recipe Pizza Dough (page 44)

1 medium onion, diced

6 rosemary sprigs, leaves chopped fine

2 tablespoons (30 ml) olive oil

2 garlic cloves, minced

1/4 cup (60 ml) parsley leaves, chopped fine

1/2 pound (225 g) mozzarella cheese, coarse-grated

1/2 pound (225 g) Italian fontina cheese, coarse-grated

6 ounces (170 g) prosciutto, sliced thin and julienned

Salt and freshly ground pepper

Olive oil

Freshly grated parmesan cheese

Divide pizza dough into six or eight portions. Roll the dough into balls, cover, and let them rest for 15 minutes.

Preheat the oven to 450° F (230° C), with a baking stone if you have one.

Sauté the onion and rosemary in the olive oil over moderate heat for 5 minutes and remove to a bowl. Stir in the garlic and parsley.

Stretch the dough gently with your hands into 6- or 8-inch (15- or 20-cm) circles, depending on how many calzone you are making. If the dough resists stretching, let it rest a few minutes longer.

When the onion and herb mixture has cooled to room temperature, add the cheese and prosciutto to it and mix well.

Fill and shape one calzone at a time, leaving the remaining dough covered. Transfer each round of dough to a lightly oiled baking pan, or to a floured bakers' peel if you have a baking stone for your oven.

Take about a sixth or an eighth of the filling and mound it on one-half of each dough round, about 1/2 inch (1 cm) from the edge. Season lightly with salt and pepper and fold the dough over the filling. Crimp the edges of the dough well.

If you are baking the calzone on a stone, transfer them as they are shaped to the oven. If you are baking on a pan, you will be able to fit three or four calzone on the pan, and can bake them together.

Bake the calzone for 10 to 20 minutes, until they are a rich golden brown. Baking time varies according to the kind of stone used, and how many calzone are baked at one time. Remove the calzone from the oven and brush them lightly with olive oil. Sprinkle with parmesan cheese, if desired. Serve the calzone as soon as they are done.

COUNTRY PEA SOUP WITH ROSEMARY

■

CAN SPLIT PEA SOUP BE IMPROVED? We think rosemary provides the answer. This is our house recipe, which we vary by adding a prosciutto bone when we have one or a smoked ham hock. Any pea soup improves in flavor when made in advance; thin it with a little water when reheating.

SERVES 8

1½ pounds (675 g) split peas	1 small onion, diced
1 rosemary sprig	1/4 cup (60 ml) olive oil
1 bay leaf	1 teaspoon (5 ml) salt
2 carrots, diced	3 garlic cloves, minced
1 large potato, diced	2 tablespoons (30 ml) minced fresh
3 celery stalks, diced	rosemary or 2 teaspoons (10 ml) crumbled dried rosemary

Wash the peas well until they no longer foam, then pick them over. Place them in a large soup pot and cover them with 2 inches (5 cm) of water. Add the rosemary sprig and bay leaf. Cover and bring to a boil, reduce the heat, and simmer for 20 minutes.

Sauté the vegetables in the olive oil for 10 minutes, and add them to the peas with the salt, garlic, and rosemary. Cook the soup over low heat for about 25 minutes, or until the peas are done, stirring occasionally. Adjust the seasoning with salt and serve hot.

ROSEMARY BISCUITS

■

THESE VERSATILE LITTLE BISCUITS go well with soups, with ham for lunch or as appetizers, at picnics, and at breakfast or teatime with jam. Because they are quick, they are good when you want something special to round out a meal. They may be made with all unbleached white flour if you prefer.

MAKES ABOUT 30 BISCUITS

2 cups (475 ml) whole wheat flour	1 tablespoon (15 ml) sugar
2 cups (475 ml) unbleached white flour	4 tablespoons (60 ml) unsalted butter
1/2 teaspoon (2 ml) salt	2 tablespoons (30 ml) rosemary, chopped fine, or 2 teaspoons (10 ml) crumbled dried rosemary
2 teaspoons (10 ml) baking powder	
1 teaspoon (5 ml) baking soda	1½ cups (360 ml) milk

Sift the flours, salt, baking powder, baking soda, and sugar together in a large bowl. Cut the butter into the dry ingredients to make pea-sized lumps. Add the rosemary and the milk and mix together to form a soft dough. Preheat the oven to 400° F (200° C).

Roll the dough out 1/2 inch (1 cm) thick on a lightly floured board. Cut into 1½-inch (4-cm) squares and place close together on a greased and floured baking sheet. Bake for 20 minutes. Serve hot or cool on racks.

TROUT BAKED IN PARCHMENT WITH ROSEMARY

■

PARCHMENT COOKING, which utilizes dry heat to capture steam in a paper package, is noted for the intensity and purity of aroma it creates. When rosemary is added to the package, the result is heady. Using heavy brown wrapping paper or brown paper bags works, though the flavor is less subtle because of the oil. We have not done this for years, however, largely because we aren't sure how paper is processed anymore. Because you want the steam and aroma to stay in the package, it is important to crimp and fold the parchment tightly. Some cooks insert a straw before the final corner is folded and inflate the package gently, which makes it puff extravagantly for an impressive presentation. For another refinement, ask the fishmonger to remove the central bones from the trout.

SERVES 2

2 12-ounce (375-g) whole trout, cleaned and scaled

1/2 pound (225 g) Florence (bulb) fennel

1 shallot, diced fine

1 tablespoon (15 ml) olive oil

6 rosemary sprigs

Salt and freshly ground pepper

2 tablespoons (30 ml) dry vermouth

Rinse the trout and pat them dry. Cut two 18-inch (46-cm) rounds of parchment paper, or cut two 18-inch (46-cm) rounds of heavy brown paper and soak them in 1/2 cup (120 ml) olive oil for 5 minutes.

Trim and discard the outer leaves from the fennel and slice it about 1/8 inch (3 mm) thick lengthwise. Soften the fennel and the shallot in the olive oil over low heat for 10 minutes. Remove from heat and set aside. Preheat the oven to 450° F (230° C).

Salt the cavity of each trout lightly and place two sprigs of rosemary inside. Place each trout on a separate piece of parchment, centering the fish on the lower half of the parchment. Divide the vegetables over the fish. Sprinkle each fish with salt, pepper, and vermouth and place a sprig of rosemary on top of the vegetables.

Fold the paper over the fish, crimping the edges and folding them over twice. Place the parchments on a baking sheet and bake for 10 minutes. Remove them to heated dinner plates. With scissors, cut the crimped edge of the paper around to the fold. Unfold and serve immediately.

ROSEMARY ROASTED CHICKEN

■

THE LEMON HERE IS FROM GREEK COOKING, and the rosemary from Italian. As well as adding perfume and flavor, lemon helps to crisp the skin, aided by the high initial roasting temperature. The chicken and its pan juices call for potatoes: baked, french-fried, mashed, or riced.

SERVES 6

5- to 6-pound (2.3- to 2.6-kg) roasting chicken

1 lemon

Salt and freshly ground pepper

1 white onion, cut in quarters

3 garlic cloves

10 rosemary sprigs

1/2 cup (120 ml) chicken stock

Rinse the chicken and pat it dry. Reserve the giblets and neck for another use.

Cut two 1-inch (2-cm) pieces of lemon peel, the yellow part only, from the lemon. Cut the lemon in half and rub the chicken inside and out with it, squeezing the juice as you rub. Salt and pepper the chicken lightly inside and out.

Preheat the oven to 425° F (220° C). Place one piece of lemon peel, the onion, garlic, and six rosemary sprigs inside the cavity. Place the remaining rosemary sprigs between the wings and breast and the thighs and back; then truss the chicken.

Place it, breast up, on a rack in a roasting pan or baking dish. Squeeze the rest of the lemon juice over it. Place the remaining lemon peel in the bottom of the pan.

Roast the chicken for 30 minutes. Remove it from the oven and reduce the heat to 350° F (180° C). Cover the breast loosely with aluminum foil and turn the chicken back side up on the rack. Roast for 30 minutes, then turn again. Remove the foil and roast about 20 minutes longer, or until thigh juices run clear.

Remove the chicken from the oven and let it rest on a carving board for 10 minutes. Drain the fat from the roasting pan and discard the lemon peel. Deglaze the pan with the chicken stock. Pour the pan juices into a sauce dish.

Carve the chicken in the kitchen, or transfer it to a serving platter to carve at the table. Pass the pan juices separately.

ROSEMARY RAGOUT

■

RAGOUTS ARE OLD-FASHIONED STEWS that deserve more attention in our fast-food era. Making them offers insights into the transformation that is cooking. The change is palpable to the nose: gradually, at each stage, a complex new aroma arises. Smelling, stirring, and tasting ragouts as they cook connects us to the history and prehistory of the skill of cooking. Try this on a weekend if you don't have time during the week; it requires little preparation or watching but must be cooked long and slow. It is good with polenta in any form—soft, fried, or grilled—and with boiled or riced potatoes.

SERVES 6

1 pound (450 g) beef stew meat	3 garlic cloves
1 pound (450 g) beef heart	1 large carrot, diced fine
1/2 cup (120 ml) flour	1 large red onion, diced fine
4 tablespoons (60 ml) olive oil	1 large celery stalk, diced fine
1 bottle full-bodied red wine	8 Italian parsley sprigs, leaves coarsely chopped
4 rosemary sprigs or 1½ teaspoons (8 ml) crumbled dried rosemary	Salt and freshly ground pepper
14-ounce (400-g) can tomatoes	

Cut the stew meat and the heart into 1-inch (2-cm) cubes. Season them lightly with salt and pepper and dredge them in the flour, shaking off the excess. Heat 3 tablespoons (45 ml) of the olive oil in a large, heavy casserole until very hot. Sear the meat for 10 minutes, stirring occasionally with a wooden spoon. Add the wine and simmer, covered, for 1 hour.

Add three rosemary sprigs, or all of the dried rosemary, the tomatoes, and the whole peeled garlic cloves. Season the sauce with salt and pepper. Simmer uncovered for 1 hour.

Sauté the carrot, onion, and celery in the remaining olive oil over moderate heat for 10 minutes. Add the vegetables to the meat, and simmer the stew uncovered for 20 minutes, stirring occasionally. Add the remaining rosemary sprig and the chopped parsley and simmer for 15 minutes more. Discard the rosemary sprigs and transfer the ragout to a warm serving dish. Serve hot.

CHICK PEA TAGINE

■

THE FULL, NUTTY FLAVOR OF CHICK PEAS is evident when you start with dried legumes. This calls for soaking them and cooking them for an hour or so before they are ready to be incorporated into a dish. A time-saving method that yields good results is cooking the soaked beans in a pressure cooker. In ours, the chick peas are done in 10 minutes, but this time may vary according to brand. A crockpot is another option; follow the manufacturer's instructions. When the chick peas are done and cooled, they may be refrigerated for a day or two before using. This tagine may be made ahead entirely, then reheated. It is our rendition of the traditional ones we so enjoyed in northern Morocco.

SERVES 6

1 cup (240 ml) dry chick peas

4 tablespoons (60 ml) olive oil

3 tablespoons (45 ml) chopped fresh rosemary or 2½ teaspoons (12 ml) crumbled dried rosemary

1 teaspoon (5 ml) turmeric powder

1 teaspoon (5 ml) curry powder, or to taste

Salt

1 large onion, halved and sliced thin

3 carrots, cut in 1-inch (2-cm) pieces

2 large white or red potatoes, cut in 1-inch (2-cm) cubes

2 garlic cloves, minced

1/4 teaspoon (1 ml) cayenne pepper, or to taste

1/4 cup (60 ml) currants, soaked and drained

Rosemary sprigs

Wash and pick over the chick peas. Cover them with 4 cups (1 litre) cold water in a large pan and soak overnight, or cover them with the water, bring them to boil, simmer 5 minutes, and soak for an hour.

Drain the chick peas and rinse them. Add fresh water to cover them by two inches (4–5 cm) and cook them for about an hour, or until they are tender.

Puree half the cooked chick peas and all of the cooking liquid in a blender or food processor with 2 tablespoons (30 ml) of olive oil, 2 tablespoons (30 ml) of the fresh rosemary, or about two-thirds of the dried rosemary, the turmeric, and the curry powder. Season lightly with salt. Combine the puree with the whole chick peas in an earthen casserole or in a large noncorrodible pot. Reheat over low heat.

Cook the onion in the remaining olive oil in a large heavy frying pan over low heat for about 5 minutes. Add the carrots and potatoes and cook, stirring occasionally, for about 5 minutes. Cover and cook for about 5 minutes more, or until the carrots and potatoes are almost done. Add the rest of the rosemary, the garlic, and the cayenne pepper to the skillet. Cook together over low heat for about 5 minutes.

Add the cooked vegetables and the currants to the chick peas. Cover and cook over low heat for about 15 minutes, stirring occasionally. Adjust the seasoning. Serve the tagine over hot couscous or rice. Garnish the dish with rosemary sprigs.

OVEN-FRIED ROSEMARY POTATOES

∎

THOUGH PERHAPS AS MUCH OIL IS ABSORBED by these potatoes as by french-fried potatoes (the recipe betrays its Tuscan farmhouse origins in the amount of olive oil), you will not have to stand over them while frying them twice. And once again, rosemary's perfume will whet everyone's appetite. The potatoes may be cut in half-rounds, in lengthwise slices, or like french fries; the important thing is to cut them about the same thickness so they cook evenly.

SERVES 4 TO 6

2 pounds (900 g) russet potatoes

1/2 cup (120 ml) olive oil

1½ teaspoons (8 ml) salt

3 tablespoons (45 ml) fresh rosemary leaves or 2 teaspoons (10 ml) crumbled dried rosemary

Preheat the oven to 350° F (180° C).

Scrub the potatoes well and cut them in half lengthwise. Cut each half into 1/4-inch (6-mm) slices. Coat the potatoes with the olive oil and salt. Place the potatoes and oil in a lightly oiled 9-by-12-inch (23-by-30-cm) baking dish. Strew the rosemary over the potatoes.

Cover the dish and bake for 30 minutes. Remove the cover, turn the potatoes and bake for 20 minutes longer, or until they are tender and golden brown. Serve hot.

OVEN-FRIED

ROSEMARY

POTATOES

H E R B E D   G R E E N   B E A N S

■

THIS ANTIPASTO OR SALAD has demonstrated to us that rather a lavish use of herbs is appealing to most people. Rosemary and sage, the only fresh herbs we had in Milano when we first made this dish, surprised us with their compatibility with green beans.

SERVES 6

2 pounds (900 g) young green beans, topped and tailed	1 sage sprig or a heaping 1/2 teaspoon (4 ml) crumbled dried sage
1/4 cup (60 ml) olive oil	1 garlic clove, crushed
1 lemon	Salt and freshly ground pepper
4 or 5 rosemary sprigs or 2 teaspoons (10 ml) crumbled dried rosemary	

If the beans are large, snap or cut them in about 1½-inch (4-cm) lengths. Pan-steam the beans in a little water until they are just tender.

Mince the fresh rosemary and sage. Combine the olive oil, lemon juice, rosemary, sage, and garlic in a small bowl or glass measuring cup. Season the dressing with salt and pepper.

Place the beans in a bowl and pour the dressing over them while they are still warm. Toss them well and marinate them for an hour or so. Adjust the seasoning and serve at room temperature.

CASTAGNACCIO

■

THIS UNUSUAL, RUSTIC SWEET CAKE is a specialty of Tuscany, where chestnuts are a much-favored seasonal delicacy. Except in the most dismal harvest years, a portion of the crop is peeled and dried, then sold whole or ground into flour. The whole chestnuts are reconstituted by simmering in water or milk, then used in confections, or stewed with polenta. The flour is used to make this cake-bread and a few sweet and savory puddings. Castagnaccio is a very old dish; some experts say its origins may be Etruscan. The flavor and aroma are rich and naturally sweet, making espresso or coffee a good accompaniment. We have enjoyed it as well with the end of dinner's red wine, and with vin santo, a Tuscan wine made of semidried grapes. In this country, chestnut flour is available at Italian food stores.

MAKES 2 FLAT CAKES, SERVING 6 TO 12

1/4 cup (60 ml) currants

1 pound (450 g) chestnut flour

4 cups (950 ml) cold water

*1 tablespoon (15 ml) chopped fresh
   rosemary leaves*

4 tablespoons (60 ml) olive oil

2 tablespoons (30 ml) honey

*1/3 cup (80 ml) unblanched
   almonds, chopped coarse*

1/2 teaspoon (2 ml) salt

*1 tablespoon (15 ml) and 1 teaspoon
   (5 ml) fresh rosemary leaves*

Soak the currants in warm water for 15 minutes, then squeeze them dry. Preheat the oven to 375° F (190° C).

Mix the chestnut flour with the water in a large bowl, breaking up any lumps with a wooden spoon. Add the currants, chopped rosemary, 2 tablespoons (30 ml) of the olive oil, the honey, almonds, and salt. Mix well and divide the batter between two 9-inch (23-cm) glass or ceramic pie dishes, each oiled with 1 tablespoon (15 ml) olive oil.

Sprinkle each castagnaccio with half of the whole rosemary leaves. Bake on the middle shelf of the oven for 1 hour and 15 minutes. The top of the castagnaccio should be cracked and crisp. Remove and cool on a rack for 30 minutes.

Cut each castagnaccio into six pieces and remove the pieces carefully with a spatula. Serve warm or at room temperature.

S AGE

SAGE *soothes both youth and age,*
and brings the cook pleasing praise.

■ The meanings of sage are linked to Latin as in English. The herb's name is from *salvere*, "to be well", "to save", while the word relating to wisdom is from *sapere*, "to taste", "to know". It is certainly wise to know sage well because, in addition to its traditional uses in sausages and with poultry, game, and liver, sage can add a rich and graceful note to vegetables, breads, and sweets.

Sage graces the garden as well, with its soft gray-green foliage providing a pleasing contrast to the bright hues of other culinary herbs. Common sages (*Salvia officinalis*) mark two corners of our herb garden handsomely throughout the season, especially when the bloom-laden spikes are in full purple flower. Varieties with pink or white flower and variegated leaves are available, as well.

Sage's use with rich dishes probably came from its reputation as a digestive. It was prized as a medicinal plant by the Greeks and Romans, primarily as a calmative for the stomach and nerves. Regular use of sage tea was said to confer an even disposition to excitable natures and a healthy old age to everyone. Sage was especially recommended to older persons to restore ailing memory and banish melancholy and depression. Swiss peasants used sage as a dentifrice, first chewing a few leaves, then brushing the gums with a twig. In England, tea made with the leaves of clary sage (*Salvia sclarea*) was a common beverage until China tea began to be imported. The English, in turn, introduced sage tea to the Chinese, who

SAGE GRACES THE

GARDEN WITH ITS SOFT

GRAY-GREEN FOLIAGE. . . .

would exchange up to five bushels of Chinese tea for one bushel of sage.

Sage as a culinary herb is much respected in England and Italy, where most country gardens have a sage bush, often more than a decade old. The flavor of sage does not deteriorate with the age of the plant, but plants vary in flavor, depending on soil and recedes and the camphor, along with a pleasant musk-

SAGE NEEDS FULL SUN AND USUALLY SURVIVES COLD WINTERS.

Still, common sage keeps its aroma and flavor through cooking and drying better than most culinary herbs. Dwarf sage, white-flowered sage, and purple sage are all handsome varieties of common sage with good flavor and aroma. Pineapple sage, fruit-scented sage, and mint-leaved sage all belong to the sage genus and have the familiar muskiness, with the added aromas that their names suggest. They lose a bit of their perfume when dried, and most of it when cooked. They do have their place in the kitchen for flavoring beverages and jellies, and with fruits and desserts. Pineapple sage (S. elegans), a lovely plant reaching 4 to 5 feet (1.2 to 1.5 m), has sweetly scented green leaves, and beautiful red flowers.

Sage will grow to about 4 feet (1.2 m) in diameter, keeping a well-rounded shape with little pruning in mild climates. It should have a well-drained or gravelly soil with adequate calcium; add some lime if calcium content is low. Sage needs full sun and usually survives cold winters. It should be pruned in the early spring to encourage new growth. Mulching sage plants with an inch or two (2 to 5 cm) of sand will limit the spread of soil-borne wilt diseases where these are a problem.

Sage is an excellent herb for tub planting, as the soil and light requirements can be controlled, and its shape is well suited to large planters. An established sage needs little care aside from occasional pruning and watering. Sage may be kept to manageable proportions in an outside window box by harvesting the leaves and trimming back the woody stems as necessary.

Like most other herbs, sage should be dried in a warm, dry place away from sun. When the leaves are completely dry, store them whole in airtight containers. Sage should be crumbled, never ground, as needed for cooking; grinding completely destroys the delicate lemony perfume, leaving the harsher resinous flavors.

GOAT CHEESE MARINATED WITH SAGE AND GARLIC

■

MOST MEDITERRANEAN PERENNIAL HERBS taste good with goat cheese: bay, rosemary, sage, and thyme. Sage also flavors some American and English farmhouse cheddars. This marinated cheese is good with toasted or untoasted bread.

SERVES 6 TO 8 AS AN APPETIZER

10 ounces (280 g) montrachet or other fresh, mild goat cheese

16 to 20 large fresh sage leaves

2 garlic cloves, sliced thin

12 to 15 black peppercorns, cracked

1/3 cup (80 ml) olive oil

Cut the cheese into 3/8-inch (8-mm) slices. Scatter half the sage leaves on a serving dish just large enough to hold the cheese. Scatter half the garlic slices over the sage leaves. Sprinkle half the cracked pepper over the herbs. Place the cheese on the herbs. Cover the cheese with the remaining sage leaves, garlic, and cracked pepper. Drizzle the olive oil over the cheese and herbs.

Marinate the cheese for 24 hours at cool room temperature or covered in the refrigerator.

If the cheese has been marinated in the refrigerator, remove it an hour or two before serving.

FOCACCIA WITH SAGE

■

FOCACCIA AND SCHIACCIATA are regional Italian terms for flatbread, similar to pizza. They are distinguished by their ancient hearthbread origins, lost to history, and by the simplicity of their toppings. Although they vary from place to place and from baker to baker, they usually carry just two or three ingredients. A full-flavored local olive oil is the main one. Sage and rosemary are common, with perhaps the addition of some onion or garlic; olives or Muscat raisins are popular, too. Olive oil with a little coarse sea salt is the simplest topping we have tried. These breads are usually thicker than pizza; in a home oven, they are best baked at a slightly lower temperature than pizza to create the crisp crust and bready, chewy interior.

SERVES 6 TO 8 AS A BREAD OR APPETIZER COURSE

1 recipe Pizza Dough (page 44), risen overnight in the refrigerator

1/3 cup (80 ml) olive oil

2 dozen fresh sage leaves, chopped

1 medium-sized sweet onion such as Vidalia, sliced thin

Salt

Remove the dough from the refrigerator in the morning and punch it down. Let it rise in a cool place for a few hours, or as long as all day.

About 2 hours before baking, punch the dough down again and divide it into two portions. About 30 minutes before baking, shape the dough into rectangles, about 12 by 9 inches (30 by 23 cm) with rounded corners, on lightly oiled baking pans.

Preheat the oven to 425° F (220° C), with a baking stone if you have one, on the bottom rack.

Just before baking, make depressions in the dough with the thumbs. Scatter the sage over the dough. Scatter the onion over the dough and season lightly with salt. Drizzle the dough with the olive oil, letting some collect in the depressions.

Place the baking sheets directly on the baking stone or on the middle rack of the oven. Bake the bread about 15 minutes. Brush some of the oil over the tops twice during the first 5 minutes of baking.

When they are done, they will be light golden brown and crisp on the outside. Remove them to racks to cool, or cut and serve warm.

S A G E   F R I T T E R S

■

TUSCANS MAKE THIS FRITTER to serve as an accompaniment to aperitifs, or as a light appetizer on its own. What makes the dish worth the effort of deep-frying is the unadorned clean flavor of the herb and an airy, melting-crisp batter. A good way to tell when oil is hot enough for deep-frying is to test the heat with bread cubes. Cut 1-inch (2-cm) cubes from day- or two-day-old bread. Day-old bread takes about 1 minute to color a medium golden brown all over in oil at 300° F (150° C). It takes about 45 seconds to color at 325° to 330° F (160° to 165° C) and about 30 seconds to color at 360° F (182° C). If the bread is very fresh, it will take longer to color.

SERVES 4 TO 6

50 sage leaves, about 2 inches (5 cm) long

3/4 cup (180 ml) all-purpose flour

1/2 teaspoon (2 ml) salt

4 tablespoons (60 ml) olive oil

2 tablespoons (30 ml) dry white wine

1/2 cup (120 ml) water

2 large egg whites

Vegetable oil for frying

Lemon wedges for serving

Brush the sage leaves clean. Wash them only if necessary, and be sure they are completely dry before battering them.

Mix the flour and salt together in a bowl. Whisk the water, then the olive oil and wine into flour to make a smooth batter. Cover the batter with plastic wrap and let it stand for an hour or two at room temperature, or in the refrigerator overnight. Let the batter come to room temperature before using it.

When you are ready to cook the fritters, heat 1 inch (2 cm) of peanut or other vegetable oil to about 360° F (182° C). Beat the egg whites until stiff but not dry.

Fold the beaten egg whites into the batter and place the batter in a shallow baking dish. Place about one-third of the sage leaves on the batter. Using kitchen tongs or a fork, coat the leaves with the batter.

Drop the leaves individually into the hot oil. Cook the fritters until they are golden brown, turning them once, about 1½ minutes. Remove from the oil and drain on paper towels. Keep warm in a 150° F (65° C) oven. Continue coating and frying the leaves until all have been cooked. Serve the fritters hot, with lemon wedges on the side.

T U S C A N - S T Y L E   C A L V E S '
L I V E R   W I T H   S A G E

■

EVEN IN THIS ERA OF cholesterol- and chemical-intake-consciousness, we occasionally try, and succeed, in gaining a wider audience for liver by cooking this dish. It is
quickly cooked, tender and pink in the center, and the sage gives it a new flavor. For our
tastes, crispy french-fried potatoes or creamy mashed potatoes are the best accompaniments to liver.

SERVES 4

1½ pounds (675 g) calves' liver	2 tablespoons (30 ml) lemon juice
4 tablespoons (60 ml) olive oil	Freshly ground black pepper
8 large fresh sage leaves	4 small sage sprigs
1 garlic clove, sliced thin	1 lemon, cut into thin wedges
1/2 teaspoon (2 ml) salt	

Trim the liver and cut it into 3/8-inch (8-mm) thick strips. The liver should be cut
to the same thickness to cook evenly; the width and length of the strips may vary.

Heat the olive oil in a large heavy frying pan over moderate heat. Add the garlic and
sage leaves. When the oil is hot, add the liver and sauté it for 2 to 3 minutes, stirring or
moving the pan constantly.

Dissolve the salt in the lemon juice and add it to the pan, stirring the juice for about
30 seconds. Season with black pepper. Transfer the liver to a warm serving platter and
pour the pan juices over it. Garnish the platter with sage sprigs and lemon wedges. Serve
immediately.

Chicken Stuffed with Corn Bread, Pecan, and Sage

■

THE UNDER-SKIN STUFFING TECHNIQUE protects the meat from dry heat, keeping it juicy, and gives it extra flavor because of direct contact with the stuffing. Of course, the stuffing can also be baked on the side; in this case, it may need more liquid. This is good with side dishes that have some acidity, such as sauerkraut or stewed tomatoes.

SERVES 4 TO 6

4- to 5-pound (2-kg) roasting chicken or fryer

Salt and freshly ground pepper

4 tablespoons (60 ml) unsalted butter

1 medium onion, diced fine

2 celery stalks, diced fine

1 ½ cups (360 ml) very dry corn bread, crumbled

1 ½ cups (360 ml) very dry whole wheat bread cubes

6 sage leaves, chopped or 1/2 teaspoon (2 ml) dried crumbled sage

1 rosemary sprig, leaves chopped or 1/4 teaspoon (1 ml) crumbled dried rosemary

2 thyme sprigs, leaves chopped, or 1/4 teaspoon (1 ml) crumbled dried thyme

2/3 cup (160 ml) pecans, lightly toasted and chopped medium-fine

1 small apple, cored and chopped medium-fine

About 1/3 cup (80 ml) half-and-half (single cream)

About 1/2 cup (120 ml) chicken stock

Rinse the chicken well and pat dry. Chop the gizzard, heart, and liver medium fine. Reserve the neck for another use.

Loosen the skin of the chicken, starting at the neck and working over the breast and thighs and drumsticks. The skin is elastic and easy to work loose, but try not to tear it. Repair any tears with a needle and thread. Salt and pepper the cavity of the chicken lightly.

Melt the butter over low heat. Cook the onion and celery with the chopped giblets in the butter for about 7 minutes. Remove to a large bowl.

Add the corn bread and whole wheat bread to the cooked vegetables and chicken.

Stir in the herbs, pecans, and apple. Season with salt and pepper. Combine the mixture thoroughly with the cream and stock. The stuffing should be somewhat moist; it will absorb more moisture from the chicken. Taste for seasoning, adding more salt, pepper, or herbs as necessary.

Preheat the oven to 375° F (190° C).

Work the stuffing under the skin in small handfuls. Reserve half of the stuffing for the cavity.

Bake the chicken for an hour, basting every 15 minutes or so with the pan drippings. Check to see if the thigh juices run clear when the joint is pierced. Bake longer if necessary. Cover the chicken loosely with foil if it begins to brown too much.

Let the chicken stand about 10 minutes before carving and serving.

P O R K   L O I N   W I T H   P R O S C I U T T O   A N D   S A G E

■

THIS IS A VERSION of the famous Roman saltimbocca ("jump in the mouth"), there made with veal scaloppine. The Italians often use sage with veal: in stews and sauces as well as with scaloppine. In this country, we have found that the veal sold as scaloppine does not begin to approach the quality of Italian veal, and is usually cut improperly as well. Pork loin makes a very tasty substitute; pork and sage are good flavor partners, the loin is tender, and can be pounded thin enough for quick cooking. But double pork? We urge you to try it; prosciutto and loin have quite different flavors and textures that work well together. The slight saltiness of the prosciutto is enough to season the dish for our taste; add salt if you like. Use the white wine for a tart sauce, the Marsala for a slightly sweeter one.

SERVES 4

1 pound (450 g) pork loin, sliced across the grain 1/4 to 3/8 inch (5 to 8 mm) thick, to yield 8 slices

8 large sage leaves

4 thin slices imported prosciutto

2 tablespoons (30 ml) olive oil

2 tablespoons (30 ml) unsalted butter

Freshly ground pepper

1/2 cup (120 ml) dry white wine or dry Marsala

Flatten the pork loin between waxed paper or plastic wrap by letting a cutlet bat or the flat of a heavy cleaver drop on each slice from about 8 inches (20 cm) above the board. Do not pound the meat or the fibers will break and the scaloppine will be uneven or develop holes. Each scaloppina should be a little less than 1/4 inch (5 mm) thick all over.

Cut the prosciutto in half crosswise. Place a sage leaf in the center of each scaloppina. Center a piece of prosciutto over the sage. Attach the sage and prosciutto to the scaloppina with a short toothpick. Finish layering the scaloppine.

Heat the olive oil and butter over medium heat in a pan large enough to hold the scaloppine without touching. Cook in two batches if necessary.

Place the scaloppine in the pan, loin side down, and cook until lightly browned, about 4 minutes. Turn the scaloppine and cook until the prosciutto is crisped, about 2 minutes. Remove to a serving platter and keep warm.

Add the wine or Marsala to the pan and scrape the browned bits while deglazing over high heat for a minute or two. Season the pan juices with pepper. Pour the sauce over the scaloppine and serve immediately.

PASTA E FAGIOLI

■

THIS IS ANOTHER COLD-WEATHER COMFORT DISH, one that we'll never tire of. With the inclusion of leftover odd-cut pieces of homemade pasta that we save for soup, a good loaf of country bread, fruity green olive oil, and a simple red wine on the side, we are eating, and living, well. When imported cannellini beans are available, we use those, but Great Northern and navy beans are good, too. For a change, replace the sage with about half as much rosemary.

SERVES 6 TO 8

1 ½ pounds (675 g) white beans

1/3 cup (80 ml) olive oil

1 ½ teaspoons (8 ml) salt

1 large onion, diced

8 garlic cloves, chopped

8 ounces small dried pasta

5 cups (1200 ml) vegetable stock or water

1/3 cup (80 ml) tomato paste

3 tablespoons (45 ml) chopped fresh sage or 2 teaspoons (10 ml) crumbled dried sage

3 tablespoons (45 ml) chopped parsley

Salt and freshly ground pepper

6 sage leaves

2–3 parsley sprigs

Olive oil

Freshly grated parmesan

Soak the beans overnight. Pour off the soaking water and transfer the beans to a large soup pot. Cover the beans with 1 inch (2 cm) of water. Add 3 tablespoons (45 ml) of the olive oil. Cook the beans until they are tender, about 1 hour, adding 1 ½ teaspoons (8 ml) salt at the end of the cooking time.

While the beans are cooking, soften the onion and garlic in the remaining olive oil over moderate heat. Bring abundant, well-salted water to a boil. Cook the pasta barely al dente and drain it. Stir the pasta, onion, and garlic into the beans. Add the vegetable stock and the tomato paste and simmer over low heat for about 5 minutes.

Add the chopped sage and parsley to the soup. Cook over low heat for 10 minutes. Adjust the seasoning with salt and pepper. Chop the sage and parsley leaves together for garnish. Ladle the soup into warm soup plates or bowls. Garnish with the herbs. Pass the olive oil and the grated cheese.

CHESTNUTS AND APPLES WITH SAGE

∎

THE ONLY THING WE DON'T LIKE about chestnuts is peeling them, unless we are roasting them over the fire after dinner. But they are such a special seasonal treat that we make a few dishes with them every fall. To roast chestnuts in the oven, cut an X on the rounded side, then place them on a baking sheet. Bake at 400° F (200° C) with a pan of water on the bottom rack until the shells and skins peel back, 15 to 20 minutes. The trick to peeling chestnuts is to do it while they are hot. Leaving them in the oven, with the heat turned off and the door open, keeps the last ones from cooling while you are peeling the first. Wear rubber gloves if your hands are sensitive to heat. This recipe is a variation of a traditional accompaniment to roast goose, duck, or chicken. If you would like to puree this dish, save some of the milk used to simmer the chestnuts. Cook the chestnut and apple mixture together a little longer than the recipe calls for, then puree it through a food mill, adding milk as necessary. The resulting puree is fit for the finest dinner. A food processor, by contrast, makes a rather unappetizing paste of chestnuts.

SERVES 4 TO 6

1 pound (450 g) chestnuts

About 2 cups (475 ml) milk

4 tablespoons (60 ml) unsalted butter

2 celery stalks, diced

1 medium red onion, diced

1 large Granny Smith apple or 2 small Pippin apples, cored and cut into 1/8-inch (3-mm) slices

8 large fresh sage leaves, shredded

Salt

Roast and peel the chestnuts. Put them in a 1-quart (1-litre) saucepan and add enough milk to barely cover them. Cook over very low heat for about 20 minutes, until they are just tender. Drain the chestnuts and chop them coarsely.

Melt the butter in a large frying pan over moderate heat. Soften the celery and onions in it. Add the chopped chestnuts and the apple slices to the pan. Reduce the heat to medium low.

Stir the sage leaves into the pan. Salt the mixture lightly and cook for about 10 minutes. Serve hot.

SAGE APPLE CAKE

■

THE PLEASANT MUSKINESS OF SAGE is enjoyable with apples in our palates, though we must say that many people don't notice an herb is used in this cake. Moist and full of flavor, the cake is very good with coffee or tea. When dark brown sugar is used, the cake is even richer and moister.

SERVES 8 TO 10

2 cups (475 ml) unbleached white flour

1 teaspoon (5 ml) baking soda

1 teaspoon (5 ml) baking powder

1/2 teaspoon (2 ml) salt

1/2 teaspoon (2 ml) cinnamon

1 cup (240 ml) packed light or dark brown sugar, plus 3 tablespoons (45 ml)

14 tablespoons (210 ml) unsalted butter, at room temperature

2 large eggs

1 tablespoon (15 ml) minced fresh sage

1 cup (240 ml) Sage Honey Applesauce (recipe follows)

1 large McIntosh, winesap, or other good cooking apple

1 tablespoon (15 ml) lemon juice

Sift the flour with the baking soda, baking powder, salt, and cinnamon. Cream 1 cup (240 ml) brown sugar with 12 tablespoons (180 ml) of the butter. Beat the eggs into the creamed sugar and butter.

Combine the sage with the applesauce and add to the butter mixture, beating well. Preheat the oven to 350° F (180° C).

Core the apple and slice it thin. Toss the slices with the lemon juice. Butter the bottom and sides of a 9½-inch (24-cm) bundt pan heavily with the remaining 2 tablespoons (30 ml) of butter. Sprinkle the bottom and sides of the pan with the remaining 3 tablespoons (45 ml) brown sugar. Arrange the apple slices around the bottom and sides of the pan.

Gradually add the flour mixture to the applesauce mixture, blending well. Pour the batter carefully into the prepared pan. Bake for 50 to 60 minutes, until the top is a deep golden brown and a cake tester comes out clean. Cool the cake to room temperature on a rack before removing it from the baking pan.

To serve the cake, loosen the sides of the pan. Invert the cake on a serving platter.

SAGE

APPLE

CAKE

S A G E   H O N E Y   A P P L E S A U C E

■

FRESH MCINTOSH APPLES make excellent applesauce. You can find these, in season, in most of the northern United States and in Canada. Use your favorite tart cooking apple if really firm McIntoshes are not available. The recipe is easily doubled.

MAKES ABOUT 2 CUPS (475 ML)

6 large McIntosh apples, about 2 pounds (1 kg)

1/3 cup (80 ml) sage honey, or 1/3 cup light honey and 2 sage leaves

1 to 2 tablespoons (15 to 30 ml) lemon juice

Core the apples and chop them roughly. Put them in a heavy saucepan and stir in the honey, sage leaves if you are using them, and lemon juice. Cover them and cook over low heat for 30 to 40 minutes, until they have softened completely. Remove the sage leaves if they were used. Puree in a food mill or food processor.

Let the sauce cool to room temperature and use, or store in the refrigerator.

SAGE TEA

■

THIS IS A COMFORTING TEA suited to quiet, cold evenings. Pineapple or fruit-scented sage gives a more perfumed aroma and a different flavor. Many herb teas are rather delicate; well or spring water without chlorine or other chemical treatments is the best medium for their subtlety.

MAKES 4 CUPS (1 LITRE)

1 quart (1 litre) spring water

1/2 cup (120 ml) packed fresh sage leaves

3 tablespoons (45 ml) sage honey

1 lemon or lime

Bring the water just to a boil and pour it over the sage leaves. Stir in the honey and lemon or lime juice to taste. Steep the tea for about 20 minutes. Bring it to a boil, then strain it into a warm teapot.

Summer and Winter Savory

WINTER, *summer, spring, and fall,*
Savory flavors over all.

The savories are some of the most amenable and useful herbs in our gardens. We've found them as adaptable in their growing requirements as in the dishes they flavor. Summer savory, especially, is one of our favorite blending herbs; it contributes its mildly piquant taste to mixtures with parsley, bay, basil, marjoram and oregano, rosemary, and thyme. Both summer and winter savories are famous for their affinity with beans; they are also excellent with cabbage and brussels sprouts, very good with meats, especially pork and veal, and wonderful with corn. They offer tomatoes a nice change from basil and marjoram or oregano and potatoes, a rest from parsley and chives.

Without changing the nature of a bouquet garni, either savory can be used to strengthen mild herbs or soften the effect of the more robust herbs. Summer savory's flavor is reminiscent of aromatic marjoram and thyme together, a blend of sweet and spicy tastes, whereas in winter savory, the peppery and resinous tones predominate, giving it a heartier character.

Although treasured mainly for their culinary excellence, the savories were also respected for their medicinal properties. We have tried the old remedy of rubbing a bruised sprig on a bee sting and found that it really does relieve the pain. In Elizabethan times the leaves were crushed into poultices for the treatment of colds and chest ailments. Savory teas were given for colic and flatulence. Perhaps this use

THE SAVORIES ARE SOME

OF THE MOST AMENABLE

AND USEFUL HERBS IN

OUR GARDENS.

influenced German cooks always to add savory, which they call *Bohnenkraut,* the bean herb, to bean dishes. But the savories offer even more virtues to the cook: versatility, affinity with other herbs, good flavor when dried, and the bonus of being easy to grow.

Both winter and summer savory (*Satureja montana* and *S. hortensia,* respectively) have a modest but pleasant appearance. Winter savory is a perennial, growing about 10 to 12 inches (25 to 30 cm) tall with thickly set, glossy, deep green leaves. It is well shaped and decorates our permanent garden, especially when covered with small blossoms that the bees hover at for hours. Summer savory, an annual, may grow as tall as 2 feet (60 cm), with tender reddish purple stems that tend to droop. The leaves are green, often lightly tinged with red, and are spaced widely apart. The delicate flowers of both species range in color from white through pale pink and lavender blue.

THE SAVORIES DRY

VERY WELL,

RETAINING MUCH OF

THEIR ESSENTIAL OILS.

Summer savory can be started from seed in flats and transplanted when the weather is quite warm and the plants are 4 to 6 inches (10 to 15 cm) tall. The seeds can be sown directly in the ground in late spring or when there is no danger of cold temperatures: *S. hortensis* germinates and grows quickly but is not resistant to cold. It flourishes in full sun with moderate water and light fertilization.

Winter savory, on the other hand, is hardy and will grow almost anywhere. A plant in full sun will produce fine growth if the roots are kept moist and the leaves dry. This bushy plant grows fairly slowly; it will start bearing fewer leaves after two or three seasons. Root division or layering (covering part of a stem with about an inch (2 cm) of soil to stimulate the growth of new roots) are the best ways to ensure a continuing supply of healthy winter savory.

The savories dry very well, retaining much of their essential oils. We dry them by spreading the sprigs on screens or in flat baskets, or by hanging several stems together upside down in a dry place out of the sun. Both savories are best harvested just before flowering. Summer savory plants may be pulled up and dried in late summer. Later harvests of winter savory may be made throughout the summer.

The savories' nature, so sweet in the garden, becomes fierce when you try to strip the sharp-pointed leaves from the stems of the winter variety. If you're not wearing gloves, you will get pricked, but the effect is not long-lasting. A winter's worth of flavor in the jars of dried herb is the reward for growing and harvesting these undemanding plants.

BLACK AND WHITE BEAN SOUP WITH SAVORY

■

THIS IS A FESTIVE AND FLAVORFUL SOUP which is really delicious with fresh corn bread. The nasturtiums, while not necessary, are a perfect garnish.

SERVES 8

1 pound (450 g) small dried black beans

1 pound (450 g) small dried white beans

12 garlic cloves, chopped

6 tablespoons (90 ml) olive oil

2 tablespoons (30 ml) minced summer savory or 1½ to 2 teaspoons (8 to 10 ml) crumbled dried savory

6 tablespoons (90 ml) red wine vinegar

4 jalapeño peppers, stemmed, seeded, and diced

1 teaspoon (5 ml) toasted and ground cumin

Salt

Nasturtium flowers

Rinse and pick over the beans. Soak them separately overnight. Drain them and rinse well. Put the beans in separate pots and cover with 3 inches (8 cm) water. Simmer them for about 1½ hours, or until they are very tender.

Soften the garlic in the olive oil over low heat. Divide the softened garlic and oil between the beans.

Add the savory to the white beans. Add the vinegar, jalapeños, and cumin to the black beans. Simmer the soups for about 10 minutes.

Puree each soup separately and return them to low heat for about 5 minutes. They should be rather thin; add a little water if necessary. Adjust the seasoning with salt.

To serve, ladle about 1/2 cup (120 ml) black bean soup in each warm soup plate. Carefully ladle 1/2 cup (120 ml) white bean soup in the center of the plate. Garnish the soup with nasturtium blossoms.

S A V O R Y   P H Y L L O   T R I A N G L E S

■

A FRENCH-GREEK FRIEND of Carolyn's says that a Greek cook's definition of happiness is when the filling and the phyllo come out the same. You might need an extra sheet or two of phyllo, depending on how large your teaspoons are. These are good candidates for making ahead and freezing in case of unexpected guests. They hold their flavor and texture well for two or three months. Place them directly on the baking sheet from the freezer, and bake as directed below.

SERVES 6 TO 8

1/2 pound (225 g) phyllo dough, about 18 sheets

3 tablespoons (45 ml) unsalted butter, melted

3 tablespoons (45 ml) olive oil

3½ ounces (100 g) fresh mild goat cheese, or feta, at room temperature

8 ounces (225 g) ricotta cheese

1 bunch green onions, sliced thin with about 4 inches (10 cm) of green

About 1 tablespoon (15 ml) minced summer savory or about 3/4 tablespoon (12 ml) minced winter savory

Salt and freshly ground black pepper

Thaw the phyllo and keep it covered according to package directions. Warm the melted butter with the olive oil. Mix the goat cheese, ricotta cheese, sliced green onions, and minced savory together well. Season the mixture to taste with salt and pepper.

Cut the phyllo into thirds along the length of the dough. Make a small cut 2 inches (5 ml) from one edge of the short side of the phyllo strips.

Work with one phyllo strip at a time on a baking sheet lightly brushed with the butter-oil mixture. Butter a 2-inch (5-cm) wide section, using the cut as a guide. Fold this section onto the phyllo strip.

Brush the strip of phyllo lightly with the butter-oil mixture. Place a heaping teaspoon (6 to 7 ml) of filling about 1 inch (2 cm) from the corner of the folded section. Fold over to form a triangle. Brush lightly with butter-oil mixture and fold to form another triangle. Repeat until the triangle is complete. Brush the top and bottom lightly with butter-oil mixture.

SAVORY

PHYLLO

TRIANGLES

Continue until all the triangles have been formed. The triangles may be baked at this point, or prepared as long as 24 hours ahead. To store them, wrap tightly with plastic wrap and refrigerate.

To serve, preheat the oven to 350° F (180° C). Bake the triangles for 15 to 20 minutes, until light golden brown, changing the position of the baking sheets halfway through the baking. Serve hot on a warm platter.

S A V O R Y   S A U S A G E

■

SAUSAGE USUALLY CONTAINS between 25 and 30 percent fat. This recipe is on the lean side because half the meat is veal. Pork raised in this country is much leaner than it was just a decade ago. Some butchers offer leaner ground pork which can be used if you are concerned about fat in your diet. In any case, you can pour off the fat that cooks out. This mild but flavorful sausage can be stuffed into casings, used as bulk sausage, or wrapped in caul fat. Rolled into 1-inch (2-cm) or smaller balls, it is good with noodles and as an appetizer. Patted into cakes, it makes a fine breakfast sausage. When the cakes are wrapped in caul fat—a lacy, visceral membrane in pigs—and grilled, you will have the centerpiece of a rustic-elegant meal. As with most sausage, the flavor is better when the sausage is made a day before it is cooked.

MAKES ABOUT 2 POUNDS (900 G)

1 pound (450 g) ground pork	3/4 teaspoon (4 ml) allspice
1 pound (450 g) ground veal	1 teaspoon (5 ml) salt
1/2 small onion, about 2 ounces (60 g), grated	1/4 cup (60 ml) dry white wine
	Freshly ground pepper
2 garlic cloves, minced	Pinch ground cloves
1½ tablespoons (22 ml) minced winter savory or 1 teaspoon (5 ml) crumbled dried winter savory	Sausage casings, optional

Place the pork and veal in a large bowl and mix them together with your hands. Blend in the onion, garlic, savory, allspice, salt, white wine, pepper and cloves.

The sausage should be well seasoned. Check by frying about a tablespoon (15 ml) of the mixture; taste and adjust the seasoning.

Stuff the sausage into casings if using a sausage stuffer; wrap the sausage tightly and store in the refrigerator. It will keep for 3 or 4 days. You may freeze it, tightly wrapped, but it will be a little drier when cooked after freezing.

S A V O R Y   P E P P E R - B R A I S E D   B E E F   A N D   V E G E T A B L E S

■

LIKE PORK, BEEF IS BEING RAISED LEANER than before; this is good for the body politic, but makes a meltingly tender pot roast harder to achieve, since the meat is not marbled with self-basting fat as it once was. Larding—inserting pieces of fat into the meat—is an option we forgo, both because of the excessive amount of fat, and the amount of time it takes. Marination and slow cooking give us good results. Because the meat must marinate overnight and the cooking takes about 3 hours, you may want to make this on a weekend and serve it during the week. Preparation time is short. Check to see that the liquid is just simmering while the meat is braising; turn the heat down, if necessary. This is a one-dish dinner, good with a salad of winter greens such as escarole or curly endive (marketed when small as frisée), and country-style bread.

SERVES 6

4- to 5-pound (2-kg) bone-in pot or chuck roast	4 medium potatoes
	4 medium carrots
3 garlic cloves, slivered	2 medium onions
12 to 15 black peppercorns, cracked	3 tablespoons (45 ml) chopped parsley
4 winter savory sprigs	Salt and freshly ground pepper to taste
1 cup (240 ml) full-flavored red wine	

Make small slits in the meat on both sides and insert the garlic slivers. Press the crushed peppercorns into the meat on both sides. Put the roast in an earthenware casserole or noncorrodible pan with a tight-fitting lid.

Bruise two sprigs of the savory and add them to the casserole. Pour the red wine over the meat. Marinate overnight in the refrigerator, turning the meat two or three times.

Remove the casserole from the refrigerator 2 hours before cooking. Preheat the oven to 300° F (150° C). Salt the meat lightly and place the casserole in the oven. After an hour, turn the meat. Cook for 1½ hours longer.

Peel the carrots, potatoes, and onions. Cut the potatoes lengthwise into sixths and the carrots lengthwise into quarters. Quarter the onions. Put the vegetables on top of the roast, salt and pepper, and baste them with the pan juices. Cover and cook for 20 minutes.

Chop the leaves from the remaining savory sprigs. Sprinkle the vegetables with the chopped savory and 2 tablespoons (30 ml) of the parsley. Cook, covered, for 15 to 20 minutes, until the vegetables are just done.

Remove the roast to a board and let rest for about 5 minutes. Skim the fat from the casserole and reduce the pan juices over high heat for a minute or two.

Slice the roast into serving pieces. Arrange the roast and vegetables on a serving platter. Spoon the pan juices over. Sprinkle with the remaining parsley and serve hot.

PORK CHOPS WITH SAVORY STUFFING

■

MOST AMERICANS HAVE BEEN TAUGHT to cook pork well done to destroy the parasitic larval nematodes (trichinae) that very rarely occur in under-cooked and raw pork. If the principle "better safe than sorry" is one that guides you, then continue this method. We have checked into the question, however, and have learned that as long as pork is cooked to an internal temperature of 150° F (65° C), the parasite is destroyed. Pork cooked to this temperature is a soft pink color, and the fiber has not dried out and toughened, rendering the meat unpalatable. This temperature, and the resulting succulent pork chop, roast, or grilled tenderloin, is best achieved by gentle heat. A brief period at medium heat for browning is fine. Then reduce the heat and cook until the meat reaches 150° F (65° C); cooking time will vary according to the cut and size of the pork. Instant-reading thermometers are fairly accurate. After you have established what pork cooked to 150° F (65° C) looks and feels like, you will be able to judge the timing without using a thermometer. These chops are good with Potato and Turnip Puree with Sour Cream and Chives (page 109), Potato Pie with Wilted Cress (page 137), or mashed potatoes.

SERVES 6

6 center loin pork chops, each about 1½ inches (3 cm) thick

1/4 pound (115 g) ground veal

1½ to 2 tablespoons (22 to 30 ml) minced summer savory or 1½ to 2 teaspoons (8 to 10 ml) crumbled dried savory

3 tablespoons (45 ml) freshly grated parmesan cheese

2 tablespoons (30 ml) fine dry bread crumbs

1 egg

Salt and freshly ground pepper

1 tablespoon (15 ml) olive oil

1 tablespoon (15 ml) unsalted butter

1/2 cup (120 ml) dry white wine

Slit each chop with a sharp knife to make a pocket for the stuffing. Mix the veal, savory, parmesan, bread crumbs, and egg. Season with salt and pepper.

Divide the stuffing among the chops and fasten the pockets with string or toothpicks.

Heat the olive oil and butter in a large frying pan over medium heat. Salt and pepper the chops and sauté them for about 4 minutes on each side, until they are nicely browned.

Add the wine, cover, and cook very slowly for 15 to 20 minutes. Turn the chops occasionally for even browning. Remove the string or toothpicks and serve very hot.

BAKED BEANS WITH SAVORY

■

THIS IS AN AMERICAN-EUROPEAN RECIPE, borrowing what we like from Boston-style baked beans and Italian slow-cooked beans, with the addition of savory, a German touch. It has no pork and is not as sweet as American beans, but the molasses makes it richer and more saucy than European baked beans. Overnight soaking improves the texture, and for many people, the digestibility of beans. Quick-soak directions are on page 249.

SERVES 8 TO 10

1½ pounds (675 g) small white (haricot) beans, Great Northern beans, or cannellini beans

1 bay leaf

1 large onion, diced

1 14-ounce (400-g) can tomatoes, seeded and diced

1/3 cup (80 ml) molasses

1/4 cup (60 ml) olive oil

4 garlic cloves, minced

1 tablespoon (15 ml) chopped winter savory or 1½ teaspoons (8 ml) crumbled dried savory

1 teaspoon (5 ml) ground mustard seed

1 teaspoon (5 ml) salt

1/8 teaspoon (0.5 ml) cayenne pepper

Freshly ground black pepper

Soak the beans overnight in 2 quarts (2 litres) cold water. Drain, rinse, and pick over the beans. Put them in a pot with the bay leaf and cover by 1 inch (2 cm) of water. Bring them to a boil, reduce the heat and simmer, covered, for 30 to 45 minutes, until they are barely tender.

Drain the beans and reserve the stock. Mix them with the onion, tomatoes, molasses, olive oil, garlic, savory, mustard seed, salt, cayenne pepper, and black pepper. Stir in 1 cup (240 ml) of bean stock. Preheat the oven to 250° F (120° C).

Put the beans in an oiled 2-quart (2-litre) bean pot and bake, covered, for 3 hours; reduce the heat to 200° F (93° C) and bake 2 hours longer. Stir the beans once an hour after the first two hours. Add bean stock, 1/2 cup (120 ml) at a time, if the beans become dry. About an hour before they are done, adjust the seasoning and uncover the beans. Serve hot from the bean pot.

Smoked Trout and Potato Salad

■

YES, THERE ARE A LOT OF potato salad recipes in this book. We have included them for two reasons: many herbs go well with potato salads, and we really like them. The practice of using savory with freshwater fish is an old and common one in Central and Eastern European cooking. We have been glad to adopt this idea; savory adds a good deal to the flavor of the aquacultured trout available in the markets.

SERVES 6

1¾ pounds (800 g) new potatoes, red, white, or gold

About 3 tablespoons (45 ml) white wine vinegar

About 1/3 cup (80 ml) olive oil

1 large shallot, diced fine

1 tablespoon (15 ml) small capers, rinsed

3 or 4 parsley sprigs, leaves chopped

2 winter savory sprigs, or 4 summer savory sprigs, leaves chopped

Salt and freshly ground black pepper

1 quart (1 litre) cleaned salad greens, such as oak leaf, red leaf, or Black-Seeded Simpson lettuce

2 smoked trout

Scrub the potatoes, cut them in half, and steam them until they are just done, about 15 minutes.

Meanwhile, put the vinegar in a bowl and whisk in the olive oil. Add the shallot and capers to the vinaigrette. Stir in the parsley and savory. Season with salt and pepper.

When the potatoes are cool enough to handle, peel them and rub them lightly all over with olive oil.

Arrange the salad greens on a serving platter. Carefully remove the skin and bones from the trout and flake them in large pieces.

Cut the potatoes in slices about 1/4 inch (5 mm) thick and arrange them on the salad greens. Drizzle about half of the vinaigrette over them. Arrange the flakes of smoked trout over the potatoes and drizzle with the remaining vinaigrette. Serve immediately.

GREEN BEANS WITH SAVORY AND SHALLOTS

■

HERE IS AN ADAPTABLE salad-cum-side dish that we have served at summer family gatherings and beach picnics. It seems to appeal to people of all ages, though children tend to pick out the olives. The recipe is easily doubled. We have served it warm to accompany many different summer main courses. Make it even if you don't have the red pepper, but do use your best olive oil.

SERVES 4 TO 6

1½ pounds (675 g) small green beans, about 1/4 inch (5 mm) thick and 3 to 4 inches (8 to 10 cm) long

1/4 cup (60 ml) olive oil

2 tablespoons (30 ml) red wine or balsamic vinegar

2 medium shallots, diced

6 to 8 sprigs summer or winter savory, leaves rough-chopped

Salt and freshly ground pepper

1 small red bell pepper, about 6 ounces (170 g), seeded and sliced thin

1/4 cup (60 ml) imported oil-cured olives, pitted

Trim and clean the beans. Pan-steam them in lightly salted water until just tender. Refresh the beans with cold water and pat dry.

Mix the olive oil with the vinegar, the diced shallots, and the chopped savory. Salt and pepper the vinaigrette lightly.

Toss the beans, red pepper strips, and olives with the vinaigrette. Marinate, covered, 3 to 4 hours, or overnight in the refrigerator.

Bring the salad to cool room temperature before serving, or heat it gently for a few minutes, until it is warm. Adjust the seasoning with oil, vinegar, salt, and pepper.

S A V O R Y   C O R N   R E L I S H

■

WITHOUT UNDERTAKING A SURVEY, we have noticed that those who like relishes eat them on the most diverse foods. We have one friend who always takes a jar of relish backpacking; the taste is worth the extra weight to him. This one is full-flavored with spices and savory but not hot. It goes in the usual relish contexts: grilled foods, Mexican or Indian meals, or any place you like relish. Sometimes we make a batch with a cup of assorted chopped chilis for a hot variation. If you do this, be sure to label the jars "chili corn relish". Either is a nice gift for relish lovers.

FILLS ABOUT 6 PINT (475-ML) JARS

24 ears fresh sweet corn, husked

2½ cups (590 ml) assorted diced sweet peppers, red, green, and yellow

2 cups (475 ml) diced onion

1½ cups (360 ml) water

1/2 cup (120 ml) olive oil

1/2 cup (120 ml) honey

1 cup (240 ml) white wine vinegar

1 tablespoon (15 ml) pickling or kosher salt

2 teaspoons (10 ml) celery seed

4 tablespoons (60 ml) winter savory, chopped fine

1 tablespoon (15 ml) yellow mustard seed

3 garlic cloves, minced

3/4 teaspoon (4 ml) ground turmeric

6 winter savory sprigs, 3 inches (8 cm) long

Bring a large kettle of water to boil and cook 12 ears of corn for 3 minutes. Remove the corn, refresh, and pat it dry. Cook the remaining 12 ears in the same way. Cut the kernels from the cob. There should be at least 10 cups (2.5 litres) of corn. An extra cup (240 ml) will not affect the recipe.

In a large noncorrodible pot, combine the peppers, onion, water, olive oil, honey, vinegar, salt, celery seed, savory, mustard seed, and garlic. Bring these ingredients to a simmer and cook for 5 minutes.

Add the corn and bring to a boil, reduce heat, and simmer for about 5 minutes, stirring occasionally so that the relish does not stick. Combine 2 tablespoons (30 ml) of the liquid with the turmeric in a small cup, then add the mixture to the pot and stir well. Simmer 2 minutes longer.

Ladle the relish into hot, sterilized pint (475-ml) jars with a sprig of savory in each jar. Seal the jars and process them in boiling water for 15 minutes. Refrigerate any unsealed jars and use them within a week or two.

S A V O R Y   B A K E D   A P P L E   C U S T A R D

■

THE SLIGHT PEPPERINESS OF SAVORY is a pleasing accent to the smoothness of custard, and the sweet-tartness of apples. Summer savory goes well with many fruits: peaches, apricots, and cherries in compotes; pears, peaches, apricots, and apples in jellies, jams, or butters. Firm-ripe peaches or pears could also be used in place of the apples in this recipe.

SERVES 6 TO 8

2 cups (475 ml) milk

9 sprigs summer savory, about 6 inches (15 cm) long

About 1 tablespoon (15 ml) butter

3 medium-sized tart cooking apples, such as Winesap, McIntosh, or Granny Smith

1/4 and 1/3 cup (60 and 80 ml) light honey

2 tablespoons (30 ml) lemon juice

1/2 teaspoon (2 ml) cinnamon

1/4 teaspoon (1 ml) freshly ground nutmeg

3 eggs

2 egg yolks

Scald the milk with 6 savory sprigs and let the mixture stand for 30 minutes. Generously butter a 10-inch (25-cm) glass pie plate or ceramic quiche dish. Peel and core the apples and slice them thinly into a bowl. Toss them with 1/4 cup (60 ml) honey, the lemon juice, cinnamon, and nutmeg.

Remove the savory from the milk and squeeze the extra liquid from the leaves. Combine the eggs, egg yolks, and 1/3 cup (80 ml) honey in a bowl. Whisk the mixture until blended. In a slow, steady stream, pour the scalded milk into the egg mixture, whisking continually. Preheat the oven to 325° F (160° C).

Drain the apples, reserving the liquid. Arrange them around the bottom of the baking dish in overlapping concentric circles. Strain the custard through a fine sieve and pour it carefully over the apples.

Place the baking dish in a larger dish and add hot water to a depth of half the custard dish. Bake about 35 minutes, testing with a cake tester for doneness. Remove the custard to a rack to cool.

After the custard has cooled to room temperature, gently loosen the edges with a spatula. Slide a flat platter over the custard dish and invert the custard onto it.

Pour the reserved apple liquid into a small saucepan and add the remaining savory sprigs. Bring the sauce to a simmer and cook on low heat for 10 minutes. Serve the custard at room temperature and pass the sauce separately.

The custard may be made ahead and refrigerated. Allow it to stand at room temperature for 30 minutes before serving. If you refrigerate the custard, reduce the sauce while the custard is standing.

S O R R E L

SORREL'S *point is well taken;*

with it the cook can wax symphonic.

Without it salmon seems forsaken

and garden salads too laconic.

It favors the palate to awaken,

and orchestrates each spring tonic.

■ Just as the French bring us haute couture each spring, they have devised one of the most elegant means to fashion a spring tonic—cream of sorrel soup. It has long been traditional in France to eat sorrel in spring to quicken the blood and enliven the appetite.

We, too, enjoy sorrel most in the spring and early summer. Its slightly sour flavor with a lemony zest sparks our palates and salads as no other herb does. As the first green to grace the herb garden, it thaws our frosted spirits with the reminder of spring to come. Although it looks a bit weedy, we think it a noble plant with inimitable flavor.

Sorrel's culinary foundation rests on two French classics: sorrel soup and sorrel sauce. It has not traveled to many other cuisines, though occasional recipes using it appear in English, Jewish, Swiss, and German cookbooks. The tender-leaved and distinctive herb has great versatility if we approach it with imagination and remember the English habit of eating it in salads. We find it good with eggs and vegetables, and in sauces or mayonnaise. Cooked dishes will need less salt when sorrel is used. To keep the bright green color in soups and sauces pay careful attention to the cooking time. We add young leaves by the handful to enliven simple salads and find that they need less vinegar or lemon juice, or none at all, when made with this herb.

Many of the old herbals mention sorrel, mainly as a pot- or salad herb. There's no long list of ailments

AS THE FIRST GREEN TO GRACE THE HERB GARDEN, SORREL THAWS OUR FROSTED SPIRITS . . .

it was purported to cure, though it did acquire a reputation for preventing scurvy and "cooling inflammation and heat of the blood." Gerard and Evelyn were extravagant in their praise, the one saying, "It is the best of sauces not only in virtue, but in pleasantness of taste," and the other, that it "renders not plants and herbs only, but men themselves, pleasant and agreeable."

Sorrel (*Rumex acetosa* and *R. scutatus*) is a hardy perennial. It grows best in full sun, in rich, well-drained soil, but will do moderately well in partial shade. The leaves appear on tall stems in dense clusters 18 to 24 inches (46 to 60 cm) high.

Cut them back periodically to stimulate new growth throughout the season. In mild climates, the herb will stay green all winter, though growth is limited. Sorrel is best used fresh; it has particularly thin leaves and does not freeze or dry well.

...SORREL ADDS "SO GRATEFUL A QUICKNESS TO SALAD THAT IT SHOULD NEVER BE LEFT OUT."

Hot weather can make the leaves taste bitter; we advise mulching to retain moisture and cutting any seed stalks back. For salads, leaves less than 6 inches (15 cm) long are best; larger ones are better cooked or combined with other foods.

Sorrel has deep roots that can be divided in spring or fall. Our original patch of sorrel, grown easily from seed, has been divided and moved about numerous times and has provided many friends and family members with their own crops. Sorrel does not thrive indoors, but ambitious gardeners might experiment with a grow light or in a greenhouse.

When we enjoy a salad of tender young sorrel leaves, we can't help but agree with Evelyn's advice that it adds "so grateful a quickness to salad that it should never be left out." We hope you will be stimulated to include sorrel in your gardens and kitchens and to relish its clear, sour accent in many dishes.

CELERY SORREL SOUP

■

THE SPRING TONIC ASPECT OF SORREL is particularly palatable in this soup, in which the celery adds body and its own mildly tonic properties. It can be served before many dishes, but is most appropriate at the beginning of an elegant spring dinner, followed by shad or salmon, asparagus and new potatoes, perhaps a salad of watercress and baby lettuces, with strawberries for dessert.

SERVES 4 TO 6

6 large celery ribs, roughly chopped

1 small onion, diced

2 tablespoons (30 ml) unsalted butter

3 cups (710 ml) chicken or vegetable stock

1 cup (240 ml) half-and-half (single cream)

1/2 cup (120 ml) packed sorrel leaves

Salt and freshly ground pepper

Soften the celery and onion in the butter, covered, over medium-low heat for 10 minutes. Meanwhile, heat the stock to simmering and heat the cream in a separate pan.

Puree the vegetables with the sorrel in a little of the hot stock. Stir in the rest of the stock and the cream. Season the soup and serve immediately.

SORREL BEET PUREE

■

WE WERE IMPRESSED when Tom DeBaggio whipped this up for us late one spring afternoon, after an herb-buying and educational excursion to his nursery. The tartness of the sorrel works with the sweetness of the beets, and the bit of butter makes it velvety smooth. For a man who knits his brow whenever we mention a recipe that takes more than 10 minutes, one who takes every known kitchen shortcut, this is pure delicious genius.

SERVES 4

1 bunch of beets (2 or 3 large beets or 4 or 5 smaller ones)

2 tablespoons (30 ml) unsalted butter

2 shallots, minced

1 cup (240 ml) packed fresh sorrel leaves, chopped, with stems removed

1 tablespoon (15 ml) white wine

Salt and freshly ground pepper

4 large sorrel leaves

Scrub the beets and cook them until tender. Peel them under cold running water while they are hot. Chop them coarsely.

While the beets are cooking, melt the butter in a heavy noncorrodible saucepan. Soften the shallots. Add the sorrel and cook for a few moments until the leaves are wilted. Add the warm beets and the wine and cook for 2 or 3 minutes.

Transfer the contents of the pan to a processor or blender and puree. Season with salt and pepper. Serve hot on large sorrel leaves.

CREAMED EGGS AND SORREL IN CROUSTADES

■

SORREL IS ONE OF THE BEST HERBS WITH EGGS; it softens the sulfur flavor in the yolks and sparks the blandness of the whites. This is a different but easy-to-prepare brunch or lunch dish. The croustades may be made the day before and kept in airtight containers. A little vinegar and salt in the poaching water helps to set the eggs; about a tablespoon (15 ml) of vinegar and a pinch of salt per quart (litre) of water is enough. Breaking the eggs, one by one, into a small teacup, then slipping them into the simmering water helps them to keep their shape. Because these eggs are covered with sauce, trimming is not necessary. Croustades are attractive, tasty containers for many first courses, especially those with cream sauce.

SERVES 6 AS A LUNCH COURSE, OR 12 AS A FIRST COURSE

12 slices of fresh, firm-textured white bread	2 cups (475 ml) packed shredded sorrel leaves
10 tablespoons (150 ml) unsalted butter	1½ cups (360 ml) half-and-half (single cream)
12 eggs	Salt and freshly ground white pepper
1 shallot, diced fine	

Preheat the oven to 350° F (180° C). Trim the crusts from the bread. Melt 7 tablespoons (105 ml) of the butter and let it cool slightly. Brush a slice of bread liberally with the melted butter on both sides and mold it in a small custard cup or muffin tin. Repeat with the rest of the bread. Bake the croustades for 10 to 15 minutes until they are light golden brown and crisp. Remove from the oven and turn them onto a cake rack.

Poach the eggs and keep them in warm water.

Soften the shallot in the remaining butter over low heat. Stir in the sorrel leaves and cook for 10 seconds. Add the cream and season with salt and pepper. Keep the sauce warm over very low heat.

Carefully drain the eggs on a tea towel, then place one in each croustade. Arrange the croustades on a warm platter or on plates, and spoon some sauce over each. Serve immediately.

SORREL SUSHI STYLE

■

WHEN THE SUSHI CRAZE came to California in the late seventies, we succumbed: to the delicious rice, which we loved; to the taste and texture of raw tuna and giant clams; to the fastidiously clean and calm open kitchens. Sushi is high culinary art in Japan; we have no pretensions about our sushi, but sorrel and laver taste right together to us, and sushi are fun to make. As accompaniments, we serve the traditional soy sauce and wasabi. Ingredients and sushi mats are available in Japanese food stores and some supermarkets.

MAKES ABOUT 32 SUSHI

1 cup (240 ml) sweet Oriental rice or short-grain Oriental rice

1½ cups (360 ml) water

1/2 teaspoon (2 ml) salt

2½ tablespoons (38 ml) rice wine vinegar

1½ teaspoons (8 ml) sugar

1 teaspoon (5 ml) toasted sesame oil

4 sheets nori seaweed (laver)

24 to 30 small sorrel leaves less than 4 inches (10 cm) long

12 to 16 strips pickled ginger, about 2½ inches (6 cm) long and 1/8 inch (3 mm) thick and wide

12 to 16 strips cucumber, cut the same size as the ginger

Place the rice, water, and salt in a pan and bring to a boil. Cover, reduce the heat to a simmer, and cook for 25 minutes. Remove from the heat and spread the rice in a shallow dish and cool to medium warm. Mix in the vinegar, sugar, and oil.

Toast the nori by passing the glossy side over a medium flame. Lay one sheet on a bamboo mat, glossy side down, with a short side facing you. Moisten your fingertips with water and rub them lightly over the seaweed.

Arrange six to eight sorrel leaves on the lower half of the seaweed. Spread almost one-quarter of the rice across the center of the leaves. Arrange one-quarter of the pickled ginger and one-quarter of the cucumber in the center of the rice. Cover the strips with 2 to 3 tablespoons (30 to 45 ml) of rice.

Begin rolling by bringing the edge of the sheet closest to you over the rice, using the mat to guide the roll. Continue until the roll is complete; hold the mat in place for 30 to 60 seconds to set the sushi. Make the remaining rolls in the same way. Cut each roll with a sharp knife into 1-inch (2-cm) slices.

SORREL

SUSHI

STYLE

S O R R E L   S P I N A C H   S O U F F L É

■

THE BALANCE OF ACIDITY from the sorrel, spinach, and cheese makes this soufflé an exceptional pleasure. The texture of soufflés is always special, but many times their flavor is a bit dull and rich with eggs and cheese. The cheese wanted here is soft and buttery with some acid; boursault, taleggio, and teleme would also be good. We think this informal soufflé is just as dramatic as the high-hat type, and it must also be served immediately. Sorrel and spinach are very complementary. Try stewing them together gently, in the water that clings to their leaves, until they are wilted; stir in some butter and season with freshly ground pepper.

SERVES 2 TO 3

2 tablespoons (30 ml) unsalted butter	3 egg yolks
1½ tablespoons (22 ml) all-purpose flour	3 ounces (85 g) St. André triple crème or other buttery cheese, at room temperature
1 cup (240 ml) milk, at room temperature	About 1 tablespoon (15 ml) butter
Salt and freshly ground pepper	About 3 tablespoons (45 ml) freshly grated parmesan cheese
1½ cups (360 ml) tender spinach leaves	4 egg whites
1 cup (240 ml) tender sorrel leaves	

Melt 2 tablespoons (30 ml) butter in a heavy-bottomed saucepan over medium-low heat. To make a thick bechamel sauce, stir the flour in all at once and cook over low heat for 2 to 3 minutes. Add the milk all at once, stirring vigorously. Cook the bechamel very slowly for about 15 minutes. Salt and pepper lightly. Remove from heat, cover and cool to room temperature.

Wash the spinach and sorrel very well. Put them in a pan with the water which clings to the leaves and wilt for 15 seconds over medium heat. Transfer them to a bowl and let them cool for 5 minutes.

Stir the egg yolks and cheese into the cooled bechamel, then add the spinach and sorrel. Butter a shallow 9-inch (23-cm) gratin dish or pie plate thickly and dust it with parmesan cheese. Preheat the oven to 450° F (230° C).

Beat the egg whites until they are stiff but not dry. Stir a little of the beaten whites into the cheese mixture. Fold in the rest of the whites in two parts.

Carefully pour the soufflé mixture into the prepared dish and bake for about 10 minutes, until the top is a rich golden brown while the center is still a little soft.

S A L M O N   W I T H   S O R R E L   B U T T E R

■

GRILLING FISH IS NO MORE DIFFICULT than grilling meats or vegetables, provided that the grill is clean and well-oiled and the fire is medium hot. Too much heat toughens the outer layers of the fish. For any grilling we recommend using wood or wood charcoal and starting the fire with kindling or newspapers so that oily, chemical flavors are not imparted to the food. Salmon and sorrel are a classic combination in French cuisine.

SERVES 4 TO 6

2-pound (900-g) piece salmon fillet	1½ cups (360 ml) finely chopped sorrel leaves
1 shallot, diced fine	
1/3 cup (80 ml) dry white wine	6 tablespoons (90 ml) unsalted butter
	Salt and freshly ground pepper

Prepare a medium-hot charcoal fire. While the grill is heating, prepare the sauce.

Add the shallot to a heavy noncorrodible saucepan with the wine and a little salt and pepper. Reduce the liquid to about 2 tablespoons (30 ml).

In another noncorrodible pan, wilt the sorrel for about 15 seconds, then remove it to a plate to cool to room temperature.

Work the cooled sorrel and the wine-shallot mixture into the butter. Season lightly with salt and pepper.

Salt and pepper the salmon lightly and grill for about 4 minutes on each side, or until it is just done. Let the salmon stand on a platter for 2 or 3 minutes before cutting and serving.

Place the salmon on a serving platter, or cut it and place on individual plates. Spread the sorrel butter over the salmon and serve.

CHICKEN AND CANTALOUPE SALAD

■

THIS IS A FANCIFUL, EXTRAVAGANT SALAD that tastes best in the heat of summer, when we have to root through the sorrel to find the tender leaves. But when flavorful cantaloupe are plentiful, it is cooling and refreshing. We usually poach the chicken the night before we plan to serve the dish, cool it to room temperature, then refrigerate it. The mayonnaise is also good with fish salads and as a garnish for cold steamed lobster, shrimp, and crab.

SERVES 6 TO 8

3- to 3½-pound (1.5-kg) chicken

1 carrot, roughly chopped

1 onion, roughly chopped

1 celery rib, roughly chopped

A bouquet garni made of 1 bay leaf, 2 thyme sprigs or 1/2 teaspoon (2 ml) dried thyme, 6 parsley sprigs, 1 teaspoon (5 ml) fennel seed, and 6 to 8 peppercorns

1/2 teaspoon (2 ml) salt

1½ cups (360 ml) tender sorrel leaves

6 Italian parsley sprigs

1 egg yolk, at room temperature

3/4 cup (180 ml) olive oil

1 or 2 limes or lemons

Freshly ground pepper

2 small or 1 large cantaloupe

Lettuce or sorrel leaves

Rinse the chicken well. Reserve the giblets for another use. Trim the chicken of excess fat.

Put the carrot, onion, celery, and bouquet garni in a stockpot and add enough water to just cover the chicken. Remove the chicken and bring the liquid to a boil. Reduce the heat and simmer for 15 minutes.

Add the chicken with 1/2 teaspoon (2 ml) salt and simmer it for 40 to 50 minutes. Remove it, drain, and cool on a rack.

Shred the sorrel leaves. Stem and roughly chop the parsley leaves. Put the leaves in a large mortar and pound them to a rough paste.

Stir an egg yolk into the mortar. Add the olive oil a few drops at a time while stirring with the pestle. Gradually increase the amount of olive oil added to a fine stream. When the oil has been used, season the mayonnaise with lime juice and salt and pepper.

To make the mayonnaise in a food processor or blender, place the shredded sorrel and parsley leaves in the processor bowl or blender jar. Add the egg yolk, a little lime juice, and a pinch of salt. With the motor running, add the oil in a very fine stream until the emulsion has formed. Adjust the seasoning with lime juice and salt and pepper.

Skin and bone the chicken and cut the meat into 1/2-inch (1-cm) dice. Remove the flesh of the cantaloupe with a melon baller. You should have 3 cups (710 ml) of cantaloupe. Toss the chicken and cantaloupe with the mayonnaise. Chill the salad, covered, for 2 or 3 hours.

Arrange the lettuce or sorrel leaves on six chilled salad plates. Taste the salad for seasoning and add more lime juice, salt, or pepper, if necessary. Divide the salad among the plates and serve chilled.

A   S I M P L E   S A L A D   W I T H   S O R R E L

■

There is nothing so appetizing to us as a salad with garden herbs and lettuce. Such a salad always reaffirms our belief that in simplicity lies the cook's highest art.

You will need handfuls of just-picked garden lettuce and sorrel: about a handful of greens for each person unless you are serving salad lovers. We like to use four parts lettuce to one part sorrel. It is good to include a variety of lettuces; lamb's lettuce (mâche), oak leaf and red leaf, and other sweet varieties taste good with sorrel. The sorrel leaves should be quite young and tender, about 2 inches (5 cm) long. If you like to tingle your taste buds, add a few leaves of rocket, or salad mustard greens such as mizuna.

The perfect dressing requires only some really good extra-virgin olive oil, a few drops of wine vinegar or lemon juice, and a little salt and pepper. Simple garnishes such as hard-cooked eggs, garlic croutons, spring beets, or summer tomatoes complement the freshness of the salad and look pretty, too.

LENTIL SALAD WITH SORREL

■

THE SMALL GREEN FRENCH LENTILS are delicious in salads and retain their shape better than most. The common brown lentils will work; be sure they are cooked until just tender. With a loaf of crusty bread and a simple, fruity red wine, this is a good main course salad for lunch, supper, or a picnic.

SERVES 6 TO 8

1½ cups (360 ml) lentils	2 garlic cloves, minced
1 small onion, diced fine	About 1/3 cup (80 ml) olive oil
2 or 3 medium-sized ripe tomatoes, diced	3 ounces (85 g) fresh mild goat cheese or feta cheese
2 or 3 cooked new potatoes, diced	Juice of 1/2 lemon, or to taste
1 cup (240 ml) shredded sorrel leaves	Salt and freshly ground pepper

Rinse and pick over the lentils. Put them in a pan with water to cover by 1/2 inch (1 cm). Bring to a boil, then reduce heat and simmer, covered, until they are just tender, from 20 to 30 minutes.

When the lentils are done, spread them on a baking sheet and toss with the olive oil. Let them cool slightly, then stir in the onion, tomatoes, garlic, and potatoes. Season with lemon juice, salt, and pepper.

When the lentils are at room temperature, stir in the sorrel leaves and crumble in the goat cheese. The flavor improves if the salad is refrigerated for 3 to 4 hours, then brought to cool room temperature before serving.

WARM POTATO AND TURNIP SALAD WITH SORREL

■

WARM SALADS ARE GOOD with many kinds of meals and as the main event of a meal. We have enjoyed this one before lemony roast chicken or cumin-scented roast pork with carrots or winter squash, beside an omelet or soufflé, and as a main-course spring salad preceded by soup. Pancetta is Italian bacon; it is not smoked but peppered, and has a rather sweet flavor. Any kind of small new potato—red, white, or gold—is good here. Baby turnips are a spring or fall treat; we save the tops to use in minestrone. The tops also make a wonderful sauce for sturdy pasta such as penne when they are sautéed with olive oil, garlic, and balsamic vinegar, and garnished with a sharp romano or pecorino cheese.

SERVES 6

1 ½ pounds (675 ml) new potatoes	3 tablespoons (45 ml) olive oil
1 pound (450 g) small turnips with tops, about 2 bunches	About 1 teaspoon (5 ml) white wine vinegar
3 ounces (85 g) pancetta or salt pork	Salt and freshly ground pepper
1 garlic clove, finely minced	1 cup (240 ml) shredded sorrel leaves

Scrub the potatoes and turnips and cook them in water to cover by 1 inch (2 cm) until they are just tender. Drain them and let them stand until they are just cool enough to peel.

Cut the pancetta into 1/2-inch (1-cm) dice. Cook it over medium-low heat until it is golden brown and there are about 2 tablespoons (30 ml) of rendered fat in the pan. Off heat, remove the pancetta from the pan. Place the garlic and olive oil in the pan.

Peel and cut the vegetables into 1-inch (2-cm) dice. Put them in the pan with the oil and sprinkle the vinegar, salt, and pepper over them. Heat the vegetables over medium heat, shaking the pan frequently. When they are heated through, transfer them to a bowl and toss with the sorrel leaves and pancetta. Serve the salad immediately.

T ARRAGON

FROM *times* of *old*,

subtle yet bold,

in sauces fine with meat or fish,

tarragon defines the dish.

■ The Romans named this herb *dracunculus* because its serpentine root structure suggested little dragons. We think the fieriness that warms the palate sparks more brilliant draconic images. Tarragon's multifaceted flavor heralds rich historical associations: glowing tapestries and paintings of dragons, their scales gleaming as greenly as the plant in the garden.

Tarragon is one of the royal herbs, in fact as well as legend. The "little dragon" was the favorite herb of Charlemagne and was cultivated in the gardens of the Tudors. Through the centuries, it has become more used and respected for its regal presence in the kitchen. The first-century naturalist Pliny thought tarragon prevented fatigue. This notion continued through the Middle Ages, when the faithful put it in their shoes before setting out on pilgrimages. Arab doctors used its pleasant flavor and numbing properties to mitigate the effects of swallowing bitter medicines. Evelyn wrote of tarragon as "good for the heart, lungs, and liver."

Tarragon's strongest champions in Europe have been cooks rather than herbalists or doctors. The French work with tarragon in the most creative way, although it also finds favor with the Sienese and with some peoples of southern Russia, where it probably originated. The rich, aniselike, peppery flavor of tarragon and its complex aroma of just-cut hay, mint, and licorice enhance a great variety of foods. Classic in sauces from béarnaise to tartar and excel-

TARRAGON IS ONE OF THE ROYAL HERBS, IN FACT AS WELL AS LEGEND.

lent with fish, eggs, and chicken, tarragon also adds much to grilled meats. A light sprinkling goes well with many simply prepared vegetables, notably peas, spinach, cauliflower, and potatoes.

Tarragon tastes best on its own or with the classic fines herbes: parsley, chervil, and chives. The strong aromatics—rosemary, sage, and thyme—do not harmonize with it. The fresh herb is subtler than the dried and may be used accordingly. As heat brings out its flavor, cooked dishes usually need less. In the late spring and early summer, tarragon is often sold in produce markets and at greengrocers.

French tarragon, *Artemisia dracunculus* var. *sativa*, is the culinary herb of choice. It must be started from cuttings or by root divisions as it does not set viable seed. The tarragon seeds of commerce are of Russian tarragon, A. *dracunculus*, a tasteless look-alike of no culinary merit. Mexican tarragon (*Tagetes lucida*) is sometimes substituted for French tarragon when the latter is dormant or where winters are too warm for tarragon to thrive. This perennial member of the marigold genus resembles French tarragon in flavor, but is coarser and more pungent. It is stronger in vinegar and milder in cooked dishes.

It is best to buy rooted cuttings or small plants of French tarragon in the spring and set them 18 inches (46 cm) apart, as this herb has a shallow lateral root system. Tarragon likes a well-drained rich soil a bit on the sandy side and a sunny spot free from the shadow of other plants. Fertilize twice a month, especially during the first few months after it has been transplanted with a 10–10–10 liquid fertilizer diluted to half the recommended strength. You will have to protect young plants if you set them out while there is still a chance of frost. Mature French tarragon, a handsome, bushy plant, is some 2 to 2½ feet (60 to 75 cm) tall. Frequent harvesting of leaves, especially in summer, and a sand mulch lessen disease problems, but do remove all yellow or brown leaves as soon as they are observed to retard the spread of fungus.

To ensure the most flavorful tarragon, the roots of established plants should be divided every two to three years in the spring, before the new growth is 3 inches (8 cm) tall. Dig up a plant and carefully separate it into pieces, each with part of last year's stem and roots. Plant divisions just as you would new plants (see above). Any extras you may have will be greatly appreciated by gardening friends who like to cook.

Tarragon dies back to the ground each winter even in mild climates; in cold climates, it should be

FRENCH TARRAGON

. . . IS THE CULINARY

HERB OF CHOICE.

well protected with mulch. Mature tarragon plants can be potted up and grown indoors, but they need artificial light for 15 hours a day to maintain vegetative growth. Choose a wide pot with good drainage and do not overwater, especially during short winter days when they are not actively growing.

By far the best way to preserve tarragon is in vinegar; the flavor is true and long-lasting (until the next season's growth), though of course the texture and color are not the same as the fresh herb. Fill quart jars loosely with cuttings and pour in white wine vinegar to cover them. Close the jars and store in the pantry. We refrigerate the jars as we open them, and use the same amount of the preserved herb as the fresh. The vinegar can be used as well. If you want a stronger tarragon vinegar, bring the desired quantity of good quality white wine vinegar just to the boil. Decant it into bottles containing several sprigs of fresh, healthy tarragon. Cap and store three weeks before using. For another method of making tarragon vinegar, see "Concentrating Herbal Flavor" (pages 24–26).

Tarragon can be harvested in several cuttings for preserving. Freezing sprigs in airtight plastic bags gives fairly good results. To dry tarragon, place sprigs on mesh screen in a shady but warm place. Drying emphasizes the hay aroma and licorice taste at the expense of the more volatile oils; the dried herb will not be as rich in flavor as the fresh leaves.

BY FAR THE BEST WAY

TO PRESERVE

TARRAGON

IS IN VINEGAR . . .

SALMON CURED WITH TARRAGON

■

ALL INGREDIENTS SHOULD BE the finest and freshest. Kosher and sea salt have no additives, and a saltier taste than table salt, so a smaller amount of them can be used for a good cure. Needle-nosed pliers are the most efficient tools for removing the bones from the salmon. This recipe is a relative of gravlax, Scandinavian salmon cured with dill and aquavit, and is very versatile. Serve it for brunch or a light supper with scrambled eggs, brioche, croissants, or rye bread. As an appetizer or dinner first course, serve it with thin slices of sourdough or rye bread, and garnish with caviar if desired. The salmon keeps for 3 or 4 days, tightly covered, in the refrigerator. If we have any left over, we grill it and use it in first-course salads, with very thin slices of sweet onion, and in pasta sauces.

SERVES 12 TO 16

2 whole fillets of salmon, each about 2 pounds (900 g), with the skin on

8 to 10 tarragon sprigs

1/4 cup (60 ml) Cognac or brandy

1 1/2 tablespoons (22 ml) kosher or coarse sea salt

Remove any bones from the fillets. Arrange the tarragon sprigs along the flesh side of one of the fillets. Sprinkle this fillet with the Cognac. Scatter the salt evenly over the tarragon sprigs. Place the other fillet, flesh side down, on the first fillet.

Place the salmon on a platter large enough to hold it without crowding and cover it with a damp tea towel. Cure in the refrigerator for 24 hours, turning the fish at least once and keeping the towel damp.

To serve, scrape the tarragon and any excess salt from the fillets. Place the salmon, skin side down, on a serving board or platter and slice it very thin. Begin slicing at the tail end and hold the knife almost parallel to the flesh.

SALMON

CURED WITH

TARRAGON

Tarragon Deviled Eggs in Celery

■

THIS WAY OF SERVING DEVILED EGGS makes them easy to handle and gives them textural contrast with the crisp celery. Imported Hungarian paprika has a deep, naturally sweet capsicum flavor that we have not noticed in domestic brands.

MAKES 26 TO 30 APPETIZERS

6 large eggs

1/4 cup (60 ml) sour cream or yogurt

2 teaspoons (10 ml) minced tarragon

2 teaspoons (10 ml) Dijon-style mustard

1 teaspoon (5 ml) tarragon vinegar

1/2 teaspoon (2 ml) paprika, preferably Hungarian

2 dashes cayenne pepper

Salt

7 celery stalks

Capers

Hard-cook the eggs, peel, and cool them. Rub them through a medium sieve into a bowl. Add the sour cream, tarragon, mustard, vinegar, paprika, and cayenne pepper. Season with salt.

Wash the celery stalks and cut them into 3-inch (8-cm) lengths. Fill the celery pieces with the egg mixture, using a pastry bag or a spoon. Garnish with capers.

CREAM OF CAULIFLOWER SOUP

∎

THE LICORICE SHARPNESS OF TARRAGON brightens the flavor of earthy cauliflower in this creamy pureed soup. Tarragon is good with other white vegetables too: parsnips, celery root, and turnips. Serve the soup before any main course except a rich one or one featuring a cream sauce.

SERVES 6

1 medium-large cauliflower, about 1½ pounds (700 g)

1 quart (1 litre) chicken or vegetable stock

2 shallots, diced fine

2 tablespoons (30 ml) unsalted butter

1 cup (240 ml) half-and-half (single cream)

1 tablespoon (15 ml) minced tarragon

1 tablespoon (15 ml) snipped chives

Salt and freshly ground white pepper

1/4 teaspoon (1 ml) freshly ground nutmeg

Wash and break the cauliflower into flowerets and put it in a soup pot with the stock. Cook until the cauliflower is just tender.

Puree the cauliflower with 1 cup (240 ml) of stock in the blender or food processor until smooth. Return the puree to the soup pot. Soften the shallots in the butter for about 5 minutes.

Add the shallots, cream, tarragon, and chives to the soup and stir well. Season with salt and pepper and add the nutmeg. Heat the soup just through and serve in warm soup bowls or a tureen.

FILLET OF SOLE WITH CRAB

■

WHEN FRESH COOKED CRAB IS AVAILABLE, this is a special fish course. Any variety of local crab will be good. Frozen crab, aside from being bland, will not work because it is too watery. For a nice presentation, we like to echo the rolled shape of the sole with rice timbales, made with some grated carrot and chives, and to serve asparagus or young green beans in the center of the plates. Crème fraîche is rather expensive to buy but is easy to make. Shake 2 cups (475 ml) of whipping cream (double cream) with 1 tablespoon (15 ml) of buttermilk in a pint (half-litre) jar. Set the jar in a warm place, such as an oven with a pilot light, for 24 hours. The crème fraîche should have thickened slightly, and taste tangy. This may take another 24 hours. The culture grows best when fresh, *not* ultrapasteurized cream and buttermilk are used. Crème fraîche reduces and whips as well as heavy cream.

SERVES 4

1 cup (240 ml) fresh cooked crab meat, about 1/2 pound (225 g)

2 tablespoons (30 ml) créme fraîche

Pinch of white pepper and cayenne pepper

4 sole fillets

1 medium shallot, diced fine

1 tablespoon (15 ml) unsalted butter

1 tablespoon (15 ml) minced tarragon

1/2 cup (120 ml) dry white wine

Salt and freshly ground white pepper

1/2 cup (120 ml) whipping cream (double cream)

Mix the crab meat gently with the crème fraîche, and add the white pepper and cayenne. Roll the sole around 1/4 cup (60 ml) of crab mixture for each fillet and tie the fillets with kitchen string or secure with toothpicks.

Soften the shallot in the butter over low heat for 5 minutes. Add the tarragon, wine, and salt and pepper to taste. Simmer for 5 minutes. Add the rolled fillets and poach gently for about 5 minutes, carefully turning them once.

Remove fillets with a slotted spoon to a warm plate and keep warm. Increase the heat under the sauce and reduce to 1/3 cup (80 ml). Add the cream and heat thoroughly. Spoon the sauce into warm serving dish, remove the string or toothpicks from the fillets and place the fillets on top of the sauce. Serve immediately.

BRAISED CHICKEN AND ARTICHOKES WITH TARRAGON

■

THIS DISH WAS INSPIRED BY Giuliano Bugialli's Rabbit Stuffed with Artichokes and Tarragon, which Carolyn tasted when she took classes with him many years ago in Florence. His dish derived from his researches into old recipes from Siena, where tarragon has long been esteemed; it is rare in most other Italian regions. Though chicken is used here rather than rabbit and the preparation has been simplified, the complex flavor elements still work together: the combination of the rich succulence of pancetta, a peppery Italian bacon, and poultry with the tanginess of wine, the peppery anise flavor of tarragon, and the nuttiness of artichokes.

SERVES 4 TO 6

3 ounces (85 g) pancetta, or salt pork

3½- to 4-pound (1.6- to 1.8-kg) chicken

1 cup (240 ml) dry white wine

1/2 cup (120 ml) chicken broth

Salt and freshly ground pepper

Few leaves chopped parsley and fresh tarragon

1 lemon

5 or 6 medium artichokes

4 garlic cloves

Leaves from 4 or 5 fresh or vinegar-preserved tarragon sprigs, or 1½ teaspoons (8 ml) dried tarragon

Dice the pancetta and render it over low heat. Remove it from the heat and drain on paper towels. Pour off all but about a tablespoon (15 ml) fat from the pan.

Joint, rinse, and pat the chicken dry; season with salt and pepper. Brown in the pancetta fat over medium-high heat. Remove from heat and pour off all but about a tablespoon of fat. Meanwhile, squeeze half a lemon into a small bowl of cold water. Trim the artichokes by removing all leaves and the dark green outer flesh. Rub them with the cut lemon as you trim. Remove the chokes, quarter the hearts, and place in the bowl of acidulated water. Sliver the garlic. Add the artichokes, garlic, tarragon, wine, and broth to the chicken. Cook covered, over low heat, for 20 to 25 minutes.

Just before serving, add the pancetta and adjust the seasoning. Sprinkle the dish with a little chopped parsley, and fresh tarragon, if available.

WILD GOOSE WITH BLUEBERRY TARRAGON SAUCE

■

SUSAN'S FATHER, ROBERT BELSINGER, goes goose hunting every season, and brings home the noble and very tasty Canada goose. Its wonderful flavor and low fat make it a good candidate for clay cooking. Blueberries and tarragon are a gentle contrast to the mildly gamy meat. If fresh blueberries are not available, use berries frozen without juice or sugar, and partially thaw them before making the sauce.

SERVES 4 TO 6

4- to 5-pound (2-kg) wild goose, plucked and cleaned

Vinegar-preserved or fresh tarragon sprigs

2 teaspoons (10 ml) salt

1 teaspoon (5 ml) cracked black pepper

2 cups (475 ml) blueberries

1/3 cup (80 ml) orange juice

2 teaspoons (10 ml) minced vinegar-preserved or fresh tarragon

Fresh tarragon or parsley sprigs

Rinse the goose and dry it well. Bruise 1 tarragon sprig and rub the bird inside and out with it. Mix the salt and pepper and rub the bird inside and out with it. Put the tarragon sprig inside the bird.

Follow manufacturer's directions for soaking a clay roaster.

Put the goose, breast up, in the roaster and roast for 15 minutes per pound (33 minutes per kilogram) at 500° F (260° C).

Remove the goose to a warm platter and keep warm. Carefully decant the juices from the roaster into a frying pan, scraping the roaster with a wooden spoon to loosen any bits of meat and skin.

Reduce the juices to 1 cup (240 ml) and strain them. Add the blueberries, orange juice, minced tarragon, and salt to taste to the strained juices. Cook over medium-high heat for 5 minutes.

Place the goose on a platter and garnish with tarragon or parsley sprigs. Pass the sauce separately.

GRILLED LAMB WITH MUSTARD TARRAGON MARINADE

■

LAMB IS GOOD WITH MANY HERBS: thyme, rosemary, marjoram, oregano, dill, and basil. Grilled, it works well with tarragon in a simple marinade. We serve this with grilled eggplant and/or squash brushed with a little olive oil and balsamic vinegar, or with Minted Tomatoes Gratiné (page 214), and a crusty country-style bread.

SERVES 6 TO 8

4- to 5-pound (2-kg) leg of lamb, boned and butterflied	4 tablespoons (60 ml) whole-grain mustard
6 tarragon sprigs or 2 teaspoons (10 ml) dried tarragon	2 tablespoons (30 ml) olive oil
2 to 3 cloves of garlic, slivered	1/2 teaspoon (2 ml) black peppercorns, cracked
2 tablespoons (30 ml) medium-dry sherry	Salt

Remove excess fat from the lamb. Make small incisions in the meat with a sharp knife. If you have fresh tarragon, insert a leaf, along with a garlic sliver, in each incision.

Stem and mince the remaining fresh tarragon, or soak the dried tarragon in the sherry. Mix the mustard, olive oil, sherry, tarragon, and pepper together. Rub the marinade all over the lamb. Cover and marinate overnight in the refrigerator.

Before cooking the lamb, remove it from the refrigerator and let it come to cool room temperature.

Prepare a medium-hot wood or wood charcoal fire. Grill the lamb about 5 inches (13 cm) above the coals, turning it four or five times. For rare lamb, check for doneness after 15 minutes. The lamb will be rare when it is firm yet springy when pressed lightly with a finger, or when the internal temperature is 125° to 128° F (52° to 53° C). Let the lamb rest for 5 minutes before carving.

To serve, slice the lamb about 3/8 inch (8 mm) thick on a diagonal across the grain of the meat. Serve immediately.

BAKED POTATOES WITH BOURSAULT AND TARRAGON

■

THE SOFT TANG and unctuousness of triple crème cheeses—boursault, St. André, explorateur—are well complemented by the anise-pepper bite of tarragon. For a blue cheese variation, try blu castello, stracchino, taleggio, or gorgonzola dolce. The potatoes are rich and best paired with simple and crisp foods: roasts and pan-steamed vegetables.

SERVES 6

3 large baking potatoes

3 ounces (85 g) boursault cheese, at room temperature

1 tablespoon (15 ml) minced tarragon

1 tablespoon (15 ml) unsalted butter

1/2 cup (120 ml) half-and-half or whipping cream (single or double cream)

Salt and freshly ground pepper

Scrub the potatoes and bake them at 425° F (220° C) for 50 minutes to 1 hour, or until the potatoes are tender. Remove from oven and cut in half lengthwise. Carefully scoop the pulp into a large bowl, leaving 1/4-inch (5-mm) shells.

Mash or rice the potato pulp. Blend in the cheese, leaving some lumps. Add the tarragon, butter, and cream, and season with salt and pepper. Mound the potato filling in the skins and place on a baking sheet. Return to the oven for 10 minutes, until the potatoes are golden brown.

SCALLOP, SHRIMP, AND ARTICHOKE SALAD

■

OF ALL CLASSES OF FOOD, seafood resonates notably with tarragon. Artichokes and tarragon are one of our favorite combinations. Adding a sprig or two to the water for steamed artichokes is one way we indulge this taste. Others are dipping sauces: a simple melted butter with tarragon and lemon juice, tarragon mayonnaise, ravigote with tarragon (page 85), or salsa verde with tarragon.

SMALL CAPS: Serves 6

1 cup (240 ml) water	1/2 pound (225 g) scallops, trimmed of fibrous tissue
1/2 cup (120 ml) dry white wine	
1 carrot, cut in pieces	1/2 pound (225 g) medium shrimp
1 onion, cut in pieces	3 tablespoons (45 ml) olive oil
1/2 teaspoon (2 ml) salt	Salt and freshly ground pepper
6 to 8 tarragon sprigs	2 lemons
12 parsley sprigs	6 medium-large artichokes
6 fennel seeds	Limestone or butter lettuce
8 black peppercorns	Thin slices of red bell pepper

Prepare a court bouillon by combining the water, wine, carrot, onion and 1/2 teaspoon (2 ml) salt in a noncorrodible soup pot. Add a bouquet garni made with one tarragon sprig, six parsley sprigs, the fennel seeds, and peppercorns. Simmer for 30 minutes, then strain into a clean pan.

If you are using bay scallops, poach them whole in the court bouillon for about a minute, until they are just done. If you are using sea scallops, cut them into 1/4-inch (5-mm) rounds and poach them until they are just done, about a minute. Remove the scallops with a slotted spoon to a plate to cool. Poach the shrimp in their shells in the court bouillon for about 2 minutes, or until they just begin to turn pink. Remove the shrimp with a slotted spoon and spread them to cool.

Skim the court bouillon and reduce it to 3/4 cup (180 ml). Off the heat, whisk in the olive oil and about 2 tablespoons (30 ml) of lemon juice. Pour the dressing into a glass bowl and set aside to cool.

Mince the leaves of the remaining tarragon and parsley. Shell and devein shrimp. Add shrimp, scallops, and herbs to the dressing and toss well. Adjust the seasoning with salt and pepper, adding lemon juice and olive oil if necessary. Cover and chill for 2 hours.

Squeeze half a lemon into a small bowl of cold water. Trim the artichokes by removing all leaves and paring the hearts of the dark green outer flesh. Remove the chokes and place the hearts in the acidulated water.

Squeeze the juice from half a lemon into a noncorrodible steamer and add water. Steam the artichokes for 10 to 15 minutes, until the hearts are tender but still firm. Cool them to room temperature, then assemble the salad.

To serve, line six salad plates with lettuce and place an artichoke heart on each plate. Divide the salad among the artichokes, spooning the remaining dressing over each. Garnish with red pepper strips.

LIMA BEANS WITH TARRAGON

■

THIS BEAN STEW, OR SALAD, came about when we had the last of the garden's tomatoes and new-crop dried limas. The fine buttery flavor and texture of dried limas make them worth looking for. Use any white bean if you can't find limas. Prepare the dish a day in advance for a full, mellow flavor. If vine-ripened tomatoes are not available, serve the dish as a salad and garnish with some thin slices of red bell pepper or with lettuce. Be sure to serve crusty bread to soak up the juices.

SERVES 6

1 pound (450 g) dried baby lima beans

1 tablespoon (15 ml) chopped tarragon or 1 teaspoon (5 ml) crumbled dried tarragon

About 1 tablespoon (15 ml) lemon juice

1/4 cup (60 ml) olive oil

3 garlic cloves, minced

Salt and freshly ground white pepper

2 medium-sized ripe tomatoes

Soak the beans overnight. Pour off the soaking water and add enough water to cover beans by 2 inches (5 cm). Cook the beans covered over medium heat until they are tender.

Add the tarragon, lemon juice, olive oil, garlic, and salt and pepper to taste. Remove from the heat and allow the beans to cool to room temperature. The beans may be prepared ahead to this point, covered, and refrigerated.

When you are ready to serve, seed and dice the tomatoes, and add them to the beans. Serve at room temperature or reheat gently until warm.

T A R R A G O N   P I C K L E S

∎

PATRICIA WELLS SHARED HER CORNICHONS, and her recipe for preparing them, with Carolyn in Paris several years ago. They were superior in flavor and appearance, and stimulated us to try an American rendition. The tiny French pickling cucumbers work best, though we have not seen them in markets here; we grow them from seed. Kirby cucumbers taste good when prepared according to the recipe. Choose the smallest ones and pack them in pint (475-ml) jars.

FILLS 8 HALF-PINT (240-ML) JARS

2½ pounds (1.1 kg) scrubbed pickling cucumbers

1/3 cup (80 ml) kosher salt

About 8½ cups (2 litres) cold water

2½ cups (590 ml) tarragon vinegar

1 tablespoon (15 ml) sugar

16 very small white pickling onions, peeled but with ends intact

16 tarragon sprigs, about 2 inches (5 cm) long

8 garlic cloves, peeled

8 small bay leaves

8 small dried hot red peppers

32 peppercorns

Trim off the stem ends of the cucumbers, rinse, and drain them. Place them in a large bowl with the salt and enough water to just cover, about 6 cups (1.4 litres). Let them stand in a cool place for 6 hours or overnight. Drain the cucumbers well.

Combine the vinegar, 2½ cups (590 ml) water, and the sugar in a noncorrodible saucepan and bring to a boil.

Have ready eight sterilized, hot half-pint canning jars with lids and rings.

Fill the jars with the drained cucumbers, layering the onions, herbs, and spices in between. Each jar should have two onions, two tarragon sprigs , one clove garlic, one bay leaf, one hot pepper, and four peppercorns.

Pour the boiling vinegar and water into each jar to 1/4 inch (5 mm) from the top. Wipe the rim of each jar and seal. Let the jars cool and seal. Store any unsealed jars in the refrigerator and use within 2 weeks.

Store the sealed jars for 3 to 4 weeks in a cool dark place before serving. Refrigerate after opening.

T H Y M E

HONEYSWEET and handsome thyme,
with what wit you bring to rhyme:
Conceits of cabbage, apple, oyster:
Advance brave cooks, braise, and roister.

Of all the classical culinary herbs, thyme is especially endearing to those who love miniatures; its handsome compact form growing close to the earth perfumes the air around it, seemingly to the heavens. It has a modest appearance, not more than 8 to 12 inches (20 to 30 cm) from the ground, but a luxurious symmetry to its plump, thickly set leaves and a charm to its rosy lavender or white flowers which do much to explain why it has entranced herbalists for so long. As the aroma intimates, it is a sweetish, though pungent, herb when fresh—a combination to scent and savor.

Thyme is another herb of Mediterranean origin. The classical Greeks, conservative in the culinary use of many common herbs, embraced this herb wholeheartedly, perhaps because they discovered thyme's attraction for bees and tasted the resulting honey. Certainly, a taste of the famous Mount Hymettus honey is a sensual recognition of the beauty and power of thyme.

Athenians did not restrict their use of thyme to the kitchen; they also made liqueurs with it, burned it in their temples, and bathed in it. The root of thyme's name is Greek, although whether it is derived from *thuo,* "to fumigate", "to perfume", or from *thumus,* "courage, without fear of death", is uncertain. Possibly both concepts come from the Egyptians, who used thyme in their embalming processes.

Later, thyme became a symbol of energy and

OF ALL THE CLASSICAL

CULINARY HERBS, THYME

IS ESPECIALLY

ENDEARING TO THOSE

WHO LOVE MINIATURES.

acuity, teas and baths of it being especially recommended for the eyes. Culpeper spoke highly of its effects on the lungs, and it is used in cough medicines today. Thyme also had a well-deserved reputation for banishing unpleasant odors, making it, with rosemary and lavender, one of the chief strewing herbs. Renaissance England respected thyme in more elegant social contexts: "to smell as sweet as thyme" was a moral as well as physical compliment. "Punning thyme" was a signal for clever wordplay among the wits and poets of the Elizabethan period.

In uses closer to the cook, the Spanish, Italians, and French grazed sheep and goats on thyme for the flavor it gave their meat. The herb was used in many rich dishes, as it was believed to alleviate the misery of gout. Thyme, if used judiciously, will add a soft, plummy fragrance and a subtle taste compounded of mint, bay, and marjoram to almost all classes of cooked foods. It is good with cereal grains, especially rice and wheat; all meats, including brains and sweetbreads; eggs; most vegetables, especially potatoes, carrots, squash, onions, and tomatoes; and it makes an exquisite marriage with fish and shellfish. Although it loses some of its fragrant quality in drying, which emphasizes an earthy aroma and pungent flavor, thyme can still enrich the simplest soup or stew and give a delectable accent to fruits and salads. It is indispensable in bouquets garnis for making stock, particularly chicken and lamb

SNIFF YOUR WAY

THROUGH THE THYMES,

TAKING A BREAK

NOW AND THEN . . .

stocks. A good part of our kitchen wealth is concentrated in freshly harvested bundles of thyme.

Thyme is easily grown from seed, though it is chancy to grow it this way because most seed sold is a mixture of varieties. For culinary use, many cultivars of *Thymus vulgaris* are available: French, English, and German thyme are common names. Their aromatic properties are similar, distinctions being made in the width of their leaves. To decide which thymes to grow, choose a nursery or herb grower that offers named varieties, such as Broad-leaf English or Narrow-leaf French. Sniff your way through the thymes, taking a break now and then, and select the one or ones that appeal to you. Interesting scented varieties include the lemon thymes and caraway thyme. These should be used fresh, with little or no cooking; they are excellent for marinades. The beautiful variegated thymes, such as Silver Thyme (*T.* 'Argenteus'), tend to have a milder flavor and aroma.

The creeping thymes, which include *T. praecox* subspecies *arcticus*, make beautiful ground covers, although they are not particularly useful in the kitchen. We grow some of these to provide magic carpets for the bees.

All thymes grow best in sandy soil, as their fine root structures are more prone to rot in heavy soil. They are hardy plants that usually survive the coldest winters.

Thymes should be cut heavily several times a year, especially where summers are hot and humid. Cut thyme by about one-third in early spring or late winter, when temperatures begin to warm. Cut again when buds form, and again in midsummer, or 45 to 60 days after flowering. The final harvest/pruning should take place about 60 days before the first frost is expected; this may coincide with midsummer cutting in some climates. Cut 3 to 4 inches (8 to 10 cm) of the stems and hang them in small bunches or spread them on screens to dry.

In the house, thyme does not require special care if it is transplanted to a wide pot with sandy soil and given plenty of sun. And now, the time has come to please the palate.

T H Y M E - C U R E D   O L I V E S

■

A JAR OF THYME-CURED OLIVES usually stands in each of our pantries to bring back Mediterranean memories of the places we have visited or lived in Italy, southern France, Greece, and Morocco. Thyme and olives are two of the oldest culinary quintessentials of this region. The olive oil becomes wonderfully thyme-flavored and is good in marinades and to brush on grilled foods. We have kept oil-packed olives as long as a year in a cool, dark pantry with no problems of spoilage or off-flavors. This makes a handsome gift for olive lovers when packed in an attractive European-style canning jar with a rubber ring and snap closure.

FILLS A 1-QUART AMERICAN CANNING JAR (750-ML EUROPEAN-STYLE JAR)

20 to 25 thyme or lemon thyme sprigs
1 pint (475 ml) oil-cured olives

1½ to 2 cups (360 to 475 ml) olive oil (You will need the larger amount if you use an American canning jar.)

Pick off any brown or moldy leaves from the thyme. Bruise the remaining leaves slightly by rubbing the sprigs gently between your palms.

Place a layer of olives in a quart canning jar, or a 750-ml European-style canning jar. Add about one-quarter of the thyme to the jar. Add more olives and thyme, ending with olives, until the ingredients have been used.

Pour the olive oil into the jar, shaking gently to distribute it. Close the jar and leave it in a cool dark place for 2 weeks before opening and using.

MUSHROOMS WITH THYME ON TOAST

■

THE AFFINITY BETWEEN MUSHROOMS and thyme has been recognized for centuries in European cooking, where wild mushrooms and thyme were used together before the cultivation of mushrooms. We serve this dish in the fall and winter as a light course, followed by any food also in season except fish.

SERVES 4

1/2 ounce (15 g) dried porcini mushrooms

1 cup (240 ml) boiling water

8 slices of bread, about 3 inches (8 cm) across, and 1/2 inch (1 cm) thick

2 garlic cloves

1/2 pound (225 g) cultivated mushrooms

2 tablespoons (30 ml) butter

1 tablespoon (15 ml) olive oil

6 thyme sprigs

1 tablespoon (15 ml) dry sherry

Salt and freshly ground pepper

1 tablespoon (15 ml) minced parsley

Pour the boiling water over the porcini and let stand for 30 minutes.

Lightly toast the bread and allow it to cool. Rub each piece of toast lightly on both sides with one of the garlic cloves. Place them on a serving dish.

If the cultivated mushrooms are large, halve them and slice thin. If they are small, slice them thin.

Trim the porcini and rinse them carefully to rid them of any sand. Strain the liquor through a sieve lined with a damp paper towel or fine-weave cheesecloth and reserve it.

Chop the porcini coarsely.

Heat the butter and oil in a sauté pan over medium heat. Add the sliced mushrooms to the pan and cook for about a minute. Add the porcini. Press the remaining clove of garlic into the pan and stir well. Add the thyme, about 1/3 cup (80 ml) of the reserved mushroom liquor, and the sherry, and stir well.

Cook, stirring occasionally, for 3 to 5 minutes, until most of the liquid has been absorbed. Season with salt and pepper. Take the pan off the heat and remove the thyme sprigs. Hold them, one at a time, over the pan and run your fingers down the stems. Stir the leaves that come off into the mushrooms. Divide the mushrooms and sauce evenly over the prepared toasts. Garnish with the parsley and serve immediately.

CARROT SOUP WITH THYME

■

THYME IS A GOOD HERB with orange vegetables: carrots, winter squash, including pumpkin, and sweet potatoes. A richer variation of this recipe adds a cup (240 ml) of cream after the soup is pureed.

SERVES 4 TO 6

2 pounds (900 g) carrots, chopped coarse

1 medium onion, diced

4 tablespoons (60 ml) unsalted butter

1½ quarts (1½ litres) chicken or vegetable stock

A bouquet garni made with 6 Italian parsley sprigs, 3 thyme sprigs or 1 teaspoon (5 ml) dried thyme, and 6 to 8 black peppercorns

Salt and freshly ground pepper

Freshly grated nutmeg

1 tablespoon (15 ml) thyme leaves, chopped fine, or thyme blossoms

2 tablespoons (30 ml) chopped parsley leaves

Soften the carrots and onion in the butter in a soup pot, covered, over low heat for about 15 minutes. Add the stock and bring the soup to a simmer. Add the bouquet garni and simmer about 20 minutes.

Remove the bouquet garni and puree the soup in batches. Season it with salt, pepper, and nutmeg. Reheat the soup over low heat and serve it in warm soup bowls garnished with a little chopped thyme or thyme blossoms and chopped parsley.

H E R B E D   C L A M   C H O W D E R

■

FISH CHOWDERS OFTEN HAVE a little thyme, whether they are cream- or broth-based; shellfish and thyme seem particularly compatible. Manila clams, despite their name, come from Pacific Northwest, Alaskan, and Canadian waters. They are small, very tender, and full of flavor. Since clams give off a goodly amount of juices when they open, we pan-steam them in a little water or wine and incorporate the juices into the dish we are making. Pan-steaming is good for many vegetables too, as they reabsorb some of the juices lost to the small amount of water.

SERVES 6

4 dozen Manila clams or the smallest littleneck clams

1 28-ounce (800-g) can tomatoes

4 thyme sprigs or 1 teaspoon (5 ml) dried thyme

2 marjoram sprigs or 1/2 teaspoon (2 ml) dried marjoram

1 bay leaf

Cayenne pepper

1 medium onion, diced

2 celery stalks, diced

3 medium new potatoes, peeled and diced

4 tablespoons (60 ml) unsalted butter

Salt

Garlic croutons, optional

Roasted Red Pepper and Basil Butter (page 51), optional

Scrub the clams and pan-steam them in 1 cup (240 ml) of water until they just open. Shuck them and rinse them if necessary. Strain the cooking juices through rinsed fine-weave cheesecloth in a sieve. Pour the strained juice over the clams and set aside.

Add the tomatoes and their juice to a soup pot and break them up with a wooden spoon. Add the thyme, marjoram, and bay leaf, and season with cayenne pepper.

Cook the onion, celery, and potatoes in the butter over low heat for about 10 minutes.

Add the vegetables to the tomatoes along with most of the juice covering the clams. Simmer until the vegetables are just done, about 10 minutes. Add the reserved clams and the rest of the juice and heat through. Serve hot in warm soup bowls accompanied by garlic croutons and Roasted Red Pepper and Basil Butter, if desired.

OATMEAL BREAD WITH THYME AND WALNUTS

■

SUSAN'S GRANDMOTHER-IN-LAW, affectionately called Bama, passed along the tradition of making these tasty, almost square little loaves. We have made her recipe less sweet, and added thyme and walnuts, but still find the look and tenderness of these irresistible, especially when they are warm, with butter and molasses or honey. This is an excellent breakfast bread; mix it the night before and let it rise overnight in a cool room. Shape it the next morning, then let it rise in a warm place before baking. Imported walnut oil adds extra nutty flavor.

MAKES 4 SMALL LOAVES

2 cups (475 ml) boiling water

1 cup (240 ml) rolled oats

2 tablespoons (30 ml) imported walnut oil or unsalted butter

1/4 cup (60 ml) honey

1 tablespoon (15 ml) molasses

1 teaspoon (5 ml) salt

1 tablespoon (15 ml) active dry yeast

4½ to 5 cups (1000 to 1200 ml) unbleached white flour

2 tablespoons (30 ml) minced thyme

2/3 cup (160 ml) coarsely chopped walnuts

Pour the boiling water over the oats and walnut oil or butter. Stir in the honey, molasses, and salt. Cool the mixture to warm. Add the yeast and sift in 4 cups (950 ml) of the flour. Stir in the thyme and walnuts.

Turn the dough onto a smooth surface and knead until smooth, working in extra flour as necessary. Cover the dough, place it in a lightly buttered bowl, and let rise until doubled in bulk. You may let the dough rise in the refrigerator overnight. Let the refrigerated dough come to cool room temperature before shaping.

Punch the dough down and knead it for two or three turns. Cut it into four pieces and shape the pieces into small loaves. Divide the loaves between two buttered 9-by-5-inch (23-by-13-cm) loaf pans.

Preheat the oven to 350° F (180° C).

When the dough has risen to the top of the pans, bake it for 50 to 60 minutes. Cool the loaves in the pans on a rack for 10 minutes, then turn them out onto the rack to cool completely.

L E M O N   T H Y M E   G R I L L E D
C H I C K E N   L E G S

■

LEMON THYME GIVES THIS DISH a special depth of flavor, but any other favorite culinary thyme is good, too. Other chicken parts can be used: wings, breasts, or a whole chicken cut in serving pieces. If you don't like the skin, the marinade works as well when the skin is removed. Prepare this dish the day before a picnic, and refrigerate the cooked chicken after it has cooled to room temperature. Take it along to the picnic in a cooler. Serve plenty of other food, or double this amount; this is one of the most popular picnic dishes we know with people of all ages.

SERVES 4 TO 6

3 pounds (1.4 kg) chicken thighs and drumsticks

12 or 15 lemon thyme sprigs

4 large garlic cloves, mashed

2 lemons, cut in thin slices

2 tablespoons (30 ml) olive oil

Freshly ground black pepper

Salt

Separate the drumsticks from the thighs if the butcher has not already done this. Place the chicken in a dish large enough to hold it in one layer.

Break the thyme sprigs in half and bruise them. Scatter the thyme, garlic, and lemon slices over the chicken. Toss with the olive oil and black pepper.

Cover the dish well and marinate in the refrigerator for 6 to 8 hours, or in a cool room—60° to 65° F (16° to 18° C) for 2 or 3 hours. Turn the chicken two or three times.

Prepare a medium-hot wood or wood charcoal fire. When ready to grill, brush the marinade off the chicken. Grill the chicken for about 20 minutes, or until it is done. Turn frequently and sprinkle it with a little salt when it is nearly done. Serve hot or at room temperature.

S P A R E R I B S   A N D   P O T A T O E S   I N   T H Y M E   T O M A T O   S A U C E

■

THIS DISH WAS SUSAN'S BIRTHDAY DINNER when she was a child, specially prepared by her mother, Audrey Belsinger. Audrey cooked this in a pressure cooker, though there was one birthday when the kitchen was redecorated with tomato sauce. Marinating helps seal in the flavor and is safer. Serve the dish when etiquette can be put aside, the spareribs eaten out of hand, and the potatoes mashed in the plates to soak up the delicious sauce.

SERVES 6

1 cup (240 ml) dry white wine

6-ounce (170 g) can tomato paste

8 to 10 thyme sprigs

3 garlic cloves, mashed

1 teaspoon (5 ml) freshly ground pepper

1/4 teaspoon (1 ml) ground allspice

3 pounds (1.4 kg) country-style spareribs

1½ pounds (675 g) white or red potatoes, peeled and quartered

2 cups (475 ml) beef or veal stock

1 teaspoon (5 ml) salt

3 tablespoons (45 ml) chopped parsley

Mix the wine, tomato paste, thyme sprigs, garlic, pepper, and allspice in a large ceramic or glass bowl. Add the spareribs and coat them with the marinade. Cover and marinate in the refrigerator overnight.

Let the spareribs come to room temperature. Spread them on a baking sheet large enough to hold them in one layer. Reserve the marinade. Preheat the oven to 450° F (230° C).

Salt and pepper the ribs lightly and bake them in the upper third of the oven for about 30 minutes, until they are well browned and tender. Turn them once while they are cooking. Transfer the ribs to a large warm platter and pour off the fat in the baking pan.

While the ribs are baking, put the potatoes in a noncorrodible saucepan along with

1½ cups (360 ml) of the stock, salt, and the reserved marinade. Bring the liquid to a boil, reduce to a simmer, and cook the potatoes until they are just done, 15 to 20 minutes. Transfer the potatoes to a platter, cover them, and keep them warm. Reduce the cooking liquid to about 1 cup (240 ml).

Deglaze the baking pan with the remaining stock and stir the liquid and the browned bits into the reduced sauce. Arrange the potatoes around the ribs, pour the sauce over the ribs, and sprinkle the dish with the chopped parsley.

BAKED TOMATOES WITH RICE AND THYME

■

A GRAPEFRUIT SPOON OR KNIFE works well to hollow out the tomatoes for this Mediterranean-flavored dish. They are good as a first or appetizer course and with grilled meat, fish, or chicken.

SERVES 6

6 medium-sized tomatoes, 2 generous pounds (1 kg)

Salt and freshly ground pepper

2 cups (475 ml) cooked rice

3 tablespoons (45 ml) minced shallots

2 tablespoons (30 ml) lightly toasted pine nuts

2 tablespoons (30 ml) olive oil

2 teaspoons (10 ml) lemon juice, or to taste

1½ teaspoons (8 ml) thyme, minced

1 tablespoon (15 ml) minced parsley

2 tablespoons (30 ml) dry bread crumbs

1 tablespoon (15 ml) lightly toasted pine nuts, ground

2 tablespoons (30 ml) grated parmesan or romano cheese

1/2 cup (120 ml) dry white wine or water

Olive oil

Thyme sprigs or flowers

Wash, core, and hollow the tomatoes. Salt and pepper them lightly.

Preheat the oven to 350° F (180° C). Lightly oil a baking dish large enough to hold the tomatoes.

Combine the rice, shallots, and whole pine nuts in a bowl. In a separate bowl, mix the oil, lemon juice, thyme, and parsley. Season with salt and pepper and toss with the rice. Fill the tomatoes with the rice mixture, dividing it evenly. Combine the bread crumbs, ground pine nuts, and cheese. Sprinkle the topping on each tomato.

Transfer the tomatoes to the baking dish, pour in the wine or water, and drizzle a bit of olive oil over each tomato.

Bake for 12 to 15 minutes, until the tops are golden brown.

Remove the tomatoes carefully to a serving plate and garnish with thyme sprigs or flowers. Serve hot or at room temperature.

B U T T E R N U T   P U R E E   W I T H   T H Y M E

■

ROAST PORK, RABBIT, CHICKEN, DUCK, and goose are particularly good with squash purees. But winter squashes are mild-mannered enough to accompany almost any dish, as long as they are not oversweetened. If we don't have the roasted garlic, we make the puree without it; the small amount of thyme adds just enough interest to entice squash avoiders. We are partial to the deep flavor and fine texture of butternut, but other winter squash can be used here: pumpkin, buttercup, or banana, for example.

SERVES 6

1½ pounds (675 g) butternut squash	1 tablespoon (15 ml) honey, optional
1 half-head of Roasted Garlic, (page 159), tender cloves squeezed out	2 teaspoons (10 ml) chopped thyme leaves
1 tablespoon (15 ml) olive oil	Salt and freshly ground white pepper to taste
2 to 3 tablespoons (30 to 45 ml) unsalted butter	

Preheat the oven to 375° F (190° C). Split the squash lengthwise. Place the halves, cut side up, on a baking sheet and cover them with aluminum foil. Bake the squash for 1 hour, or until a fork pierces it easily.

Remove the squash from the oven and set aside until it is cool enough to handle. Remove the seeds. Scoop out the meat and puree it, with the roasted garlic cloves, through a food mill, or carefully in a food processor.

Stir the butter, optional honey, and chopped thyme into the puree. Season with salt and pepper. Increase the oven temperature to 400° F (200° C).

Bake the puree in a buttered ovenproof serving dish for 20 to 25 minutes. Serve hot.

GREEK SALAD WITH THYME VINAIGRETTE

■

ALTHOUGH THIS IS NOT A TRADITIONAL Greek salad, the flavors and textures remind us of eating in Greece. It is a quick and popular potluck supper dish.

SERVES 6 TO 8

1 1/2 pounds (675 g) green cabbage, shredded

1 medium red onion, halved and sliced thin

6 ounces (170 g) kalamata olives, pitted and halved

8 ounces (225 g) feta cheese, crumbled

1/2 cup (120 ml) olive oil

About 3 tablespoons (45 ml) red or white wine vinegar, or lemon juice to taste

2 tablespoons (30 ml) chopped thyme leaves

1 teaspoon (5 ml) salt

1 medium bunch spinach

Freshly ground black pepper

Toss the cabbage, onion, olives, and cheese together in a large bowl.

Whisk the olive oil, vinegar or lemon juice, chopped thyme leaves, and salt together and toss with the salad. Let the salad stand at cool room temperature for 2 hours. Adjust the seasoning if necessary.

Refrigerate the salad for about 30 minutes before serving. Wash and stem the spinach. Just before serving, toss the spinach with the salad and season with pepper.

GREEK SALAD

WITH THYME

VINAIGRETTE

THYME MUSTARD

∎

THE TEXTURE OF THE MUSTARD will depend on how fine the seed is ground. The mortar and pestle and spice mill are the best tools for grinding seeds. If you want to use a food processor, you will need to soak the seed in water to cover for 2 or 3 hours before grinding; the grind will not be as even. The basic recipe can be varied in many ways. If a sweeter mustard is desired, add more honey. Try chives, oregano, savory, or tarragon in place of the thyme. You may divide the mustard into two batches, flavoring one batch with half the thyme and the other with another herb. The mustard is hot when it is first prepared; plan to mellow it for 3 to 4 weeks before using.

MAKES ABOUT 2½ CUPS (600 ML)

1½ cups (360 ml) mustard seed, freshly ground

1/2 cup (120 ml) water

1/4 cup (60 ml) white wine vinegar

1/4 teaspoon (1 ml) salt

1/4 teaspoon (1 ml) freshly ground white pepper

1½ teaspoons (8 ml) honey

1 tablespoon (15 ml) minced thyme

Blend the mustard with the water and vinegar in a bowl. The mustard will absorb the liquid as it stands. Add the salt, pepper, honey, and thyme and blend well. Add a little water if necessary to bring the mustard to a spreading consistency.

Pack into jars and keep refrigerated until ready to use.

F A L L   F R U I T   C O M P O T E

■

THE IDEA OF STEWING FRUIT in wine with herbs is an old one that still appeals to us. The full flavor of such compotes can round out many autumn and winter meals. Preparing the compote a day in advance of serving is a good idea; be sure to remove it from the refrigerator so that it is served at cool room temperature. The whipped cream balances the slight acidity of the wine and furnishes an unctuous contrast to the tender-crisp fruit.

SERVES 6 TO 8

3 Bosc or Comice pears

2 Winesap or McIntosh apples

1 Granny Smith or other tart green apple

1/4 pound (115 g) pitted and halved prunes

6 thyme sprigs

1½ cups (360 ml) full-flavored red wine

1/2 cup (120 ml) port wine

1 tablespoon (15 ml) lemon juice

1/4 cup (60 ml) light honey

1/2 pint (240 ml) whipping cream (double cream), whipped

Freshly grated nutmeg

Peel and core the pears and apples. Cut them into quarters, or sixths if they are very large. Place them in a large noncorrodible pan. Add the prunes, thyme, red wine, port, lemon juice, and honey. Cover the fruit and bring the liquid to a boil. Reduce the heat to a simmer and cook the fruit uncovered for about 15 minutes, until it is just done.

Transfer the fruit to a large bowl to cool. Strain the poaching liquid and reduce it by about half. Remove from the heat and let the syrup cool. Pour it over the fruit.

Cover the compote and refrigerate for 3 to 4 hours. Allow the compote to stand at room temperature for 30 minutes before serving. Serve with whipped cream and freshly grated nutmeg.

BIBLIOGRAPHY

Bertolli, Paul, with Alice Waters. *Chez Panisse Cooking*. New York: Random House, 1988.

Boxer, Arabella, and Phillipa Back. *The Herb Book*. London: Octopus Books, 1980.

Bugialli, Giuliano. *The Fine Art of Italian Cooking*. New York: Quadrangle/New York Times, 1977.

Claiborne, Craig. *Cooking with Herbs and Spices*. New York: Harper and Row, 1963.

Collin, Mary A. *Everyday Cooking with Herbs*. New York: Doubleday, n.d.

David, Elizabeth. *Elizabeth David Classics*. New York: Alfred A. Knopf, 1980.

DeBaggio, Thomas. *T. DeBaggio Herbs Plant Catalogs*. Arlington, Virginia: T. DeBaggio Ltd., 1989, 1990, 1991.

Dille, Carolyn, and Susan Belsinger. *New Southwestern Cooking*. New York: Macmillan, 1986.

Foster, Gertrude, and Rosemary Louden. *Park's Success with Herbs*. Greenwood, South Carolina: George W. Park Seed Co., 1980.

Fox, Helen Morgenthau. *Gardening with Herbs for Flavor and Fragrance*. New York: Dover, 1972.

Garland, Sarah. *The Complete Book of Herbs and Spices*. New York: Viking, 1979.

Grieve, Maud. *Culinary Herbs and Condiments*. New York: Dover, 1971.

————. *A Modern Herbal*. New York: Dover, 1971.

Hatfield, Audrey Wynne. *A Complete Culinary Herbal*. Wellingborough, Northants, England: Thorsons, 1978.

Hazan, Marcella. *The Classic Italian Cookbook*. New York: Alfred A. Knopf, 1979.

Hersey, Jean. *Cooking with Herbs*. New York: Charles Scribner's Sons, 1972.

Hoffmann, Irene Botsford. *The Book of Herb Cookery*. Boston: Houghton Mifflin, 1975.

Howarth, Sheila. *Herbs with Everything*. New York: Holt, Rinehart and Winston, 1976.

Hylton, William H., editor. *The Rodale Herb Book*. Emmaus, Pennsylvania: Rodale Press, 1979.

Mallos, Tess. *The Complete Middle East Cookbook*. Sydney, Australia: Landsdowne Press, 1979.

Mazza, Irma Goodrich. *Herbs for the Kitchen*. Boston: Little, Brown, 1975.

McNair, James K. *The World of Herbs and Spices*. San Francisco: Ortho Books, 1979.

Meyer, Joseph E. *The Herbalist*. Glenwood, Illinois: Meyerbooks, 1976.

Moosewood Collective. *Sundays at Moosewood Restaurant*. New York: Simon and Schuster, 1990.

Rohde, Eleanour Sinclair. *A Garden of Herbs*. New York: Dover, 1969.

Root, Waverley. *The Food of Italy*. New York: Atheneum, 1971.

Simeti, Mary Taylor. *Pomp and Sustenance*. New York: Alfred A. Knopf, 1989.

Simmons, Adelma Grenier *Herb Gardening in Five Seasons*. New York: Hawthorn, 1964.

_____. *Herb Gardens of Delight*. New York: Hawthorn Books, 1974.

Solomon, Charmaine. *The Complete Asian Cookbook*. Sydney, Australia: Paul Hamlyn, 1976.

Sounin, Léonie de. *Magic in Herbs*. New York: Pyramid, 1977.

Stobart, Tom. *Herbs, Spices, and Flavorings*. New York: Overlook Press, 1982.

Waters, Alice. *The Chez Panisse Menu Cookbook*. New York: Random House, 1982.

Wolfert, Paula. *Couscous and Other Good Food from Morocco*. New York: Harper and Row, 1973.

Woodward, M., editor. *Leaves from Gerard's Herball*. New York: Dover, 1969.

INDEX